Sensationally light
pasta
& grains

Sensationally light
pasta
& grains

Rose Reisman

Penguin Books

PENGUIN BOOKS

Published by the Penguin Group
Penguin Books Canada Ltd., 10 Alcorn Avenue, Toronto, Ontario, Canada M4V 3B2
Penguin Books Ltd., 27 Wrights Lane, London W8 5TZ, England
Penguin Putnam Inc., 375 Hudson Street, New York, New York 10014, U.S.A.
Penguin Books Australia Ltd., Ringwood, Victoria, Australia
Penguin Books (NZ) Ltd., cnr Rosedale and Airborne Roads, Albany, Auckland 1310, New Zealand

Penguin Books Ltd., Registered Offices: Harmondsworth, Middlesex, England

First published 1999
10 9 8 7 6 5 4 3 2 1

Manufactured in Canada

Canadian Cataloguing in Publication Data

Reisman, Rose, 1953–
   Sensationally light pasta and grains

Includes index.
ISBN 0-14-028810-4

1. Cookery (Pasta).   2. Cookery (Cereals).   3. Low-fat diet – Recipes.
I. Title.

TX809.M17R44 1999   641.8'22   C99-931381-9

The National Breast Cancer Fund does not represent or warrant that the use of the recipes contained in this book will either reduce the risk of developing breast cancer or improve the prognosis for those who have been treated for breast cancer. Any questions regarding the impact of diet and health should be directed to your physician. The National Breast Cancer Fund specifically disclaims any liability, loss or risk, personal or otherwise, which is incurred as a consequence, directly or indirectly, of the use and application of any of the contents of this book.

Cover photo: Grilled fruit salad over rotini with shrimp (page 90)

Visit Penguin Canada's web site at **www.penguin.ca**

contents

credits

Design, editorial and production:	Matthews Communications Design Inc.
Photography:	Mark T. Shapiro
Art direction, food photography:	Sharon Matthews
Food stylist:	Kate Bush
Prop stylist:	Charlene Ericson
Managing editor:	Peter Matthews
Indexer:	Barbara Schon
Color scans & film:	PointOne Graphics

PHOTO PROP CREDITS

The publisher and author wish to thank the following suppliers of props used in the food photography appearing in this book:

PIER 1 IMPORTS, TORONTO   DISHES, GLASSWARE, LINENS AND ACCESSORIES

My love of life is inspired and nourished by my incredible family:

My husband, Sam, unfailing in his support of my work and my passion for what I do;

My children — Natalie, David, Laura and Adam — with whom I treasure every moment, even as they grow up too fast;

And my loving and faithful German shepherds, Aspen and Miko.

Only with my family can I do what I love.

To the sensational group of people who have made this book possible.

Bob Dees, my mentor, friend and business partner, whose dedication, hard work and diligence has made our company, Robert Rose Inc., a number-one success.

Penguin Books Canada, for their overwhelming support and enthusiasm for this book, with particular thanks to Cynthia Good, Kevin Hanson, Jackie Kaiser and Julie Traves.

Matthews Communications Design Inc., with particular thanks to Peter and Sharon Matthews, Elaine Thompson and Petrice Custance; this is the amazing team who somehow pull together all the editorial, design, art direction and production work on my books.

Mark Shapiro, for his magical touch with capturing food on film; his careful, meticulous approach may drive us crazy ("Just shoot it, Mark!"), but the results are extraordinary and can be seen in the beautiful photos that appear in this book.

Jay Town, for his invaluable assistance in the studio, keeping Mark organized and otherwise making life on set more enjoyable for everyone.

Leslie Beck, RD, for her introductory "Straight talk on healthy eating" (see page 13), and for the wonderfully approachable nutritional information ("Nutrition Watch" and "For the Record" sections) that has so enhanced the content of this book.

Kate Bush, food stylist extraordinaire.

Charlene Erricson, for her work in obtaining the props that appear in the photographs.

Lesleigh Landry, my assistant testing chef, for her remarkable professional skills in the kitchen, and for her help in refining the recipes that appear in this book.

To Ruby and Lily for their assistance in my home and with the preparation and shopping for literally hundreds of recipes tested.

Lori Bartholomew at Robert Rose, for her excellent execution of all matters relating to books and products.

And finally, to my lifelong buddy Kathy — now published author of the children's book, *The Secret of Gabi's Dresser* — who is always there for me, ready to offer a listening ear, some honest opinions, or to try the umpteenth version of any recipe!

I love all my books. But honestly, I can't remember the last time I was so excited about a new project!

Because this really *is* new — a new look, a new feel and over 150 new recipes that are absolutely packed with flavor, but without a lot of fat.

Okay, so maybe the part about more taste and less fat isn't so new. In fact, it's the approach I took with my first light pasta book, *Rose Reisman Brings Home Light Pasta* — to create recipes with all the wonderfully satisfying flavor of traditional pasta dishes, but without all the fat and calories. No more boring spaghetti and sauce. No more artery-clogging fettuccine Alfredo!

Well, that was five years ago. And *Light Pasta*, with sales of over 200,000 copies to date, has shown I must be doing something right!

So now, with **Sensationally Light Pasta & Grain**s, it's time to take the next step! Why? For one thing, the food market in North America has been changing with unbelievable speed. It seems that almost every week I find some new ingredient in my grocery store. Pasta products, which five years ago were all plain-old durum semolina, are now available in a rainbow of colors and flavors, such as spinach, whole wheat and tomato. And with the influx of all things Asian, noodles have exploded onto the scene — including soba, udon, chow mein, bean thread, and countless types of rice noodles.

And if we're talking about pasta, then we really need to be talking about grains (which are part of the same food group). Here, too, the world has changed. Five years ago, we were all familiar with rice, barley, cornmeal (if not polenta) and couscous. But what about kasha, bulgur, millet, quinoa and wheat berries? Unless you were a *serious* patron of health food stores, probably not! But today these grains are widely available and are recognized as excellent sources of fiber, complex carbohydrates, protein, vitamins and minerals.

So here we are, in a world of new ingredients and, with it, a whole range of exciting new ideas for light, flavorful cooking. And that's what you'll find in this book — great recipes presented in a fresh, open design with dynamic images and plenty of information that's truly useful to you.

Frankly, I think you'll love these recipes. They're all low in fat and calories (as you'd expect), yet packed with wonderful flavors and textures. To start your meal, try **Fettuccine Baskets with Zucchini Parmesan** (plenty of visual and taste appeal) or **Beef Potstickers with Coconut Sauce** (yes, you can make a low-fat dish with coconut milk). Choose one of my super soups, whether as an accompaniment or as a substantial meal on its own, such as **Orzo Soup with Caramelized Onions and Cheese**. Discover all the wonderfully satisfying salads you can make with pasta and grains (who says a salad can't fill you up?) with dishes such as **Chicken Bulgur Niçoise**.

Wondering what to do with that chicken in the fridge? In no time, you can cook up taste sensations like **Curried Chicken Coconut Pasta with Apricots and Cranberries** (yes it's rich, no it's not high in fat). Fish and seafood fans will love dishes such as **Caesar Tortellini with Smoked Salmon** and **Shrimp Salsa over Rice Fettuccine**. And for all you meat-eaters out there — come on, don't be shy! — here's some good news: Despite what you may have heard, meat can still be part of a healthy diet; just enjoy it in moderation. And enjoy it you will, in dishes like **Polenta Lasagna with Meat Tomato Sauce**. But if meatless is the way you'd prefer to go, then you'll find plenty of sensational combinations here, including **Tomatoes with Barley and Pesto Stuffing**.

Now, this is normally where you'd expect to run out of categories in a cookbook devoted to pasta and grains. But not this one! Would you believe a *dessert* section? Well, it's true — 10 desserts, in fact, including **Baklava Wonton Pouches with Honey Lemon Sauce**. They're a delight for any sweet tooth!

What else is new in this book? Well, in addition to the bolder, more energetic presentation, you'll find a lot more useful background information (in the "Ask Rose" sections that accompany each recipe), as well as cooking tips ("Cooking 101"), suggestions for different ingredients ("Variations"), and advice on preparing recipes for family and friends ("Lifestyle").

All of this comes in response to what I've experienced over the years with my busy family (one almost-always-understanding husband, four wonderful-when-I-don't want-to-kill-them kids and two

semi-vicious but otherwise loving and loyal dogs), in promoting my books, in developing my line of commercial food products, in writing a monthly newspaper column, and in hosting my cooking show, broadcast nationwide on The Life Network. What I've discovered in talking to my readers and viewers is that, when it comes to food, they just can't get enough information. (Kind of like me, who has cookbooks and food magazines strewn throughout the house, and exercises while watching food shows on television.) So I've made every page as information-packed as possible.

I know how important it is to have expert nutritional facts and advice, so I enlisted the help of Leslie Beck, RD, who shares her professional knowledge in the "Nutrition Watch" and "For the Record" segments found throughout this book. In addition to supplying a nutritionist's perspective on my recipes, Leslie also identifies those foods that scientific studies are showing to be measurably effective in preventing or lowering the risk of heart disease, stroke, and certain types of cancer. There's nothing clinical here; it's all tremendously readable!

I'm also glad to be helping once again in the fight against breast cancer, with a portion of proceeds from the sale of this book going to the National Breast Cancer Fund. In the past, with the support of readers like you, and through the personal efforts of my husband and myself, over $1 million has been raised for the cause of breast cancer research, prevention and treatment. It's a great demonstration of what's possible when we all work together.

Finally, I'd love to hear from you. E-mail me at **rosier@idirect.com** or write to 156 Duncan Mill Road, Unit 12, Toronto, Canada M3B 3N2.

Well, that's enough from me. Now it's up to you — to make some new choices, to get going and get healthy with the exciting new recipes in ***Sensationally Light Pasta & Grains***.

Enjoy!

Rose Reisman

Dear Friends and Supporters,

With one in nine Canadian women diagnosed with breast cancer each year, representing over 18,000 women, clearly it is
likely you know someone living with breast cancer. It could be
you, your mother, daughter, sister, aunt, wife, friend or col-
league. Breast cancer profoundly affects the entire family.

The National Breast Cancer Fund (NBCF) is a volunteer organi-
zation that raises money and seeks to improve the quality of life
for women and their families. NBCF was established to provide
direct financial support for breast cancer research and all
aspects of the management of the disease, targeting programs
in committees across Canada. The ultimate goal is to ensure
that funds are placed where they will have the most immediate
benefit to locally administered facilities.

Our motto is *"We're not just helping women survive, we're helping them live."*

Again with the publishing of this cookbook, Rose Reisman
shows her strong commitment and support for the women living
with cancer and we thank her. Food plays a major role in all of
our lives — so enjoy the recipes. You might even want to share
one of her meals with a family who could use the help.

Thank you for helping and giving hope to the women living
with this disease.

Sincerely,

Monica Wright-Roberts

President
National Breast Cancer Fund
(toll free 1-877-788-NBCF)

straight talk

about healthy eating

LESLIE BECK, RD

Today, we're bombarded with an overwhelming amount of nutrition information. At the best of times it can be confusing, even for a nutritionist like myself. One day oat bran is in, the next day it's out. (It's now back in, for good, I'm pleased to say.) And just when you've gotten into the habit of taking vitamin C, you hear it might not be good for you after all. (Yes, there was such a study, but small and poorly done.) After reading the morning paper, you're left wondering if margarine really is better than butter (the debate continues). And the latest food in the nutritional doghouse — starch (more about this later). See what I mean? It can be downright frustrating if you're trying to stick to a healthy eating plan.

making sense of nutrition advice

To help you sort the fact from the fiction, Rose has given me the opportunity in this book to tell you how the foods you eat can affect your health. In this introductory section, you'll learn what key components make up a healthy diet. I'll tell you what you should be eating and how much. And, accompanying recipes throughout the book, you'll find additional information under the headings "Nutrition Watch" and "For the Record." Each of the Nutrition Watch sections relates to a particular ingredient or nutrient in the recipe. Here, you'll read about studies that link nutrients and antioxidants in fruits, vegetables and grains to reduced risks of cancer and heart disease, for example, or how eating more fish and less meat can help keep you healthier. As well, you'll learn about the latest scientific findings and nutrition recommendations. For the Record sections are intended to dispel myths and clear up nutrition controversies. No, shrimp are not bad for your heart. Yes, too much starch can make you fat. Who would have thought that a bagel is equivalent to 4 slices of bread (or more)? And so on. I hope you find these food facts useful — if sometimes surprising!

what does healthy eating really mean?

For years, we have been inundated with diet books, all offering different (sometimes even contradictory) prescriptions for health. And some may have proven to be helpful to some people. But I should point out that there is no single diet that will work for everyone. In fact, every person has a different metabolism, different nutrient needs and different food preferences. So, I don't believe in a "one size fits all" approach. Based on the scientific evidence, however, I *do* believe that a plant-based diet is the healthiest way to eat. Over and over again, nutrition researchers are finding that an increased intake of vegetables, fruits and whole grains is associated with a lower risk of heart disease, stroke, and many types of cancer.

Now, before all you meat-eaters get up and leave the room, let me say that eating a plant-based diet does not mean following a strict vegetarian diet. Rather, it means simply shifting *the focus* of your meals to grains, vegetables, fruit and legumes, and placing less emphasis on animal foods, like meat and poultry. For some people, making the transition to a plant-based diet could be nothing more complicated than eating a 4-oz (125 g) piece of grilled steak, instead of their usual 10-oz (325 g) portion. For others it means replacing the cheese in a turkey sandwich with romaine lettuce, cucumbers and tomato. And for you, it might mean adding a few pieces of fruit to your daily diet. It can be that simple.

Let's take a closer look at what makes up a plant-based diet.

grain foods – 5 to 12 servings a day

The recipes throughout this book focus on the goodness of grains. Whole wheat, rice, corn, oats, barley, millet and quinoa provide carbohydrates, dietary fiber, and important vitamins and minerals. Now, 12 servings a day may sound like a lot, but when you consider what a serving size is, you might think twice. (See box: "What's in a serving?", page 16.) For example, take that large bagel you ate for breakfast — it was at least 3 (and possibly as many as 5) servings. Most of my clients don't have a problem with eating too few grain servings. Often the reverse is true. (More about that later.) How many servings should you be eating every day? Well, that depends on your energy needs which, in turn, are largely determined by your age, body size and activity level. Here's a rough guide I often use in my practice.

Growing teenage boys	12 servings (or more)
Women, moderate exercise (3 to 4 times/week)	6 to 8 servings
Women, heavy exercise (more than 4 times/week)	8 to 10 servings
Women, little or no exercise	4 to 6 servings
Men, moderate exercise (3 to 4 times/week)	8 to 12 servings
Men, heavy exercise (more than 4 times/week)	12 servings (or more)
Men, little or no exercise	7 to 8 servings

vegetables and fruits – 5 to 10 servings a day

It's hard to argue the fact that these foods are good for us. Study after study has found that eating plenty of vegetables and fruit lowers the risk of heart disease and many types of cancer. In fact, over 200 international epidemiological studies have found that a diet high in fruits and vegetables reduces the risk of cancer. The protective power of produce has been attributed to vitamins A, C, and E, beta carotene, dietary fiber, as well as a host of phytochemicals that occur naturally in plant foods.

Many of these protective compounds can be classified by color. For example, orange fruits and vegetables (such as sweet potato, squash, cantaloupe and nectarines) are full of beta carotene. The dark green leaves of rapini, romaine, kale and spinach indicate there's a fair amount of vitamin A, folate and calcium. Tomatoes, watermelon and strawberries house a red phytochemical called lycopene. And the list goes on. My advice is to choose at least 3 different colored vegetables and 3 different colored fruits every day. That way you'll be getting a wide variety of vitamins and phytochemicals.

Despite all the evidence for the healthy properties of fruits and vegetables, many of us still fall short of the recommended 5 to 10 servings a day. We grab a bagel instead of an orange; we throw together pasta with tomato sauce instead of eating a salad with a baked potato. Some of us think that a strawberry cereal bar counts as a fruit serving. Or, when it comes right down to it, many of us would rather have French fries than a bowl of steamed spinach. Well, no more excuses! It's time to start mapping these healthy foods into your diet. Include 1 or 2 fruit servings at breakfast (banana, berries, raisins, unsweetened fruit juice), 1 vegetable serving at lunch (tomato juice, baby carrots, green salad), fruit for between-meal snacks (apples, pears, dried apricots), and at least 2 different vegetables at dinner. There, you're already at 7 servings. It's easy if you plan for it.

protein foods – 5 to 9 servings a day

Foods like poultry, meat, fish and soy foods supply our body with amino acids that are used to build all our body proteins, including muscle, hormones, immune compounds and enzymes. Protein foods also make an important contribution to our daily requirements for vitamins B6 and B12, iron, zinc and other trace minerals.

What's in a serving?

Ever wonder what they mean when they talk about a serving of rice? Or pasta? Here's a selected list to help you determine your daily portions. All serving sizes are based on measures *after* cooking.

Grain foods

Whole grain bread	1 slice
Bagel	Quarter
Roll, large	Half
Pita pocket	Half
Tortilla, 6-inch (15 cm)	1
Cereal, cold	3/4 cup (175 mL)
Cereal, 100% bran	1/2 cup (125 mL)
Cereal, hot	1/2 cup (125 mL)
Crackers, soda	6
Corn	1/2 cup (125 mL)
Popcorn, plain	3 cups (750 mL)
Grains	1/2 cup (125 mL)
Pasta	1/2 cup (125 mL)
Rice	1/3 cup (75 mL)

Vegetables and fruits

Vegetables, cooked or raw	1/2 cup (125 mL)
Vegetables, leafy green	1 cup (250 mL)
Fruit, whole	1 piece
Fruit, small (plums, apricots)	4
Fruit, cut up	1 cup (250 mL)
Berries	1 cup (250 mL)
Juice, unsweetened	1/2 to 3/4 cup (125 mL to 175 mL)

Milk and alternatives

Milk	1 cup (250 mL)
Yogurt	3/4 cup (175 mL)
Cheese	1.5 oz (40 g)
Rice beverage, calcium fortified	1 cup (250 mL)
Soy beverage, calcium fortified	1 cup (250 mL)

Protein foods

Fish, lean meat, poultry	1 oz (25 g)
Egg, whole	1
Egg whites	2
Legumes (beans, chickpeas, lentils)	1/3 cup (75 mL)
Soynuts	2 tbsp (25 mL)
Tempeh	1/4 cup (50 mL)
Tofu, firm	1/3 cup (75 mL)
Texturized vegetable protein	1/3 cup (75 mL)
Veggie dog, small	1

Fats and oils

Butter, margarine, mayonnaise	1 tsp (5 mL)
Nuts, seeds	1 tbsp (15 mL)
Peanut and nut butters	1.5 tsp (7 mL)
Salad dressing	2 tsp (10 mL)
Vegetable oil	1 tsp (5 mL)

Protein plays another important role: it helps keep our energy levels up during the day. Protein in meat, poultry, fish, legumes and dairy products takes longer to digest. So the rice or potato you eat along with your protein food gets converted to blood glucose more slowly. And a slow, steady rise in blood sugar results in longer-lasting energy levels. Compare that with the quick energy crash you feel after drinking a can of sugary pop. Since the sugar gets into your bloodstream very quickly, it causes your pancreas to secrete lots of insulin. And since insulin's job is to lower your blood sugar, you'll feel sluggish much sooner. You'll have more energy during the day if you include 2 or 3 ounces (50 or 75 g) lean protein with your meals.

When choosing protein foods, opt for low-fat choices like chicken breast, turkey, lean beef and pork tenderloin. (For a no-fat source, try egg whites.) Make fish a part of your diet at least three times a week. And start incorporating more vegetarian protein foods into your diet. Try white kidney beans in pasta sauce, black beans in tacos, firm tofu in a stir-fry, texturized vegetable protein in chili, and veggie burgers on the grill.

milk and milk products – 2 to 4 servings a day

Since we were kids we've been told that to get our calcium we need to drink our milk. It's true that a serving of milk, yogurt or cheese gives you 300 milligrams of calcium. Fluid milk also has vitamin D, a nutrient needed to help absorb calcium from foods. For many people, milk is an easy way to ensure they're meeting their daily calcium needs, which can range from 1000 to 1500 milligrams. Milk products are also a good source of protein, vitamin A, riboflavin, magnesium, zinc and potassium.

Yogurt and kefir (a kind of drinkable yogurt) are fermented milk products I often recommend. They have less lactose than milk, so they're more easily digested. And the live bacterial cultures in these foods may play an important role in disease prevention. Now, it might seem strange that a daily dose of bacteria can keep you healthy, but we've actually been consuming such organisms for centuries. Historical records show that yogurt was used by doctors in the 1500s to treat intestinal infections. More recently, scientists have found that the lactic acid bacteria (acidophilus and bifidobacteria) in fermented milk products may lower blood cholesterol, enhance the body's immune system, and prevent colon cancer.

I often see people in my practice who are unable to get their daily recommended milk servings. Some are lactose intolerant and can't digest the natural sugar in milk, others are vegetarian, and some may not like the taste of milk or yogurt. I encourage these clients to use fortified soy or rice beverages to help meet their calcium and vitamin D requirements. These products have 300 to 340 mg calcium per 8-oz (250 mL) serving and can be used on cereal, in fruit smoothies, in cooking and in baking. I also recommend eating high-calcium vegetables like broccoli, kale and bok choy. But it's unlikely you'll meet your calcium requirements on broccoli alone — that is, unless you plan on eating 10 cups (2.5 L) of the stuff each day! I often recommend calcium citrate supplements with added vitamin D for individuals who have difficulty meeting their calcium needs through food. As a general rule, it's a wise idea to take a 300 mg calcium supplement for every milk serving you're not getting.

fats and oils – 3 to 5 servings a day

It's true: we do need some fat for good health. We just don't need a lot. Fat is needed to transport vitamins A, D, E and K in the body. Eating a little bit of fat allows the body to uses these vitamins properly. Certain types of fat also provide two essential fatty acids — linoleic acid and alpha linolenic acid — which cannot be manufactured by the body and must therefore be supplied from the foods we eat. Both fatty acids are needed to maintain our body's immune system, circulation, hormones and our skin.

A guide to whole grains

Eating foods made from whole grains means you're getting *all* parts of the grain — the outer bran layer where nearly all the fiber is, the germ layer (which is rich in nutrients like vitamin E), and the endosperm (which contains the starch). When whole grains are milled, scraped, refined and heat-processed into flakes, puffs or white flour, all that's left is the starchy endosperm. That means you get significantly less vitamin E, B6, magnesium, potassium, zinc, fiber....the list goes on. Use the following guide to help you get more nutrient-rich whole grains in your diet.

Whole grains		Refined grains
Barley	Oat bran	Cornmeal
Brown rice	Quinoa	Pearled barley
Bulgur	Whole wheat bread*	Unbleached flour
Flaxseed	Whole rye bread	Pasta
Kamut	Spelt	White rice
Oatmeal		

* When buying bread, look for the words "whole wheat flour" on the list of ingredients; "wheat flour" and "unbleached wheat flour" mean it's refined.

The key, as I mentioned earlier, is to use only a small amount of added fat. For a healthy woman, this means about 3 tsp (15 mL) oil each day. A healthy man might consume 5 tsp (25 mL) added fat. In an effort to ward off heart disease or lose weight, some of us have already reduced our intake of added fats and oils. And while you might be adding less fat to your foods, think about how often you eat restaurant or fast food meals, processed snack foods or sweets. It's often these "hidden oils" that account for a hefty portion of our daily fat intake.

Now you know how much added fat you need each day. The next question is, what kind of fat? Before I answer that, here's a quick primer on dietary fat.

1 **Saturated fat** includes all animal fat found in meat, poultry and dairy products, as well as tropical oils like palm and coconut. Saturated fat in animal foods is the number-one dietary factor that can raise your blood cholesterol level. Saturated fat may also play a role in the development of certain cancers. Added fats that are saturated include butter, cream cheese, and full-fat cream in your coffee.

2 **Polyunsaturated fat** is the type found in vegetable oils (corn, sunflower, safflower and sesame), flaxseed oil and oily fish. Diets that contain too much polyunsaturated vegetable oils have been linked to certain cancers. The type of polyunsaturated fat in flaxseed oil and fish is needed for proper brain development and may reduce the risk of heart disease and cancer.

3 **Monounsaturated fat** is found in olive, canola, and peanut oils. Populations who get most of their fat from monos, especially olive oil, have lower rates of heart disease and cancers. Is this because these people eat little saturated fat? Maybe. But scientists have also learned that olive oil contains antioxidant compounds which may be beneficial for the heart.

4 **Trans fat,** also known as hydrogenated vegetable oil, is found in stick margarine, potato chips, crackers, cookies, doughnuts and fried fast food. This type of fat raises LDL (bad) cholesterol and lowers HDL (good) cholesterol. What's more, too much trans fat may adversely affect fetal development and possibly increase the risk of breast cancer.

When it comes to choosing types of fat, use the following guide:

1 Regardless of type, use fat or oil sparingly; don't exceed 4 to 5 servings a day.

2 Get at least one-half of your added fat as flaxseed oil (use in salad dressings) and/or canola oil (use in cooking).

3 Get the rest of your fat from extra virgin olive oil (this type has been processed the least).

4 Try to reduce your consumption of foods that contain "partially hydrogenated vegetable oil."

5 If you use margarine, choose a brand that has at least 6 grams of unsaturated fat (total of polyunsaturated and monounsaturated fat) per serving.

sensational grains

I'm thrilled that Rose chose to develop this cookbook around grains. Grains truly are the staff of life. They provide the fuel our brain, nervous system and muscles rely on. What's more, they're naturally low

Uncommon grains

Need a change from pasta? Getting bored of rice with your chicken? Maybe it's time to add a little adventure (and nutrition) to your meals with these tasty grains.

Buckwheat. You'll find this pancake staple in Japanese soba noodles and kasha. Kasha, also sold as roasted buckwheat groats, is quick cooking and very versatile. Try it in soups, stews, stuffing, and stir-fries. It has a nutty taste that boosts the flavor of any meal.

Bulgur. If you've eaten Middle Eastern cuisine, chances are you've met bulgur in taboulleh salad. It's high in iron, calcium and fiber and great in pilafs, soups and stuffings. It's another quick-cooking grain.

Kamut. This grain is related to the wheat family, but it has less potential for causing an allergic reaction. It's about two or three times the size of wheatberries and has more fiber and protein than most grains. It's chewy texture and buttery flavor makes it great for salads. It's also ground into flour and made into baked goods, cereals and pasta.

Quinoa. Sacred to the Incas, this fluffy grain is sold as whole grain or as pasta. It's lower in carbohydrate and higher in protein that most grains. Try it in pilafs, salads, casseroles and stir-fries.

Spelt. Touted as a type of grain well tolerated by people with a wheat allergy (like kamut), you'll find this age-old staple sold as whole grain, flour, bread, breakfast cereal and pasta. Try using spelt flour in baking and cooking. It adds a delicious nutty taste to pizza crusts and multi-grain breads.

in fat and they're an important source of dietary fiber, as well as many nutrients like iron, folate, vitamin E and other protective compounds. To get the most nutrition possible from grain foods, choose *whole* grain more often. At least one-half of your daily grain servings should be whole grain. But knowing what's whole grain and what's not can be a challenge, because you won't always find this information on labels. Take couscous, for instance; depending how it's processed, it might be whole grain and it might not. That loaf of oatmeal bread might sound wholesome, but if it's made with white flour then it's not whole grain. (To help you stock your pantry with whole grains, see box: "A guide to whole grains," page 18).

If your routine includes white toast at breakfast, a bagel at lunch and white rice at dinner, the recipes in this book will encourage you to incorporate a variety of whole grains into your diet. If you've never heard of quinoa or millet, then you're in for a new taste experience. (See box: "Uncommon grains," page 20). Besides adding variety to your meals, whole grains just might make a difference to your health!

whole grains and heart disease

Many studies have found that whole grains offer protection from heart disease, diabetes and cancer. Researchers at Harvard University studied more than 40,000 men and learned that those who ate 29 grams of fiber each day had a 41% lower risk of heart attack compared to those who ate only 12 grams. What's more, it was the fiber from grains, not fruits and vegetables, that was most strongly associated with protection. The Iowa's Women Health Study followed close to 35,000 women, aged 55 to 69 years, and found that the more whole grains eaten, the lower the risk of heart disease.

Until recently, the secret to whole grains was attributed to their fiber content. While fiber may play an important role in protecting the heart, scientists have identified other protective compounds in whole grains. Antioxidant compounds like vitamin E, tocotrienols and flavonoids may reduce heart disease by preventing blood cells from clumping together. They may also prevent LDL cholesterol from sticking to artery walls. Whole grains are also important sources of minerals like zinc, selenium, copper, and iron, which may also protect the heart.

If you want to reduce your chances of getting diabetes, you'd be wise to eat more whole grains. These foods are digested and absorbed into the bloodstream more slowly than refined grains like white bread and pasta. A gradual rise in blood glucose means less insulin is secreted and this subjects the body to less wear and tear. A Harvard study found that women who ate the most sugar and refined starches had the highest risk of getting type 2 (non-insulin dependent) diabetes compared to women who ate more whole grains.

Grains and fiber: by the numbers

If you're like most people, you probably need to double your fiber intake. Keep this list handy to help you make higher-fiber grain choices. To achieve the recommended 25 to 35 grams of fiber each day, slowly add new foods to your diet and replace lower-fiber foods you're eating now with choices higher in fiber. It does make a difference — you'll see how little fiber the white (refined) version gives you in square brackets.

FOOD	FIBER, g [REFINED VERSION]
Cereals	
100% bran cereals, 1/2 cup (125 mL)	10.0
Bran Flakes, 1 cup (250 mL)	5.0
Corn Bran, 1 cup (250 mL)	7.6
All-Bran Bran Buds, 1/3 cup (75 mL)	11.0
Oatmeal, 1 cup (250 mL), cooked	5.2
Oat Bran cereal, hot, 1 cup (250 mL), cooked	5.1
Red River Cereal, 1 cup (250 mL), cooked	5.0
Shreddies, 1 cup (250 mL)	4.0
Breads	
Bran muffin, 1 medium	2.5
Pita pocket, whole wheat, 1	4.5 [0.5]
Ryvita or Wasa crackers, 2	3.0
Whole wheat bread, 100%, 2 slices	3.0 [0.8]
Other grains	
Barley, 1 cup (250 mL), cooked	6.2
Buckwheat, kasha, 1 cup (250 mL), cooked	4.5
Bulgur, 1 cup (250 mL), cooked	6.1
Millet, 1 cup (250 mL), cooked	1.7
Pasta, whole wheat, 1 cup (250 mL), cooked	6.0 [1.2]
Rice, brown, 1 cup (250 mL), cooked	2.5 [0.5]
Wheat bran, 1 tbsp (15 mL)	1.2

When it comes to diabetes, it's the fiber in whole grains that counts. Because fiber slows down digestion, whole grains enter the blood-stream more slowly, reducing insulin secretion. Experts recommend we get 25 to 35 grams of dietary fiber each day from grains, vegetables, fruit and legumes. If you're like most North Americans, you're proba-bly getting only half this much. So boost your intake from grains, use the chart on page 22.

whole grains and cancer

Plenty of studies have found a protective link between whole grains, fiber and colon cancer. By absorbing water and adding bulk, fiber helps move food through the digestive tract faster. This may reduce the expo-sure of colon walls to cancer-causing substances, or it may be that fiber deactivates these harmful compounds in some way. The anti-cancer properties of whole grains may also come from the natural antioxidants found in these foods. Vitamin E, selenium and phytochemicals may pro-tect the genetic material inside intestinal cells from damage.

Scientists are also studying whole grains for their protective effect against breast cancer. One study found that wheat bran was able to lower blood estrogen levels in pre-menopausal women. Since it's believed that a woman's exposure to her own estrogen may be involved in the development of breast cancer, a diet high in fiber (wheat bran) may be sufficient to reduce breast cancer risk when con-sumed for a long period of time. Researchers at the University of Toronto are studying the ability of flaxseed to reduce breast cancer risk in women. Animal studies have found that phyto (plant) estrogens and lignans in flaxseed can reduce breast tumors by blocking estrogen binding to breast cells. Until we know more about whole grains and breast cancer, it makes good sense to add higher-fiber grains and ground flaxseed to your daily diet.

grains and weight control

After reading about all the health benefits of whole grains, you might wonder why any diet book would declare them to be dietary taboos. Yet a number of bestsellers have done exactly that — recommending that you eliminate grains and other carbohydrates from your diet for a period of time to help lose weight. Many of these diets claim that car-bohydrates make you fat. Well, folks, it's time for a little reality check.

First of all, carbohydrate-rich foods will cause you to gain weight only if you're eating a lot of them, or you're slathering them with high-fat spreads or sauces. Sure, I see many clients, particularly women, who eat too many grain foods — and despite the fact they have very little fat, dense bagels, fat-free muffins, baked pretzels and bowls of pasta all add calories to your diet. (By the way, fat-reduced foods are often not much lower in calories than the original full-fat version.) It's portion size and exercise that counts. Period.

There is new research to suggest that certain types of starchy foods might make it easier to gain weight by making you feel hungry sooner. An American study offered overweight teenage boys unlimited snacks for five hours after giving them one of three different types of meals: low-glycemic (vegetable omelet and fruit); medium-glycemic (regular oatmeal); or high-glycemic (instant oatmeal). The boys ate nearly twice as much after the high-glycemic meal as after the low-glycemic meal. The researchers also found that the boys' blood sugar and insulin rose the highest and fastest after a high-glycemic meal, but then crashed. A crash in blood sugar can lead to hunger and overeating.

To make your meals and snacks last longer, consider the following:

1 Choose carbohydrate foods with a low glycemic index. Reach for pumpernickel, whole grain rye bread, legumes, barley, brown rice, yams, pasta, All Bran, Red River cereal, Cream of Wheat, apples, oranges, pear, apricots, milk and yogurt. Eat less white rice, instant rice, boiled potatoes, white bagels, white bread, crackers, Corn Flakes, muesli, puffed rice, bananas, raisins.

2 Eat some protein with your meals. Adding protein to your food will lower the glycemic index of the meal and lead to a slow rise in blood sugar and insulin levels. Try including a 2- to 3-oz (50 to 75 g) portion of chicken breast, lean meat, fish, eggs and egg whites or soyfoods at mealtimes.

3 Watch the quantity of starch you eat, regardless of its glycemic index. Too much starch will cause a large rise in blood glucose. And that means your body will respond by secreting more insulin into your bloodstream. Keep in mind that most bagels are the equivalent of 4 or 5 slices of bread! Pasta in a restaurant is at least 4 slices of bread — and that's even before you've dipped into the bread basket!

time to enjoy!

I certainly hope this introductory section has helped to clear up at least some of the confusion that so many people experience when trying to get facts about healthy eating. Nutrition is a constantly evolving field and we're learning every day how food affects our health. To help you get your diet on the right track, you might want to consider consulting a professional. Look for a registered dietitian (RD) in your community in the Yellow Pages under "dietitian" or "nutritionist." Or try contacting the Dietitians of Canada (www.dietitians.ca).

Well, now it's time to put the nutrition information aside and start cooking. You'll find the recipes in *Sensationally Light Pasta & Grains* follow the fundamental principles of healthy eating. They're low in fat, chock full of energy-giving carbohydrates and, as you'll see from the nutrient information that accompanies each recipe, many of them are high in fiber, vitamins and minerals. And more importantly, they taste great!

Yours in good health,

Leslie Beck, RD

nutrient analysis notes

Nutrient analysis of the recipes in this book was performed with Food Processor Version 7.2 (adapted for Canadian foods), ESHA Research, Salem OR

The members of the nutrition team that provided recipe analysis for this cookbook are all Nutritional Scientists and Registered Dietitians and are instructors in the Nutrition Program of Brescia College at the University of Western Ontario in London, Ontario, Canada:

Leonard A. Piché PhD RD (Nutrition Team Coordinator),
   Associate Professor

Alicia C. Garcia PhD RD CFE, Assistant Professor

Carol J. Henry RD MSc, Lecturer

1 Cook pasta in a large pot of boiling water. Use 12 to 16 cups (3 to 4 L) water for each pound (500 g) of pasta. Add a little oil to prevent pasta from sticking. Stir pasta occasionally while cooking.

2 Cook pasta *al dente*, or firm to the bite. Never overcook or it will become soft and lose all its texture. When cooked, drain in colander, then transfer to a serving dish. If pasta is to be eaten right away, add sauce immediately and toss. If not, add a little sauce, water or chicken stock (so pasta does not stick), then cover and set aside. Do not add sauce to pasta until just ready to serve, or pasta will absorb the sauce, leaving the appearance of not enough.

3 Prepare the sauce while the pasta is cooking. Plan ahead so the sauce will be completed at the same time the pasta is cooked.

4 As a rule, 8 oz (250 g) dry pasta serves 4 people, 12 oz (375 g) serves 6 people, and 1 lb (500 g) serves 8 people.

5 You can prepare the pasta early in the day if necessary. Drain cooked pasta, rinse with cold water and add 3 tbsp (45 mL) of stock or 3 tbsp (45 mL) of the sauce to be used, or 3 tbsp (45 mL) of the water in which the pasta was cooked. (This will ensure that pasta strands do not stick.) Let sit at room temperature. Before serving, either warm slightly in a microwave for 1 minute at High (be careful not to overcook the pasta), or heat sauce well and pour over pasta immediately.

6 Heavier pasta such as rigatoni or jumbo shells need a heavier, more robust sauce. Lighter pasta such as fettuccine, linguine or spaghetti need a finer sauce and more finely diced vegetables. Sauces for rotini or penne should be somewhere between fine and robust.

7 Homemade pastas can be delicious (see next page for information on making fresh pasta), but most of the time I prefer to use dried pasta. There are several reasons for this:

It is easier to find, store, and costs much less than fresh.

It lacks the fat and cholesterol of the fresh types, which have eggs added.

There are more varieties of dried pasta readily available.

Dried pastas have consistent flavor and texture. Fresh pasta can stick, even if cooked properly, and is best only if cooked immediately after the pasta is made.

It can be stored at room temperature for up to 1 year.

8 If reheating leftover pasta, add more stock or tomato sauce to provide extra moisture.

making your own pasta

As pasta has grown in popularity, many people have started to make their own pasta. It takes time and patience, but for the true pasta gourmet, it is well worth the effort.

1 In a bowl, beat eggs and oil. Sift the flour and salt over the eggs. Mix with a fork and form into a ball. If it is too sticky, add some flour until it is easy to handle. If too dry, add some water.

2 Knead for approximately 8 minutes, until smooth. Wrap in a slightly moistened towel and let rest approximately 30 minutes on the counter before rolling and cutting into various pasta shapes.

Instructions continue on page 28...

Basic Pasta Dough

MAKES 3 TO 4 SERVINGS, ABOUT 12 OZ (375 G)

2	large eggs	2
2 tsp	oil	10 mL
1 1/2 cups	all-purpose flour	375 mL
Pinch	salt	Pinch

If using a food processor or electric mixer, add flour and salt to bowl; with motor running, add the eggs and oil. Mix until the dough becomes a ball. If too sticky, add more flour; if too dry, add a few drops of water. Knead for approximately 5 minutes until smooth. Let rest for 30 minutes.

The classic way of making pasta is to sift the flour and salt together, mounding it on a table. Make a well in the center of the mound and break the eggs into it. Add oil. With a fork begin to gather the flour slowly from the sides into the middle until all is incorporated. Follow the same kneading directions as above.

pasta variations

Some flavorful and colorful variations to the pasta can be added quite simply. Just add the following ingredients and continue with the same method of making the basic pasta dough.

Tomato pasta: Add 2 tbsp (25 mL) tomato paste to basic pasta dough. Add more flour if too sticky.

Green pasta (pasta verdi): Make basic pasta dough using only one egg. Add 8 oz (250 g) finely chopped, cooked spinach, well drained. If dough is too wet, add extra flour.

Herb pasta: Chop 2 tbsp (25 mL) of any herb of your choice, and add to basic pasta dough.

Whole wheat pasta: Use 1 cup (250 mL) whole wheat flour and 1/4 cup (50 mL) white flour in place of white flour in the basic pasta dough recipe. Note that this produces a heavier pasta. For a lighter version, substitute half whole wheat flour and half white flour.

Black pepper pasta: Add 2 tsp (10 mL) freshly ground black pepper to basic recipe.

Garlic pasta: Finely chop 5 cloves of garlic and add to basic pasta dough along with 1 tbsp (15 mL) water.

making your own pasta

... *by hand*

1 A long rolling pin and fairly large working space is essential. Work quickly or the pasta will crack and dry.

2 Roll the dough away from you, stretching it as you roll. After each roll, give the dough a quarter turn to keep the circular shape.

3 If the dough is sticking to your working surface, dust it with a little flour. Pull and stretch the dough instead of rolling it. To stretch it, place the dough on top of the rolling pin and pull carefully.

4 Once the dough covers a large area, let it hang over the counter to stretch more. In a few minutes the dough will look smooth and should be very thin, about 1/8 inch (2 mm) thick.

5 If the dough is to be used for unfilled pasta, spread it on a towel to dry for approximately 30 minutes. Use it immediately for filled pasta such as ravioli or tortellini.

6 Now the dough is ready to cut into shapes of your choice.

...*with a pasta machine*

Two types of wringer-style pasta machines are available. One has a motor and the other is turned by hand.

For manual machines:

1 After the dough is rested, divide into 3 or 4 pieces. Keep the pieces not being used wrapped in plastic.

2 Flatten a piece of dough with your hand just so that it will fit through the pasta machine at the widest setting. Feed the pasta into the machine with one hand while working the machine with the other hand.

3 After the pasta comes out, fold it over and feed it again into the machine. When the dough begins to get smooth and elastic, start to narrow the roller openings. Continue this process until the dough achieves the desired thickness.

4 Lay the pieces on a well-floured surface. If the dough is to sit for any length of time, cover it with a towel. Now attach the cutting attachment desired to the pasta machine. Follow the manufacturer's instructions.

5 Sprinkle the freshly cut pasta with some flour. Toss in a pile, or gather in strands. Now you can lay the pasta on a drying rack. Alternatively, you can place it in the refrigerator, where it will stay fresh for up to 1 week, or in the freezer for up to 2 months.

using an electric pasta machine

An electric machine pushes the dough through a die that creates the desired pasta shape. Some of the more elaborate machines will also mix and knead the dough. After a few minutes, it comes out of the other end in various shapes, depending upon the attachment affixed.
The biggest problem with these machines is that the various attachments are easily clogged with flour, and the time cleaning them can be considerable.

Fettuccine (tagliatelle) or any flat noodle

1 Roll up the dough like a jelly roll and cut in even widths to desired shape, approximately 1/4 inch (5 mm) thick. Cook immediately or let dry for a few days before storing.

Manicotti, cannelloni, lasagna

1 Cut flat sheets of pasta to width and length desired. The most common size for manicotti or cannelloni is 4 by 5 inches (10 by 12.5 cm).

2 In boiling water with a little oil added to prevent sticking, cook pasta for about 2 to 3 minutes. Do not place too many pieces in pot, or they may stick together. Drain and rinse with cold water.

3 The pasta sheets can then be filled with meat, cheese or vegetable stuffing; later, they can be covered and baked with a sauce over top so the pasta does not dry out.

4 To store the pasta sheets, layer them with plastic or wax paper. Fresh pasta is best cooked immediately, but can be stored in the refrigerator for up to 1 week, or in the freezer for as long as 2 months.

Ravioli and tortellini

1 Prepare the desired filling and set aside. Roll the pasta dough into strips approximately 12 inches (30 cm) long and 4 inches (10 cm) wide. Keep unused strips covered with a damp towel.

2 Brush each strip of dough with a little beaten egg. Place a small amount of filling (approximately 1/2 tsp [2 mL]) at intervals of 1 1/2 inches (4 cm) on the pasta.

3 Lay a second sheet over top and press down firmly. For square shapes, cut between the fillings with a knife, pastry wheel, or special pasta cutter.

4 For round shapes, cut circles about 1 to 2 inches (2.5 to 5 cm) in diameter. For tortellini, cut 2-inch (5 cm) circles, and place a small amount of filling in one half of the circle. Fold the pasta and crimp the edges together.

starters

pasta pizza
with goat cheese and caramelized onions

1 In a large nonstick saucepan sprayed with vegetable spray, cook onions and garlic over medium heat for 10 minutes. Add brown sugar and balsamic vinegar; reduce heat to medium-low. Cook, stirring occasionally, for 25 minutes or until golden brown and tender.

2 Meanwhile, in a large pot of boiling water, cook rice noodles for 5 minutes or until tender; drain. Rinse with cold water; drain well. In a bowl combine noodles, egg, milk and Parmesan cheese; stir well. Pour into prepared springform pan. Bake in preheated oven for 20 minutes; remove from oven. Set oven heat to broil.

3 Spread onion mixture over baked noodles; dot with goat cheese. Broil for 8 minutes or until cheese is melted.

PREHEAT OVEN TO 375° F (190° C)
9-INCH (2.5 L) SPRINGFORM PAN SPRAYED WITH VEGETABLE SPRAY

2	large sweet white onions (such as Spanish, Vidalia or Bermuda), sliced	2
2 tsp	minced garlic	10 mL
2 tbsp	packed brown sugar	25 mL
1 tbsp	balsamic vinegar	15 mL
6 oz	wide rice noodles, broken	175 g
1	large egg	1
1/3 cup	low-fat milk	75 mL
3 tbsp	grated low-fat Parmesan cheese	45 mL
2 oz	goat cheese	50 g

starters

32

essential numbers

PER SERVING

Calories	185
Protein	7 g
Fat, total	4 g
Fat, saturated	2.5 g
Carbohydrates	30 g
Sodium	119 mg
Cholesterol	44 mg
Fiber	2 g

ask ROSE

What's a pasta pizza? Simple — a pizza with a crust of pasta, not bread!

The success of this dish depends on using the sweetest onions you can find. Try varieties such as Spanish, Bermuda or Vidalia. They're all perfect — strong in flavor but not as pungent as standard yellow onions, and sweet enough to be eaten raw. Remember to store onions in a dry, dark and cool place; avoid using plastic bags.

nutrition watch

Onion power

Onions may do more than bring a tear to your eye. Natural chemicals in this vegetable may help prevent heart disease and certain cancers. These strong-smelling sulfur compounds (the ones that make you cry) may prevent the formation of blood clots and raise the level of HDL (good) cholesterol in your bloodstream. It seems they can also block the action of cancer-causing substances. A Dutch study found that people who ate at least half an onion each day had a 50% lower risk of stomach cancer than people who didn't eat any onions.

fettuccine baskets with zucchini parmesan (page 34)

prosciutto risotto
with chicken and oyster mushrooms

1 In a nonstick frying pan sprayed with vegetable spray or on a preheated grill, cook chicken over medium-high heat, turning once, for 12 minutes or until cooked through. Shred or cube chicken; set aside.

2 In a saucepan sprayed with vegetable spray, cook leeks and garlic over medium-high heat for 3 minutes or until softened. Add mushrooms; cook, stirring occasionally, for 5 minutes or until vegetables are tender. Add rice; cook, stirring, for 1 minute. Add wine; cook for 1 minute or until liquid is absorbed. Add 1/2 cup (125 mL) hot stock; cook, stirring, until liquid is absorbed.

3 Continue to add stock 1/2 cup (125 mL) at a time, stirring constantly, for 18 minutes or until rice is tender and liquid is absorbed. Reduce heat as necessary to maintain an active but slow simmer. Add chicken, prosciutto and Parmesan cheese. Serve immediately.

4 oz	boneless skinless chicken breast	125 g
1 1/2 cups	chopped leeks	375 mL
1 1/2 tsp	minced garlic	7 mL
3 cups	sliced oyster mushrooms	750 mL
1 cup	Arborio rice (risotto rice)	250 mL
1/2 cup	dry white wine	125 mL
3 1/2 cups	hot CHICKEN STOCK (see recipe, page 50)	875 mL
1 1/2 oz	prosciutto, cut into thin strips	40 g
2 tbsp	grated low-fat Parmesan cheese	25 mL

starters

33

essential numbers		
PER SERVING		
Calories	330
Protein	16 g
Fat, total	2 g
Fat, saturated	1.1 g
Carbohydrates	57 g
Sodium	354 mg
Cholesterol	25 mg
Fiber	3 g

ask ROSE

Oyster mushrooms are one of my favorites. This fan-shaped mushroom can be wild or cultivated; its color varies from pale gray to dark brown.

These mushrooms have a robust yet mild flavor and a silky texture. I always use them when regular mushrooms are called for. When sautéed, they release very little liquid and have an almost meat-like texture.

Best of all, oyster mushrooms are among the more affordable wild varieties.

for the record

Rich rice

A creamy, rich risotto doesn't have to be high in fat! As you can see here, one serving of this tasty dish contains less than 1 tbsp (15 mL) added fat. The key to success is using the right rice, not cream or butter. The short, fat kernels of Arborio rice are higher in starch than long grain rice. It's the high starch content that makes the rice moist and sticky, giving risotto a wonderful creaminess without the fat.

udon noodle soup with chicken and dried mushrooms (page 68)

fettuccine baskets
with zucchini parmesan

1. In a pot of boiling water, cook fettuccine for 8 to 10 minutes or until tender but firm; drain. In a bowl combine pasta, egg, 1 tbsp (15 mL) Parmesan cheese, basil and oil. Spoon mixture into prepared muffin cups. Bake in preheated oven for 20 minutes. Transfer pasta baskets to baking sheet.

2. Meanwhile, in a nonstick frying pan sprayed with vegetable spray, cook zucchini over medium-high heat for 5 minutes or until golden and tender.

3. Spoon tomato sauce over pasta baskets. Top with zucchini slices; sprinkle with mozzarella cheese and remaining Parmesan cheese. Bake in preheated oven for 5 minutes or until cheese melts.

starters

34

PREHEAT OVEN TO 400° F (200° C)
12 MUFFIN CUPS SPRAYED WITH VEGETABLE SPRAY
BAKING SHEET

6 oz	fettuccine (regular or spinach), broken into pieces	175 g
1	large egg	1
2 tbsp	grated low-fat Parmesan cheese	25 mL
1/2 tsp	dried basil	2 mL
2 tsp	vegetable oil	10 mL
Half	small zucchini, thinly sliced	Half
1/2 cup	tomato pasta sauce	125 mL
1/2 cup	shredded low-fat mozzarella cheese	125 mL

essential numbers

PER SERVING

Calories	188
Protein	8 g
Fat, total	6 g
Fat, saturated	1.9 g
Carbohydrates	26 g
Sodium	197 mg
Cholesterol	32 mg
Fiber	1 g

ask ROSE

Watching your fat and cholesterol intake? Be careful of eggs! Sure, they're great sources of nutrition, but a large whole egg has 75 calories, 5 g fat and 213 mg of cholesterol. The culprit here is the yolk, which accounts for 59 of the calories and all of the fat and cholesterol. Egg whites, on the other hand, are pure protein and zero fat. So just substitute 2 egg whites for 1 whole egg and you'll never know the difference. Of course, you can still use whole eggs in moderation — as we do here, dividing one between 6 servings.

variations

For a totally different flavor and texture, try replacing the fettuccine with linguine or spaghetti and the zucchini with diced red or green bell peppers. In place of the tomato sauce, try 1/3 cup (75 mL) pesto or sun-dried tomato pesto and replace the mozzarella cheese with 1 oz (25 g) goat cheese. Mmmm — these new flavors are fantastic!

pasta pizza egg rolls

1. In a nonstick frying pan sprayed with vegetable spray, cook onions and garlic over medium-high heat for 3 minutes or until starting to brown. Add beef; cook, stirring to break up meat, for 3 minutes or until no longer pink. Add tomato sauce, basil and pepper; reduce heat to medium-low and cook for 5 minutes. Remove from heat.

2. In a pot of boiling water, cook pasta for 8 minutes or until tender but firm; drain. Rinse under cold running water; drain. In a bowl combine pasta and sauce; stir well. Add mozzarella cheese.

3. Place 1 egg roll wrapper on work surface with a corner pointing towards you. (Cover others with a cloth to prevent drying.) Brush edges of wrapper with water. Place about 3 tbsp (45 mL) filling in center. Fold lower corner up over filling; fold 2 side corners in over filling. Roll bundle away from you. Repeat with remaining wrappers.

4. Bake in preheated oven, turning at halfway point, for 15 to 20 minutes or until golden.

PREHEAT OVEN TO 425° F (220° C)
BAKING SHEET SPRAYED WITH VEGETABLE SPRAY

1/3 cup	chopped onions	75 mL
1 tsp	minced garlic	5 mL
6 oz	lean ground beef or chicken	175 g
3/4 cup	tomato pasta sauce	175 mL
1/2 tsp	dried basil	2 mL
1/4 tsp	freshly ground black pepper	1 mL
1/2 cup	small pasta (such as orzo, ditali or tubetti)	125 mL
1/2 cup	shredded low-fat mozzarella cheese	125 mL
12 to 14	large (5 1/2-inch [13.5 cm] square) egg roll wrappers	12 to 14

starters

35

PER EGG ROLL

Calories	140
Protein	7 g
Fat, total	3 g
Fat, saturated	1.0 g
Carbohydrates	21 g
Sodium	260 mg
Cholesterol	11 mg
Fiber	1 g

essential numbers

ask ROSE

For this recipe, should you use ground beef or ground chicken? Well, consider this: 4 oz (125 g) regular ground beef has 351 calories and 30 g fat, while the same amount of ground chicken has 180 calories and 12 g fat. What a difference! So if you really prefer the taste of beef, at least buy the extra-lean variety, which contains only 265 calories and 19 g fat per 4 oz (125 g).

nutrition watch

A clove a day...

Of more than 200 natural chemicals that may protect your health, garlic contains a sulfur compound called S-allyl cysteine (SAC), which has been shown to protect the heart and enhance the body's immune system. SAC is found in raw garlic in small amounts but increases dramatically when garlic is aged. Researchers at Penn State University found that if you let chopped garlic sit at room temperature for 10 minutes before cooking, the SAC content rises. Try cooking with a clove of garlic each day.

spinach egg rolls
with feta and rice

1 In a nonstick frying pan sprayed with vegetable spray, cook onions and garlic over medium heat for 3 minutes or until softened. Add spinach and mushrooms; cook, stirring, for 4 minutes. Remove from heat; add feta cheese, rice, ricotta cheese, lemon juice and oregano.

2 Place 1 egg roll wrapper on work surface with a corner pointing towards you. (Cover others with a cloth to prevent drying.) Brush edges of wrapper with water. Place about 3 tbsp (45 mL) filling in center. Fold lower corner up over filling; fold 2 side corners in over filling. Roll bundle away from you. Repeat with remaining wrappers.

3 Bake in preheated oven, turning at halfway point, for 15 to 20 minutes or until golden. Meanwhile, make the sauce: In a bowl combine sour cream, dill, water and lemon juice. Serve egg rolls with dipping sauce.

PREHEAT OVEN TO 425° F (220° C)
BAKING SHEET SPRAYED WITH VEGETABLE SPRAY

1/2 cup	chopped onions	125 mL
1 tsp	minced garlic	5 mL
Half	pkg (10 oz [300 g]) frozen spinach, cooked, squeezed dry and chopped	Half
1 1/4 cups	finely chopped oyster mushrooms	300 mL
2 1/2 oz	light feta cheese, crumbled	65 g
1 cup	cooked white rice (about 1/3 cup [75 mL] uncooked)	250 mL
1/2 cup	5% ricotta cheese	125 mL
1 tbsp	fresh lemon juice	15 mL
1 tsp	dried oregano	5 mL
12	large (5 1/2-inch [13.5 cm] square) egg roll wrappers	12

Sauce

1/3 cup	low-fat sour cream	75 mL
2 tbsp	chopped fresh dill (or 1/4 tsp [1 mL] dried)	25 mL
1 tbsp	water	15 mL
1 tsp	fresh lemon juice	5 mL

essential numbers

PER EGG ROLL

Calories	136
Protein	5 g
Fat, total	3 g
Fat, saturated	2.4 g
Carbohydrates	20 g
Sodium	222 mg
Cholesterol	12 mg
Fiber	1 g

ask ROSE

If you want to boost your fiber intake, substitute brown rice for white rice. It's the most nutritious because it is whole grain and contains bran. It's also high in B vitamins, has a nutty flavor and takes approximately 40 minutes to cook.

for the record

Attention egg roll lovers
Wow, what a difference from traditional egg rolls! Each of these has only 3 grams of fat — and that includes a little dipping sauce. Order your typical deep-fried egg roll at a Chinese restaurant and you'll be getting 11 grams of fat (56% calories from fat)! That's almost 3 tsp (15 mL) of oil in just one appetizer. The next time you order an egg roll, save a little fat by soaking up some of the grease with your napkin. And don't forget to order rice and steamed veggies!

tortilla bites
stuffed with chicken, pasta and peanut sauce

1 In a nonstick frying pan sprayed with vegetable spray or on a preheated grill, cook chicken over medium-high heat, turning once, for 12 minutes or until cooked through; cut into thin slices.

2 In a pot of boiling water, cook noodles for 5 minutes or until soft; drain. Rinse under cold running water; chop noodles.

3 In a nonstick frying pan sprayed with vegetable spray, cook red peppers and snow peas over medium-high heat for 3 minutes or until tender-crisp. Remove from heat; add chicken, noodles, green onions and coriander.

4 In a bowl combine peanut butter, water, vinegar, honey, sesame oil, soya sauce, garlic, ginger and chili sauce; whisk well. Add 1/4 cup (50 mL) sauce to vegetable-noodle mixture.

5 Spread about 3/4 cup (175 mL) vegetable-noodle mixture evenly over each tortilla; roll up. Cut each tortilla diagonally into 4 pieces. Wrap in plastic and chill or serve warm with remaining peanut sauce for dipping.

4 oz	boneless skinless chicken breast	125 g
2 oz	wide rice noodles	50 g
1 1/4 cups	julienned red bell peppers	300 mL
1 1/4 cups	julienned snow peas	300 mL
1/2 cup	chopped green onions	125 mL
1/3 cup	chopped fresh coriander	75 mL

Peanut sauce

3 tbsp	peanut butter	45 mL
3 tbsp	water	45 mL
1 1/2 tbsp	rice wine vinegar	20 mL
1 1/2 tbsp	honey	20 mL
1 tbsp	sesame oil	15 mL
1 tbsp	light soya sauce	15 mL
1 1/2 tsp	minced garlic	7 mL
1 1/2 tsp	minced ginger root	7 mL
3/4 tsp	hot Asian chili sauce (optional)	4 mL
6	8-inch (20 cm) flour tortillas	6

starters

37

essential numbers

PER SERVING

Calories	276
Protein	11 g
Fat, total	10 g
Fat, saturated	1.8 g
Carbohydrates	37 g
Sodium	350 mg
Cholesterol	12 mg
Fiber	3 g

ask ROSE

If peanut allergies are a concern, there are a number of good substitutes for the peanut butter used in the sauce. Try soya nut butter, which is made from dry-roasted soya beans. It's "soya good," you won't know the difference! Other great-tasting nut butters include those made from almonds, pecans — even macadamias! Try making your own nut butters by puréeing roasted dried nuts with some oil until the mixture forms a smooth consistency.

lifestyle

Don't think of these tortilla bites just as party appetizers — they make a great dinner for the entire family. Don't bother slicing them; just "wrap and roll" and enjoy. Make early in the day, cover and serve at room temperature or heat in the oven at 400° F (200° C) for 10 minutes.

hoisin beef egg rolls

1 In a bowl combine ground beef, bread crumbs, coriander and egg; set aside.

2 In a food processor or blender, combine hoisin sauce, coriander, honey, mayonnaise, vinegar, soya sauce, sesame oil, garlic and ginger; process until smooth. Add 1/3 cup (75 mL) sauce to beef mixture.

3 Place 1 egg roll wrapper on work surface with a corner pointing towards you. (Cover others with a cloth to prevent drying.) Brush edges of wrapper with water. Place about 1 tbsp (15 mL) filling in center. Fold lower corner up over filling; fold 2 side corners in over filling. Roll bundle away from you. Repeat with remaining wrappers.

4 Bake in preheated oven, turning at halfway point, for 15 to 20 minutes or until golden. Serve with remaining sauce for dipping.

PREHEAT OVEN TO 425° F (220° C)
BAKING SHEET SPRAYED WITH VEGETABLE SPRAY

12 oz	lean ground beef	375 g
3 tbsp	plain dried bread crumbs	45 mL
2 tbsp	chopped fresh coriander	25 mL
1	large egg	1

Sauce

1/4 cup	hoisin sauce	50 mL
2 tbsp	chopped fresh coriander	25 mL
2 tbsp	honey	25 mL
2 tbsp	light mayonnaise	25 mL
2 tbsp	rice wine vinegar	25 mL
2 tbsp	light soya sauce	25 mL
1 tbsp	sesame oil	15 mL
2 tsp	minced garlic	10 mL
1 1/2 tsp	minced ginger root	7 mL
32	small (3-inch [8 cm] square) egg roll wrappers	32

essential numbers

PER SERVING

Calories	365
Protein	18 g
Fat, total	15 g
Fat, saturated	4.6 g
Carbohydrates	38 g
Sodium	674 mg
Cholesterol	75 mg
Fiber	0 g

ask ROSE

Hoisin sauce, also called "Peking sauce," is a thick, reddish-brown, sweet-and-spicy sauce widely used in Chinese cooking. It's a mixture of soybeans, garlic, chili peppers and various spices. The sauce keeps indefinitely in the refrigerator and can be purchased in the international section of your supermarket.

nutrition watch

Wok your way to health

North Americans can certainly learn a few nutrition pointers from the Chinese. Compared with our typical "meat and potatoes" fare, the traditional Chinese diet provides half the fat and triple the fiber. Studies show that the Chinese also enjoy lower blood cholesterol levels, fewer heart attacks and less colon cancer. The secret? More starch (like rice or noodles) and only small amounts of meat, with plenty of vegetables and fruits, and flavor-boosters like ginger, garlic, hoisin, oyster, bean and plum sauce — instead of fat-laden gravies, butter or sour cream.

shrimp risotto
with artichoke hearts and parmesan

1. In a saucepan over medium-high heat, bring stock to a boil; reduce heat to low. In another nonstick saucepan sprayed with vegetable spray, cook onions and garlic over medium-high heat for 3 minutes or until softened. Add rice and basil; cook for 1 minute.

2. Using a ladle, add 1/2 cup (125 mL) stock to rice; stir to keep rice from sticking to pan. When liquid is absorbed, add another 1/2 cup (125 mL) stock. Reduce heat if necessary to maintain a slow, steady simmer. Repeat this process, ladling in hot stock and stirring constantly, for 15 minutes, reducing amount of stock added to 1/4 cup (50 mL) near end of cooking time.

3. Add artichokes and shrimp; cook, adding more stock as necessary, for 3 minutes or until shrimp turn pink and rice is tender but firm. Add green onions, Parmesan cheese and pepper. Serve immediately.

3 cups	SEAFOOD STOCK *or* CHICKEN STOCK (see recipes, page 50)	750 mL
1/2 cup	chopped onions	125 mL
2 tsp	minced garlic	10 mL
1 cup	Arborio rice (risotto rice)	250 mL
1 tsp	dried basil	5 mL
Half	can (14 oz [398 mL]) artichoke hearts, drained and chopped	Half
8 oz	raw shrimp, shelled and chopped	250 g
1/4 cup	chopped green onions	50 mL
1/4 cup	grated low-fat Parmesan cheese	50 mL
1/4 tsp	freshly ground black pepper	1 mL

starters

39

essential numbers

PER SERVING

Calories	174
Protein	19 g
Fat, total	3 g
Fat, saturated	1.4 g
Carbohydrates	15 g
Sodium	300 mg
Cholesterol	93 mg
Fiber	1 g

ask ROSE

If you haven't got the time or ingredients necessary to make seafood stock from scratch, you can buy it canned or in powdered form (1 tsp [5 mL] in 1 cup [250 mL] boiling water yields 1 cup [250 mL] stock). Keep in mind, however, that these stocks are often loaded with sodium. To cut back on the sodium, try using only 1/2 tsp (2 mL) powder — or try my SEAFOOD STOCK (see recipe, page 50), which has no added salt at all!

for the record

Bring on the shellfish

If you have high blood cholesterol, don't worry about enjoying shrimp! Yes, they are fairly high in cholesterol. But for most people, cholesterol in foods has little or no effect on blood cholesterol. What counts the most is *saturated fat* (found in animal foods and processed foods with hydrogenated oils) which your body uses as a building block for blood cholesterol. And seafood contains very little saturated fat. In fact, a 3-oz (75 g) serving of shrimp has less than 1 g fat. The same goes for lobster!

greek couscous cakes

1   In a saucepan over high heat, bring stock to a boil. Add couscous; remove from heat. Let stand, covered, for 5 minutes or until liquid is absorbed and grain is tender. Fluff with a fork; set aside to cool.

2   In a bowl combine cooled couscous, red peppers, green onions, red onions, black olives, garlic, oregano, feta cheese, egg whites, whole egg and lemon juice. Form each 1/3 cup (75 mL) mixture into a flat patty, squeezing together in your hands. Place patties on prepared baking sheet. Bake in preheated oven, turning at halfway point, for 20 minutes or until golden.

3   Meanwhile, make the sauce: In a bowl combine sour cream, dill, lemon juice and garlic. Serve warm patties with sauce.

PREHEAT OVEN TO 425° F (220° C)
BAKING SHEET SPRAYED WITH VEGETABLE SPRAY

1 1/2 cups	VEGETABLE STOCK or CHICKEN STOCK (see recipes, pages 51 and 50)	375 mL
1 cup	couscous	250 mL
1/2 cup	minced red bell peppers	125 mL
1/3 cup	minced green onions	75 mL
1/3 cup	minced red onions	75 mL
1/4 cup	minced black olives	50 mL
1 tsp	minced garlic	5 mL
1 tsp	dried oregano	5 mL
1 1/2 oz	light feta cheese, crumbled	40 g
2	large egg whites	2
1	large egg	1
2 tbsp	fresh lemon juice	25 mL

Sauce

1/2 cup	low-fat sour cream	125 mL
2 tsp	chopped fresh dill (or 1/8 tsp [0.5 mL] dried)	10 mL
1 tsp	fresh lemon juice	5 mL
1/4 tsp	minced garlic	1 mL

starters

40

essential numbers

PER SERVING

Calories	216
Protein	9 g
Fat, total	6 g
Fat, saturated	2.8 g
Carbohydrates	31 g
Sodium	150 mg
Cholesterol	49 mg
Fiber	2 g

ask ROSE

While relatively new in the U.S. and Canada, couscous has been a staple of North African cuisine for centuries. It is made with coarsely ground semolina — a hard wheat flour used for pasta.

Couscous is loaded with fiber, vitamins and minerals. For extra flavor, try cooking it with stock or tomato sauce. It's a wonderful replacement for pasta, rice or other grains.

lifestyle

These cakes make terrific vegetarian burgers! Just place in a pita lined with lettuce, tomatoes and onions. Drizzle with sauce and serve.

shrimp potstickers
with peanut sauce

1. Peanut sauce: In a food processor or in a bowl with a whisk, combine peanut butter, water, coriander, honey, vinegar, soya sauce, sesame oil, ginger and garlic; set aside.

2. Filling: In a food processor combine shrimp, garlic, green onion, coriander and 2 tbsp (25 mL) of the peanut sauce; pulse on and off 10 times or until well-mixed.

3. Place 2 tsp (10 mL) filling in center of each wrapper. Pull edges up, pleating and bunching; press together to seal.

4. In a large nonstick frying pan sprayed with vegetable spray, cook potstickers, flat-side down, over medium-high heat for 3 minutes or until golden brown on bottom. Add stock; reduce heat to low. Cook, covered, for 2 minutes or until cooked through. Remove from pan; discard any remaining liquid. Serve with remaining peanut sauce for dipping.

Peanut sauce

2 tbsp	peanut butter	25 mL
2 tbsp	water	25 mL
2 tbsp	chopped fresh coriander	25 mL
1 tbsp	honey	15 mL
1 tbsp	rice wine vinegar	15 mL
2 tsp	light soya sauce	10 mL
1 tsp	sesame oil	5 mL
1/2 tsp	minced ginger root	2 mL
1/2 tsp	minced garlic	2 mL

Filling

8 oz	raw shrimp, peeled, deveined and diced	250 g
1	clove garlic, minced	1
1	medium green onion, chopped	1
2 tbsp	chopped fresh coriander	25 mL
26	3-inch (8 cm) square small egg roll wrappers	26
3/4 cup	SEAFOOD STOCK or CHICKEN STOCK (see recipes, page 50)	175 mL

starters

41

essential numbers

PER SERVING	
Calories	496
Protein	22 g
Fat, total	6 g
Fat, saturated	1.0 g
Carbohydrates	88 g
Sodium	753 mg
Cholesterol	72 mg
Fiber	0 g

ask ROSE

Fresh coriander leaves — also known as cilantro or Chinese parsley — has an intense flavor that is common in Indian, Mexican, Caribbean and Asian cuisine. It's a flavor you either love or hate. And if you love it, chances are you can't get enough. If it's not to your taste, substitute fresh parsley, dill or basil.

cooking 101

When you purchase frozen shrimp in the shell, be sure to buy a little more than is called for in the recipe. By the time you defrost and devein the shrimp, it will weigh less.

chicken cacciatore

over crisp barley crust

1 Crust: In a nonstick saucepan over high heat, bring stock to a boil. Add barley; reduce heat to medium-low. Cook, covered, for 45 to 50 minutes or until grain is tender and liquid absorbed; cool for 10 minutes. Add milk, egg whites, Parmesan cheese and basil. Press mixture into bottom of prepared springform pan. Bake in preheated oven for 25 minutes or until golden at edges and firm on top; remove from oven.

2 Meanwhile, make the topping: In a nonstick saucepan sprayed with vegetable spray, cook onions and garlic over medium-high heat for 3 minutes or until softened and lightly browned. Add mushrooms and green peppers; cook for 3 minutes or until softened. Add crushed tomatoes, stock, tomato paste, bay leaf, brown sugar, chili powder and Italian seasoning. Bring to a boil; reduce heat to medium. Cook, uncovered, for 20 minutes, stirring occasionally. Add chicken; cook for 3 minutes or until cooked through. Spread mixture over baked crust. Sprinkle with Parmesan cheese. Bake in preheated oven for 10 minutes.

PREHEAT OVEN TO 400° F (200° C)
9-INCH (2 L) SPRINGFORM PAN SPRAYED WITH VEGETABLE SPRAY

Crust

3 cups	CHICKEN STOCK (see recipe, page 50)	750 mL
3/4 cup	pearl barley	175 mL
3 tbsp	low-fat milk	45 mL
2	large egg whites	2
1 tbsp	grated low-fat Parmesan cheese	15 mL
1/2 tsp	dried basil	2 mL

Topping

1 cup	chopped onions	250 mL
1	clove garlic, minced	1
1 cup	chopped mushrooms	250 mL
1 cup	chopped green bell peppers	250 mL
1	can (19 oz [540 mL]) tomatoes, crushed	1
1/2 cup	CHICKEN STOCK	125 mL
2 tbsp	tomato paste	25 mL
1	bay leaf	1
2 tsp	packed brown sugar	10 mL
1/2 tsp	chili powder	2 mL
1 tsp	dried Italian seasoning	5 mL
4 oz	boneless skinless chicken breast, cut into 1/2-inch (1 cm) cubes	125 g
2 tbsp	grated low-fat Parmesan cheese	25 mL

essential numbers

PER SERVING

Calories	177
Protein	12 g
Fat, total	3 g
Fat, saturated	1.1 g
Carbohydrates	28 g
Sodium	200 mg
Cholesterol	15 mg
Fiber	6 g

ask ROSE

People have been enjoying barley since 7000 B.C. Now there's a food with history! And while it is traditionally associated with soups, barley is (as we see here) much more versatile.

Pearl barley, the most common variety, has the bran and germ removed, and cooks relatively fast. Pot barley has more of the bran left on and requires a longer cooking time.

nutrition watch

Fiber 101

Looking for a delicious source of fiber? Just one serving of this recipe provides 25% of your recommended daily fiber intake (25 to 35 g). Insoluble fibers in wheat bran and whole grains help prevent bowel disorders, while soluble fibers in oats, barley, legumes and citrus fruit can help to lower blood cholesterol levels.

pizza pasta
with savory wild mushrooms

1. In a pot of boiling water, cook fettuccine for 8 to 10 minutes or until tender but firm; drain. In a bowl combine pasta, egg, milk and 3 tbsp (45 mL) Parmesan cheese. Spread over bottom of prepared springform pan. Bake in preheated oven for 20 minutes or until golden and set.

2. Meanwhile, in a large nonstick frying pan sprayed with vegetable spray, cook onions and garlic over medium-high heat for 3 minutes or until softened. Add mushrooms; cook, stirring often, for 5 minutes or until golden. Add evaporated milk, black olives, basil and feta cheese; reduce heat to low. Simmer for 2 minutes, stirring occasionally.

3. Spread vegetable mixture over baked crust; sprinkle with Parmesan cheese. Bake in preheated oven for 10 minutes.

PREHEAT OVEN TO 400° F (200° C)
9-INCH (2.5 L) SPRINGFORM PAN SPRAYED WITH VEGETABLE SPRAY

6 oz	fettuccine (regular or whole wheat), broken into pieces	175 g
1	large egg	1
1/3 cup	low-fat milk	75 mL
3 tbsp	grated low-fat Parmesan cheese	45 mL
1/2 cup	chopped onions	125 mL
1 1/2 tsp	minced garlic	7 mL
3 cups	chopped wild mushrooms	750 mL
1/2 cup	low-fat evaporated milk	125 mL
1/3 cup	sliced black olives	75 mL
1 tsp	dried basil	5 mL
2 oz	light feta cheese, crumbled	50 g
1 tbsp	grated low-fat Parmesan cheese	15 mL

starters

43

PER SERVING

essential numbers

Calories	233
Protein	11 g
Fat, total	8 g
Fat, saturated	3 g
Carbohydrates	30 g
Sodium	335 mg
Cholesterol	51 mg
Fiber	1 g

ask ROSE

For the wild mushrooms called for here, I'd recommend varieties such as portobello, oyster, brown or cremini. Yes, they're more expensive than the common mushroom, but they're still affordable. If you want real luxury, try the crème de la crème of mushrooms: porcini, chanterelles, shiitake or morels. Now these really are pricey! But they have an incredible flavor and texture. Use them if you can.

for the record

Evaporating the fat
You can cut huge amounts of fat in any recipe that calls for whipping (35%) cream by substituting evaporated milk. One-half cup (125 mL) evaporated 2% milk has only 2.5 g fat. Compare that to 1/2 cup (125 mL) of whipping cream at 44 g fat. Yikes! And here's another reason to use evaporated milk instead of cream — it has almost 3 times more calcium. In fact, just one serving of this recipe has 205 mg of calcium. It's good for your heart and good for your bones!

noodle pancake
with sun-dried tomatoes, goat cheese and basil

1 In a bowl cover sun-dried tomatoes with boiling water. Let sit for 15 minutes; drain and chop.

2 In a bowl cover noodles with boiling water. Let stand for 5 minutes; drain. Add egg white, sesame oil and green onion; mix well.

3 In a nonstick frying pan sprayed with vegetable spray, cook noodle mixture over medium-high heat, flattening with a spatula, for 4 minutes or until golden on bottom. Carefully turn pancake; cook for 3 minutes or until golden. Transfer to baking sheet.

4 In a bowl combine goat cheese, sun-dried tomatoes and basil; mash with a fork. Spread mixture over pancake. Bake in preheated oven for 5 minutes or until cheese melts. Cut into wedges; serve.

PREHEAT OVEN TO 400° F (200° C)
NONSTICK BAKING SHEET

1/2 cup	dry-packed sun-dried tomatoes	125 mL
4 oz	fresh thin chow mein noodles	125 g
1	large egg white, beaten	1
1 tsp	sesame oil	5 mL
1	large green onion, thinly sliced	1
2 1/2 oz	goat cheese	65 g
1/2 tsp	dried basil	2 mL

starters

44

essential numbers

PER SERVING

Calories	175
Protein	7 g
Fat, total	9 g
Fat, saturated	3.3 g
Carbohydrates	18 g
Sodium	366 mg
Cholesterol	7 mg
Fiber	1 g

ask ROSE

Chow mein noodles are thin, yellow wheat noodles made with eggs. They are available in the refrigerated section of Asian markets and grocery stores. Don't confuse these noodles with the deep-fried chow mein sold in packages — they contain a *lot* of oil. Be sure to read the labels!

nutrition watch

Tomato power

Ounce for ounce, sun-dried tomatoes pack more nutrients and antioxidants than their fresh counterparts. One such antioxidant is lycopene, a natural chemical that makes tomatoes bright red and protects them from disease. It appears that a lycopene-rich diet might also keep us healthy. A Harvard study found that men who ate 10 or more servings of tomato-based foods a week had a 35% lower risk of prostate cancer compared to those who ate only one serving.

rice paper wraps

with creamy crabmeat

1 In a bowl combine crabmeat, celery, red onions and red peppers. In another bowl combine sour cream, dill, mayonnaise, lemon juice, garlic and mustard; add to crab mixture. Set aside.

2 Fill a shallow baking dish with cold water. Soak 4 rice paper wrappers at a time for 3 minutes; transfer to work surface. Pat dry. Lay 1 lettuce leaf over wrapper; top with about 2 tbsp (25 mL) filling. Fold bottom third of rice paper up over center. Tightly roll from left to right. Repeat with remaining wrappers.

8 oz	cooked crabmeat or surimi *or* cooked shrimp, chopped	250 g
1/3 cup	finely chopped celery	75 mL
1/3 cup	finely chopped red onions	75 mL
1/3 cup	finely chopped red bell peppers	75 mL
1/4 cup	low-fat sour cream	50 mL
3 tbsp	chopped fresh dill (or 1/2 tsp [2 mL] dried)	45 mL
2 tbsp	light mayonnaise	25 mL
2 tsp	fresh lemon juice	10 mL
1/2 tsp	minced garlic	2 mL
1/2 tsp	Dijon mustard	2 mL
16	6-inch (15 cm) rice paper wrappers	16
16	Boston lettuce leaves, washed	16

starters

45

essential numbers	PER SERVING	
	Calories	345
	Protein	17 g
	Fat, total	6 g
	Fat, saturated	1.5 g
	Carbohydrates	58 g
	Sodium	175 mg
	Cholesterol	23 mg
	Fiber	6 g

ask ROSE

Rice paper is a flat, dry sheet of rice pasta — perfect for rolling. These sheets are thin and fragile, however, so you need to handle them carefully. The best way to prepare them is to lay 4 at a time in a pan of cold water for 3 to 4 minutes or until softened. (If you soak them in hot water, they tend to crack.) Pat dry, add filling and start rolling immediately.

lifestyle

These wraps make gorgeous looking appetizers for your next dinner party. Wrap them tightly, making sure to expose the lettuce leaf. These can be made early in the day. Cover with plastic wrap.

smoked salmon
wrapped in rice paper with cheese and chives

starters

1. In a food processor combine ricotta cheese, cream cheese, chives, dill, mayonnaise, lemon juice and garlic; process until smooth. Add smoked salmon; set aside.

2. Fill a baking dish with cold water. Soak 4 rice paper wrappers at a time for 3 minutes; place on work surface. Pat dry. Spread 2 tbsp (25 mL) filling over surface; top with 1 lettuce leaf. Fold bottom third of wrapper up over center; tightly roll from left to right. Repeat process with remaining wrappers.

Amount	Ingredient	Metric
1 cup	5% ricotta cheese	250 mL
3 tbsp	light cream cheese, softened	45 mL
3 tbsp	chopped fresh chives	45 mL
2 1/2 tbsp	chopped fresh dill (or 1/2 tsp [2 mL] dried)	35 mL
1 1/2 tbsp	light mayonnaise	20 mL
1 1/2 tbsp	fresh lemon juice	20 mL
1/2 tsp	minced garlic	2 mL
3 oz	smoked salmon, chopped	75 g
12	6-inch (15 cm) rice paper wrappers	12
12	Boston lettuce leaves, washed	12

46

essential numbers

PER SERVING	
Calories	336
Protein	17 g
Fat, total	12 g
Fat, saturated	5.0 g
Carbohydrates	42 g
Sodium	383 mg
Cholesterol	32 mg
Fiber	4 g

ask ROSE

Ricotta cheese is a rich, fresh cheese that is smoother than cottage cheese. It's white, moist and has a slightly sweet flavor. Available in 5% and 10% varieties, I use it as a substitute for cream cheese. (Regular cream cheese is 35% fat!)

I like to use ricotta cheese from a tub because it's smoother. If you buy a drier version, add a little low-fat milk to give it a smoother consistency.

for the record

Where's the cheese?

If you've been spreading your bagels with cream cheese thinking you're adding protein and calcium to your diet, think again! One tbsp (15 mL) of regular cream cheese gives you 1 measly gram of protein and only 12 mg calcium. Compare that to 1 oz (25 g) of real cheese at 7 g protein and 216 mg calcium. With 86% of its calories coming from fat (and mostly saturated fat), treat cream cheese like a spreadable fat. A good reason to use light cream cheese!

beef potstickers

with coconut sauce

1 In a bowl combine ground beef, green onions, oyster sauce, rice wine vinegar, sesame oil, garlic and ginger. Place 2 tsp (10 mL) filling in center of each wrapper. Pull edges up, pleating and bunching. Press edges together to seal.

2 In another bowl, combine coconut milk, green onions, water, coriander, rice wine vinegar and oyster sauce; whisk well.

3 In a large nonstick frying pan sprayed with vegetable spray, cook potstickers, flat-side down, over medium-high heat for 3 minutes or until golden brown on bottom. Add sauce; reduce heat to low. Cook, covered, for 3 minutes or until cooked through. Serve with sauce remaining in pan.

6 oz	lean ground beef	175 g
1/4 cup	finely chopped green onions	50 mL
1 tbsp	oyster sauce	15 mL
2 tsp	rice wine vinegar	10 mL
1 tsp	sesame oil	5 mL
1 tsp	minced garlic	5 mL
1/2 tsp	minced ginger root	2 mL
18 to 20	small (3-inch [8 cm]) egg roll wrappers	18 to 20

Sauce

1/3 cup	light coconut milk	75 mL
1/4 cup	chopped green onions	50 mL
3 tbsp	water	45 mL
2 tbsp	chopped fresh coriander	25 mL
1 tbsp	rice wine vinegar	15 mL
1 tbsp	oyster sauce	15 mL

starters

47

essential numbers

PER SERVING

Calories	330
Protein	16 g
Fat, total	2 g
Fat, saturated	1.1 g
Carbohydrates	57 g
Sodium	654 mg
Cholesterol	25 mg
Fiber	3 g

ask ROSE

Oyster sauce is a dark brown sauce made from oysters (big surprise there), brine seasoning and soya sauce, which is cooked until thick. It's a staple of Asian cooking and adds richness to any dish.

for the record

A high-fat milk

It sure pays to use light coconut milk when you consider that 1/2 cup (125 mL) of the regular stuff packs 307 calories and 30 g fat! That's equivalent to 7 1/2 tsp (38 mL) of added fat. And here's more bad news: 90% of the oil in coconut milk is saturated. The good news is that you'll save 20 g fat by substituting light coconut milk. And use a little less. After all, who needs a lot when it adds so much flavor?

ps

super stocks

for chicken, beef or seafood

1. In a saucepan over medium-high heat, combine water, chicken pieces (or beef bones or fish/seafood pieces), carrot, onion, celery, garlic, pepper, salt, parsley and bay leaves. Bring to a boil, skimming any foam that rises to the top. Cover, reduce heat to low; simmer for 1 1/2 hours.

2. Pour mixture through a strainer; discard solids. Refrigerate stock until cold; skim fat off surface. Stock can be refrigerated for up to 3 days or frozen in an air-tight container.

6 cups	water	1.5 L
2	large chicken pieces (breasts or thighs) *or* 1 1/2 lbs (750 g) beef bones or 1 1/2 lbs (750 g) fish or seafood pieces*	2
1	large carrot, peeled and chopped	1
1	medium onion, quartered	1
1	large celery stalk, chopped	1
3	large cloves garlic	3
1/4 tsp	freshly ground black pepper	1 mL
1/8 tsp	salt	0.5 mL
1/2 cup	chopped parsley	125 mL
2	bay leaves	2

ask ROSE

The advantage of making your own stock is that the flavor is richer and more intense. As well, there is virtually no sodium — particularly when compared to commercially prepared bouillon, which contains about 780 mg sodium per 1 cup (250 mL) serving!

cooking 101

* For fish or seafood stock, use whatever pieces you can find — including fish heads and bones, shrimp shells, or unused pieces of flesh.

vegetable stock

1. In a saucepan over medium-high heat, combine water, potato, celery, leeks, onion, parsley, garlic, bay leaves, pepper and salt; bring to a boil. Reduce heat to low; simmer, covered, for 1 1/2 hours.

2. Pour mixture through a strainer; discard solids. Refrigerate stock until cold. Stock can be kept, refrigerated, for up to 3 days or frozen in an air-tight container.

6 cups	water	1.5 L
1	large sweet potato, diced	1
2	large celery stalks, chopped	2
2	large leeks, cleaned and sliced	2
1	large onion, chopped	1
1/2 cup	chopped parsley	125 mL
2	large cloves garlic	2
2	bay leaves	2
1/4 tsp	freshly ground black pepper	1 mL
1/8 tsp	salt	0.5 mL

soups

51

ask ROSE

Here's the perfect stock for all you vegetarians out there. It keeps for up to 6 months if frozen in air-tight containers.

for the record

Fill 'er up!

If you're looking for a snack to keep you going until dinner, try heating a mug of broth. What about fat and calories? Well, here's a nice surprise — 1 cup (250 mL) chicken or vegetable stock contains only 31 calories and zero fat. (Beef broth has just 1 g fat.) Broth is more filling than snacking crackers, and much better for you. Use homemade broth or a can of the sodium-reduced variety.

sweet potato soup

with split peas and ham

1 In a nonstick saucepan sprayed with vegetable spray, cook onions, carrots and garlic over medium-high heat for 3 minutes or until softened. Add stock, sweet potatoes and split peas; bring to a boil. Reduce heat to medium-low; cook, covered, for 40 minutes or until split peas are tender.

2 Transfer mixture to a food processor; purée until smooth. Return soup to saucepan. Add pasta and ham; cook over medium heat, covered, for 8 minutes or until pasta is tender.

3/4 cup	chopped onions	175 mL
3/4 cup	chopped carrots	175 mL
1 1/2 tsp	minced garlic	7 mL
6 1/2 cups	CHICKEN STOCK or BEEF STOCK (see recipes, page 50)	1.625 L
1 1/2 cups	diced sweet potatoes	375 mL
3/4 cup	dried yellow split peas	175 mL
1/3 cup	small soup pasta (such as orzo or ditali)	75 mL
1 cup	diced cooked ham	250 mL

soups

52

essential numbers

PER SERVING

Calories	289
Protein	17 g
Fat, total	2 g
Fat, saturated	2.4 g
Carbohydrates	41 g
Sodium	200 mg
Cholesterol	28 mg
Fiber	2 g

ask ROSE

When buying ham for this recipe, make sure it's described on the label as "fully cooked" or "ready-to-eat." Most store-bought cooked ham has been smoked to give it a rich and juicy flavor, yet it takes on other flavors when added to soup — or any other recipe. For economy's sake, buy a large ham and freeze any unused portions.

nutrition watch

Grade-A soup

Thanks to the carrots and sweet potato, one serving of this soup supplies 130% of your daily vitamin A requirement. These foods contain beta carotene, which your body converts to vitamin A — an essential nutrient for normal vision, cell division and growth, building immune compounds that fight infections, as well as healthy skin, bones and teeth. Beta carotene also acts as an antioxidant, protecting cells from damage caused by unstable free radical molecules, which scientists believe to play a role in the development of some cancers.

corn chowder

with wild rice and roasted peppers

1 In a nonstick saucepan sprayed with vegetable spray, cook onions and garlic over medium-high heat for 4 minutes or until softened. Add stock and wild rice; bring to a boil. Reduce heat to medium-low; cook, covered, for 15 minutes. Add potatoes, salt and pepper; cook, covered, for 20 minutes or until rice and potatoes are tender.

2 In a bowl whisk together evaporated milk and flour; add to soup. Add corn and roasted red peppers; cook for 3 minutes or until slightly thickened. Serve garnished with coriander.

1 cup	chopped onions	250 mL
1 1/2 tsp	minced garlic	7 mL
4 cups	VEGETABLE STOCK *or* CHICKEN STOCK (see recipes, pages 51 and 50)	1 L
1/3 cup	wild rice	75 mL
1 cup	diced peeled potatoes	250 mL
1/8 tsp	salt	0.5 mL
1/8 tsp	freshly ground black pepper	0.5 mL
3/4 cup	low-fat evaporated milk	175 mL
1 tbsp	all-purpose flour	15 mL
1	can (12 oz [341 mL]) corn, drained *or* 2 cups [500 mL] frozen corn, thawed	1
1/3 cup	chopped roasted red bell peppers	75 mL
1/3 cup	chopped fresh coriander, basil or dill	75 mL

soups

53

essential numbers

PER SERVING

Calories	218
Protein	10 g
Fat, total	3 g
Fat, saturated	1.0 g
Carbohydrates	42 g
Sodium	400 mg
Cholesterol	5 mg
Fiber	3 g

ask ROSE

Roasted red peppers taste wonderful, but they require some time to prepare. So when a recipe (like this one) calls for just a small amount, do what I do — use bottled roasted peppers. Look for those packaged in water (not oil) to avoid excess fat. Once opened, a jar of these peppers does not keep for very long, so freeze any unused peppers in small airtight containers.

nutrition watch

Beta carotene's kissing cousin

Corn is rich in lutein, an antioxidant compound related to the famous beta carotene. Research has linked a lutein-rich diet with reduced breast cancer risk: according to the Harvard Nurse's Health Study, higher intakes of lutein offered a strong protective effect for breast cancer in premenopausal women. Other good sources of lutein include kale, collard greens, spinach, Romaine lettuce and red bell peppers.

orzo soup
with caramelized onions and cheese

1 In a saucepan sprayed with vegetable spray, heat oil over medium heat. Add onions, brown sugar and garlic; reduce heat to medium-low. Cook, uncovered and stirring occasionally, for 30 minutes or until browned and tender.

2 Increase heat to medium-high. Add stock and thyme; bring to a boil. Add orzo; reduce heat to medium. Cook, covered, for 10 minutes or until pasta is tender.

3 Ladle soup into bowls; sprinkle evenly with Swiss cheese. Serve immediately.

2 tsp	vegetable oil	10 mL
2	large white onions, thinly sliced	2
1 tbsp	packed brown sugar	15 mL
2 tsp	minced garlic	10 mL
6 cups	VEGETABLE STOCK *or* CHICKEN STOCK (see recipes, pages 51 and 50)	1.5 L
3/4 tsp	dried thyme leaves	4 mL
2/3 cup	orzo or small-shaped pasta	150 mL
1/2 cup	shredded low-fat Swiss or mozzarella cheese	125 mL

soups

54

essential numbers

PER SERVING

Calories	168
Protein	8 g
Fat, total	5 g
Fat, saturated	2.0 g
Carbohydrates	24 g
Sodium	200 mg
Cholesterol	10 mg
Fiber	1 g

ask ROSE

Caramelizing onions slowly over low heat gives them a deliciously sweet intensity — and allows us to use less cheese than in traditional onion soup. While brown sugar is used here as the caramelizing agent, sweet vinegar (such as balsamic) also works. Want even more sweetness? Try using extra-sweet onion varieties such as Vidalia or Walla Walla. No matter what type of onions you use, be sure to stir occasionally to avoid burning.

for the record

Calcium heavyweights
Looking for a calcium-rich, hard cheese? Well, you can't go wrong with Swiss or Gruyère. Ounce for ounce, they both have more calcium than any other cheese. Compare the following calcium figures (per 1.5-oz [40 g] serving):

Gruyère	455 mg
Swiss	432 mg
Cheddar	325 mg
Mozzarella	242 mg
Feta	229 mg
Camembert	174 mg

Serves 4

hummus soup
with couscous and vegetables

1. In a nonstick saucepan sprayed with vegetable spray, cook onions and garlic over medium-high heat for 5 minutes or until softened. Add stock, 2 cups (500 mL) chickpeas, potatoes, carrots and tahini; bring to a boil. Reduce heat to medium-low; cook, covered, for 15 minutes or until potatoes are tender.

2. In a food processor or blender, purée soup in batches until smooth. Return to saucepan; bring to a boil. Remove from heat; add couscous and remaining 1/2 cup (125 mL) chickpeas. Let stand, covered, for 5 minutes. Add coriander; serve immediately.

3/4 cup	chopped onions	175 mL
2 tsp	minced garlic	10 mL
4 cups	VEGETABLE STOCK *or* CHICKEN STOCK (see recipes, pages 51 and 50)	1 L
2 1/2 cups	canned chickpeas, rinsed and drained	625 mL
1 cup	diced peeled potatoes	250 mL
1/2 cup	chopped carrots	125 mL
2 tbsp	tahini (sesame paste)	25 mL
3 tbsp	couscous	45 mL
1/2 cup	chopped fresh coriander	125 mL

soups

55

PER SERVING

essential numbers

Calories	314
Protein	15 g
Fat, total	6 g
Fat, saturated	1.1 g
Carbohydrates	53 g
Sodium	200 mg
Cholesterol	1 mg
Fiber	7 g

ask ROSE

Tahini is used in Middle Eastern cooking. It is a thick paste made of ground sesame seeds. Its texture is very much like peanut butter — in fact, peanut butter or any nut butter can be used as a replacement. You can usually find tahini in health food stores, Middle Eastern groceries or in the specialty section of larger supermarkets.

nutrition watch

Fiber-up with beans

Want to boost your fiber intake? Try chickpeas — they're a great alternative to meat or chicken in soups, pasta sauces and salads. One cup (250 mL) of cooked chickpeas packs 14 g fiber. That's one-half the recommended daily intake. Like other legumes (such as kidney beans, black beans and lentils), chickpeas contain mostly soluble fiber, which delays stomach emptying and keeps you feeling full longer. It also keeps your blood sugar stable and can help to lower elevated blood cholesterol.

alphabet soup

with hearty roasted vegetables

1. In a bowl combine tomatoes, red onion, carrots, potato and olive oil; toss well. Place vegetables and garlic on baking sheet. Bake in preheated oven, turning at halfway point, for 50 minutes or until tender.

2. When cool enough to handle, squeeze skins off garlic head. In a food processor, combine garlic, vegetable mixture and any accumulated juices; purée. Transfer to a saucepan over medium-high heat. Add stock, evaporated milk and salt; bring to a boil. Add pasta; reduce heat to medium-low. Cook, stirring occasionally, for 10 minutes or until pasta is tender. Garnish with basil; serve.

PREHEAT OVEN TO 425° F (220° C)
LARGE BAKING SHEET SPRAYED WITH VEGETABLE SPRAY

2 lbs	plum tomatoes, cut crosswise into halves	1 kg
1	large red onion, cut into wedges	1
2	large carrots, thinly sliced	2
1	large potato, cut into eighths	1
1 tbsp	olive oil	15 mL
1	large head garlic, top 1/2 inch (1 cm) cut off, wrapped loosely in foil	1
3 cups	VEGETABLE STOCK or CHICKEN STOCK (see recipes, pages 51 and 50)	750 mL
2 tbsp	low-fat evaporated milk	25 mL
1/2 tsp	salt	2 mL
1/3 cup	alphabet soup pasta or other small pasta	75 mL
1/2 cup	chopped fresh basil, dill or parsley	125 mL

soups

56

essential numbers

PER SERVING

Calories	209
Protein	6 g
Fat, total	5 g
Fat, saturated	1.0 g
Carbohydrates	37 g
Sodium	350 mg
Cholesterol	1 mg
Fiber	6 g

ask ROSE

Think of any vegetable you love and chances are it will taste even better roasted. Just toss them in a pan, drizzle with olive oil and spices, and roast until tender and sweet. Simple, yes, but oh so good! And good for you, too. Roasted vegetables keep their nutrients and have more intense flavors. When roasting, I prefer to cut vegetables into large chunks, leaving the skin on to maintain moisture. Cook in a 400° F (200° C) oven for about 1 hour.

cooking 101

Want a great way to thicken a soup without using cream or butter? Try the low-fat alternative — evaporated milk. One-half cup (125 mL) of 2% evaporated milk has only 2.5 g fat. Compare that with 44 g fat for an equal quantity of whipping (35%) cream. Scary! Evaporated milk also has more calcium than cream. And now, with skim evaporated milk, you get half the calories of 2% and virtually no fat.

lentil soup

with sausage and tiny pasta

1 In a nonstick frying pan set over medium heat, cook sausage, stirring to break up meat, for 5 minutes or until no longer pink. Drain excess fat; set aside.

2 In a large nonstick saucepan sprayed with vegetable spray, cook onions and garlic over medium-high heat for 2 minutes or until softened. Add carrots; cook for 2 minutes. Add stock, tomatoes, lentils, brown sugar, Italian seasoning, bay leaf and sausage; bring to a boil. Reduce heat to medium-low; cook, covered, for 35 minutes.

3 Add pasta; cook, covered and stirring occasionally, for 10 minutes or until pasta and lentils are tender.

6 oz	medium-spicy Italian sausage, casings removed	175 g
1 cup	chopped onions	250 mL
1 1/2 tsp	minced garlic	7 mL
1/2 cup	finely chopped carrots	125 mL
5 cups	BEEF STOCK or CHICKEN STOCK (see recipes, page 50)	1.25 L
1	can (19 oz [540 mL]) tomatoes, crushed	1
1/2 cup	green lentils	125 mL
1 1/2 tsp	packed brown sugar	7 mL
1 tsp	Italian seasoning	5 mL
1	bay leaf	1
1/3 cup	small pasta (orzo, ditali, stelline or tubetti)	75 mL

soups

57

PER SERVING	
Calories	223
Protein	10 g
Fat, total	8 g
Fat, saturated	2.0 g
Carbohydrates	29 g
Sodium	150 mg
Cholesterol	12 mg
Fiber	4 g

essential numbers

ask ROSE

On their own, lentils are pretty b-o-o-o-r-ing. But when tossed into salads, soups or mixed with other grain dishes, they're sensational! What's more, lentils contain nutritional goodies like calcium, vitamins A and B, as well as plenty of iron. Here we use green lentils — not only do they cook faster, but they hold their shape better than red and yellow varieties (which have a tendency to dissolve as they cook).

for the record

Same great taste, less fat

OK, so we know that sausages are high in fat: a 1-oz (25 g) serving of beef or pork sausage has 10 g saturated fat (that's 2.5 tsp [12 mL] worth!). But we also know how much flavor they can add to a hearty bean soup or spicy tomato sauce. So here's the deal. Try removing the casing before browning and drain all the fat afterwards; you'll save 2 grams of fat for every sausage!

six-root vegetable soup
with maple syrup

1 In a nonstick saucepan sprayed with vegetable spray, cook onions and garlic over medium-high heat for 3 minutes or until softened. Add stock, sweet potatoes, parsnips, rutabaga, turnips, carrots and tarragon; bring to a boil. Reduce heat to low; cook, covered, for 20 minutes or until vegetables are tender. Transfer mixture to a food processor or blender; process until smooth.

2 Return soup to saucepan over medium-high heat; bring to a boil. Add pasta; reduce heat to medium. Cook for 8 minutes or until pasta is tender; add maple syrup. Serve.

2/3 cup	chopped onions	150 mL
2 tsp	minced garlic	10 mL
4 cups	VEGETABLE STOCK *or* CHICKEN STOCK (see recipes, pages 51 and 50)	1.125 L
1 1/2 cups	chopped peeled sweet potatoes	375 mL
3/4 cup	chopped peeled parsnips	175 mL
3/4 cup	chopped peeled rutabaga	175 mL
3/4 cup	chopped peeled turnips	175 mL
1/2 cup	chopped peeled carrots	125 mL
1 tsp	dried tarragon	5 mL
1/3 cup	small pasta (orzo, ditali, stelline or tubetti)	75 mL
1 tbsp	maple syrup	15 mL

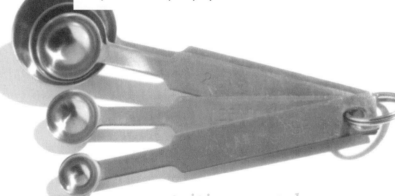

essential numbers

PER SERVING

Calories	221
Protein	6 g
Fat, total	1 g
Fat, saturated	0.2 g
Carbohydrates	48 g
Sodium	50 mg
Cholesterol	0 mg
Fiber	6 g

ask ROSE

Root vegetables are just about the perfect comfort food. As you might expect, they include just about anything that is grown underground. Good choices for this recipe include beets, radishes, regular potatoes, leeks, celeriac, daikon or salsify. Be imaginative!

nutrition watch

The right roots

As members of the cruciferous vegetable family, turnip and rutabaga are being studied for their ability to reduce the risk of breast, colon and kidney cancers. Cruciferous veggies contain more than 30 natural chemicals that can trigger the formation of enzymes that detoxify cancer-causing substances in the body. Want more crucifers on your dinner plate? Try bok choy, broccoli, Brussels sprouts, cabbage, cauliflower, kale, kohlrabi and mustard greens.

barley minestrone

with pesto

1 In a large nonstick saucepan sprayed with vegetable spray, cook onions and garlic over medium-high heat for 2 minutes or until softened. Add zucchini, eggplant and carrots; cook for 5 minutes, stirring occasionally.

2 Add stock, tomatoes (with juice), potatoes, kidney beans, barley, basil and bay leaf. Bring to a boil, breaking tomatoes with back of a spoon. Reduce heat to medium-low; cook, covered, for 45 minutes or until barley is tender.

3 Ladle soup into bowls. Spoon a dollop of pesto in center of each serving; garnish with Parmesan cheese.

1 cup	chopped onions	250 mL
1 1/2 tsp	minced garlic	7 mL
1 1/2 cups	diced unpeeled zucchini	375 mL
1 cup	diced unpeeled eggplant	250 mL
1/2 cup	diced carrots	125 mL
4 3/4 cups	VEGETABLE STOCK or CHICKEN STOCK (see recipes, pages 51 and 50)	1.175 L
1	can (19 oz [540 mL]) whole tomatoes, with juice	1
1 1/2 cups	diced peeled potatoes	375 mL
1 cup	canned cooked white kidney beans, rinsed and drained	250 mL
1/3 cup	pearl barley	75 mL
2 1/2 tsp	dried basil	12 mL
1	bay leaf	1
2 tbsp	pesto (see recipe, page 204, or use store-bought variety)	25 mL
3 tbsp	grated low-fat Parmesan cheese	45 mL

soups

59

essential numbers

PER SERVING

Calories	153
Protein	7 g
Fat, total	3 g
Fat, saturated	1.1 g
Carbohydrates	26 g
Sodium	100 mg
Cholesterol	3 mg
Fiber	3 g

ask ROSE

Pesto is one of my all-time favorite sauces. The problem is that traditional pesto, whether store-bought or homemade, is laden with fat and calories because of all the oil, nuts and cheese. In fact, 2 tbsp (25 mL) can contain as much as 150 calories and 15 g fat. Not for me, thanks! My low-fat recipe (see recipe, page 204) uses stock to replace some of the oil, and contains less cheese and nuts. The results are delicious and the fat and calories are reduced by more than half. Freeze leftover pesto in ice cube trays and use one cube per plate of pasta.

cooking 101

If you have to watch your salt intake, keep in mind that store-bought canned bouillon, powder and cubed stocks are high in sodium. Making your own stock is a much healthier alternative. Take a look at my stock recipes on pages 50-51 and give them a try. For chicken and beef stocks, refrigerate overnight, remove any layers of fat and freeze in containers for later use.

black bean soup

with wild rice and corn

1 In a large nonstick saucepan sprayed with vegetable spray, cook onions, corn, carrots and garlic over medium-high heat for 5 minutes or until starting to brown. Add stock, tomatoes, black beans, wild rice, brown sugar, cumin and basil; bring to a boil, breaking tomatoes with back of a spoon. Reduce heat to medium-low; cook, covered, for 30 minutes or until rice is tender.

2 Ladle soup into bowls. Season to taste with pepper; garnish with chopped coriander. Serve.

1 cup	chopped onions	250 mL
1 cup	canned corn or frozen corn, thawed	250 mL
1/2 cup	finely chopped carrots	125 mL
1 1/2 tsp	minced garlic	7 mL
3 1/2 cups	VEGETABLE STOCK or CHICKEN STOCK (see recipes, pages 51 and 50)	875 mL
1	can (19 oz [540 mL]) tomatoes, with juice	1
1 cup	canned cooked black beans, rinsed and drained	250 mL
1/3 cup	wild rice	75 mL
1 tbsp	packed brown sugar	15 mL
1 1/2 tsp	ground cumin	7 mL
1 1/2 tsp	dried basil	7 mL
	Freshly ground black pepper	
3 tbsp	chopped fresh coriander or parsley	45 mL

essential numbers

PER SERVING

Calories	130
Protein	6 g
Fat, total	1 g
Fat, saturated	0.3 g
Carbohydrates	30 g
Sodium	63 mg
Cholesterol	0 mg
Fiber	5 g

ask ROSE

Did you know that wild rice isn't really a rice at all? It's actually a long-grain marsh grass, characterized by a distinctively nutty flavor and chewy texture. It takes longer to cook than white rice — approximately 45 minutes. Avoid overcooking or it will become starchy.

Wild rice is expensive, so you may want to use it only for special meals — or use less by combining it with white rice, brown rice or mixed greens.

for the record

Fresh or frozen?

Have you always thought that frozen vegetables were inferior to fresh? Well they're not! In fact, they're often *more* nutritious than fresh because they're processed immediately after harvest and their nutrients are "locked in." As a result, there's no change to their nutrient content over their shelf life — whereas that bunch of broccoli sitting in your crisper might have been picked 2 or 3 weeks ago, during which time the vitamins and minerals have diminished steadily.

Serves 4

hearty beef soup
with lentils and barley

1 In a bowl coat beef with flour; shake off excess. In a nonstick saucepan sprayed with vegetable spray, cook beef over medium-high heat for 5 minutes or until browned on all sides. Remove meat to a plate; respray pan. Add onions and garlic; cook for 2 minutes. Add carrots and green peppers; cook, stirring occasionally, for 4 minutes or until vegetables are softened.

2 Add browned beef, lentils, tomatoes, stock, barley, brown sugar, basil, bay leaves and pepper; bring to a boil, breaking up tomatoes with back of a spoon. Reduce heat to medium-low; cook, covered, for 45 minutes or until lentils and barley are tender. Ladle soup into bowls. Serve.

6 oz	boneless round steak, cut into 1/2-inch (1 cm) cubes	175 g
2 tbsp	all-purpose flour	25 mL
1/2 cup	chopped onions	125 mL
1 tsp	minced garlic	5 mL
1/2 cup	chopped carrots	125 mL
1/2 cup	chopped green bell peppers	125 mL
1/2 cup	green lentils	125 mL
1	can (19 oz [540 mL]) tomatoes, with juice	1
4 1/2 cups	BEEF STOCK or CHICKEN STOCK (see recipes, page 50)	1.125 L
1/3 cup	pearl barley	75 mL
2 tsp	packed brown sugar	10 mL
1 1/2 tsp	dried basil	7 mL
2	bay leaves	2
1/4 tsp	freshly ground black pepper	1 mL

soups

61

essential numbers

PER SERVING

Calories	300
Protein	26 g
Fat, total	6 g
Fat, saturated	2.3 g
Carbohydrates	42 g
Sodium	300 mg
Cholesterol	41 mg
Fiber	9 g

ask ROSE

Stewing beef is often used in a soup like this. But I find that it takes a *lot* of cooking time before it becomes tender — and I'm always in a hurry. So I use more tender cuts of beef: either round or loin. Remember, too, that the smaller the cubes, the faster the meat tenderizes.

nutrition watch

Pumping iron
This soup is a great source of iron. At 5 mg per serving, it goes a long way towards meeting your daily iron requirements (women need 14 mg each day; men require 10 mg). Iron is used by your red blood cells to form hemoglobin, the molecule that transports oxygen from your lungs to your cells. If your body is deficient in iron, you'll feel lethargic, weak and you'll tire easily during exercise. This soup gets its iron boost from stewing beef, lentils and barley. For more on iron, see page 159.

split-pea soup

with sausage and orzo

1 In a nonstick saucepan sprayed with vegetable spray, cook onions and garlic over medium-high heat for 3 minutes or until softened. Add carrots; cook for 2 minutes. Add potatoes, split peas and stock; bring to a boil. Reduce heat to medium-low; cook, covered, for 35 minutes or until split peas and potatoes are tender.

2 Meanwhile, in a nonstick frying pan set over medium-high heat, cook sausage, stirring to break up meat, for 5 minutes or until no longer pink. Drain excess fat; set aside.

3 Transfer soup mixture to a food processor or blender; purée. Return soup to saucepan over medium-high heat; bring to a boil. Add sausage and orzo; reduce heat to medium-low. Cook, stirring occasionally, for 10 minutes or until pasta is tender. Season to taste with pepper. Serve.

1 cup	chopped onions	250 mL
1 tsp	minced garlic	5 mL
1/2 cup	chopped carrots	125 mL
1 cup	diced peeled potatoes	250 mL
3/4 cup	yellow or green split peas	175 mL
6 cups	BEEF STOCK or CHICKEN STOCK (see recipes, page 50)	1.5 L
4 oz	sausage, casings removed	125 g
1/2 cup	orzo or small-shaped pasta	125 mL
	Freshly ground black pepper	

essential numbers

PER SERVING

Calories	287
Protein	13 g
Fat, total	9 g
Fat, saturated	3.1 g
Carbohydrates	40 g
Sodium	150 mg
Cholesterol	19 mg
Fiber	3 g

ask ROSE

Sausage is made from ground meat mixed with fat and seasonings. And while it tastes great, the added fat is a problem. In fact, just 1 oz (25 g) has 90 calories and 7 g fat. Look as hard as you like in your grocery store; chances are you won't find anything called "low-fat sausages." So what I do is use small amounts to highlight my recipes. And here's a tip for eliminating 20% of the fat — sauté the sausages in a nonstick skillet and drain the fat.

cooking 101

Orzo is the Italian word for "barley," although it is actually a small rice-shaped type of pasta. I love using it to highlight soups and often substitute orzo for rice or other grains. Be sure to cook it as you would pasta — firm to the bite or "al dente."

purée of beans
and sweet potatoes with capellini

1. In a nonstick saucepan sprayed with vegetable spray, cook carrots, onions and garlic over medium-high heat for 5 minutes or until softened. Set aside 1/2 cup (125 mL) beans; add remaining beans, stock and sweet potatoes to saucepan. Bring to a boil; reduce heat to medium-low. Cook, covered, for 15 minutes or until potatoes are tender.

2. In a food processor or blender, purée soup in two batches. Return soup to saucepan over medium-high heat; bring to a boil. Add reserved beans and capellini; reduce heat to simmer. Cook for 7 minutes or until pasta is tender; add dill. Serve.

1/2 cup	chopped carrots	125 mL
1/2 cup	chopped onions	125 mL
1 1/2 tsp	minced garlic	7 mL
1	can (19 oz [540 mL]) white kidney beans, rinsed and drained	1
5 cups	VEGETABLE STOCK or CHICKEN STOCK (see recipes, pages 51 and 50)	1.25 L
1 1/2 cups	diced peeled sweet potatoes	375 mL
2/3 cup	broken capellini (thin strand pasta) or bean thread noodles	150 mL
1/4 cup	chopped fresh dill (or 1 1/2 tsp [7 mL] dried)	50 mL

soups

63

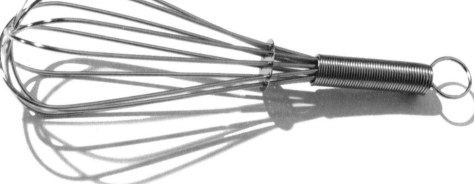

essential numbers

PER SERVING

Calories	180
Protein	7 g
Fat, total	1 g
Fat, saturated	0.3 g
Carbohydrates	35 g
Sodium	100 mg
Cholesterol	1 mg
Fiber	6 g

ask ROSE

Capellini, or angel hair pasta, consists of very thin strands, making it perfect for soup or delicate light sauces. Other substitutes include vermicelli and spaghettini.

It's not always easy to measure pasta in a cup. The most reliable method is to weigh it on a food scale, an inexpensive (and indispensable) kitchen tool.

cooking 101

If you want the freshest taste in your recipes, it's always best to use fresh herbs. But if they're not in season or just not available, substitute dried. The standard ratio is 3 parts fresh to 1 part dried.

I typically use lots of fresh herbs and only a small amount of dried. The best policy is to begin with smaller amounts and increase according to taste.

clam & swordfish chowder
with small shell pasta

1   In a nonstick frying pan sprayed with vegetable spray or on a preheated grill, cook swordfish over medium-high heat, turning once, for 10 minutes per 1-inch (2.5 cm) thickness or until cooked through. Cool completely; cut into 1/2-inch (1 cm) cubes. Set aside.

2   In a bowl combine reserved clam juice and enough stock to make 3 cups (750 mL) liquid; set aside.

3   In a large nonstick saucepan sprayed with vegetable spray, heat oil over medium heat. Add leeks, onions and garlic; cook for 3 minutes or until softened. Add potatoes, carrots, clams and stock mixture; bring to a boil. Reduce heat to low; cook, covered, for 15 minutes.

4   Add pasta; increase heat to medium-high. Cook, uncovered, for 5 minutes. In a bowl, whisk together milk and flour; add to chowder. Cook for 4 minutes or until pasta and potatoes are tender and soup is slightly thickened. Add swordfish and dill. Serve.

8 oz	swordfish steak	250 g
1	can (5 oz [150 g]) clams, drained (reserve juice)	1
2 1/2 cups	SEAFOOD STOCK or CHICKEN STOCK, approximate (see recipes, page 50)	625 mL
1 tsp	vegetable oil	5 mL
1 cup	chopped leeks	250 mL
1/2 cup	chopped onions	125 mL
2 tsp	minced garlic	10 mL
1 cup	diced peeled potatoes	250 mL
3/4 cup	chopped carrots	175 mL
1/3 cup	small shell pasta	75 mL
1 cup	low-fat milk	250 mL
1 tsp	all-purpose flour	5 mL
1/3 cup	chopped fresh dill (or 1 tsp [5 mL] dried)	75 mL

essential numbers

PER SERVING

Calories	188
Protein	17 g
Fat, total	4 g
Fat, saturated	1.0 g
Carbohydrates	19 g
Sodium	150 mg
Cholesterol	29 mg
Fiber	1 g

ask ROSE

Swordfish is one of my absolute favorite types of fish. It's delicious grilled, baked or sautéed. The only way to ruin the taste and texture of swordfish is to overcook it. So I prefer swordfish cooked just so the center remains slightly pink. Remember that the fish will continue to cook for a few minutes after it is removed from the heat.

for the record

Chow(der) down on less fat
What a difference! By using milk instead of cream, this delicious soup has 30% fewer calories and 75% of the fat found in most canned chowders. Compare this recipe's nutrient content to 1 cup (250 mL) of a canned chunky version of New England chowder — a whopping 267 calories and 16.5 g fat (4 tsp [20 mL] worth!) in every serving. What's more, this recipe also gives you 40% more protein. Now, that's a real meal in a bowl.

grilled fruit salad over rotini with shrimp (page 90)

polenta meatballs

with black bean soup

1. In a nonstick saucepan over high heat, bring 1 cup (250 mL) stock to a boil. Reduce heat to low; gradually whisk in cornmeal, Parmesan cheese and garlic. Cook, stirring, for 5 minutes. Remove from heat; let stand another 5 minutes. With wet hands, form 1 tbsp (15 mL) of mixture into a "meatball." Repeat to make about 16 balls; set aside.

2. In a large nonstick saucepan sprayed with vegetable spray, cook onions and garlic over medium-high heat for 5 minutes or until browned. Reserve 1/2 cup (125 mL) beans; add remaining beans, sweet potatoes, carrots, chili powder, pepper and stock to saucepan. Bring to a boil; reduce heat to low. Cook, covered, for 15 minutes or until vegetables are tender.

3. In a food processor or blender, purée bean mixture in batches. Return soup to saucepan over medium-high heat; bring to a boil. Reduce heat to simmer; add polenta balls and reserved black beans. Cook for 5 minutes or until heated through. Add coriander; serve.

Polenta meatballs

1 cup	VEGETABLE STOCK *or* CHICKEN STOCK (see recipes, pages 51 and 50)	250 mL
1/3 cup	cornmeal	75 mL
1 tbsp	grated low-fat Parmesan cheese	15 mL
1/2 tsp	minced garlic	2 mL

Black bean soup

1 cup	chopped onions	250 mL
2 tsp	minced garlic	10 mL
1	can (19 oz [540 mL]) black beans, rinsed and drained	1
1 cup	chopped peeled sweet potatoes	250 mL
3/4 cup	chopped carrots	175 mL
1 1/2 tsp	chili powder	7 mL
1/8 tsp	freshly ground black pepper	0.5 mL
3 3/4 cups	VEGETABLE STOCK *or* CHICKEN STOCK	950 mL
1/3 cup	chopped fresh coriander	75 mL

soups

65

essential numbers

PER SERVING

Calories	273
Protein	12 g
Fat, total	3 g
Fat, saturated	0.5 g
Carbohydrates	52 g
Sodium	130 mg
Cholesterol	1 mg
Fiber	12 g

ask ROSE

Cornmeal is nothing more complicated than ground dried corn kernels. It is often used as a cereal, but can also be added to give a crunchy texture to breads, cookies and muffins. Cornmeal can also be substituted for rice, potatoes or pasta — or, as here, to make polenta.

Polenta is essentially a thick cornmeal porridge. It hardens as it cools, so don't make it too far in advance of forming the "meatballs" in this recipe. If it gets too hard, just reheat and add extra liquid, mixing until smooth.

nutrition watch

Orange food for a healthy heart

Sweet potatoes are an excellent source of beta carotene — and, it appears, an important food for anyone 55 or older. A comprehensive study of older people conducted in the Netherlands concluded that those with the highest beta carotene intake had a 45% lower risk of heart attack compared to those who ate the least. Beta carotene acts as an antioxidant, protecting cells from damage caused by harmful free radical molecules. Other beta carotene boosters include carrots, winter squash, spinach, broccoli, peaches, apricots and cantaloupe.

southwest barley salad (page 73)

tomato rice soup
with mushrooms and beef

1 In a nonstick saucepan sprayed with vegetable spray, cook beef over medium-high heat, stirring occasionally, for 3 minutes or until browned on all sides. Remove from pan; set aside.

2 Respray pan; add mushrooms, onions and garlic. Cook for approximately 5 minutes or until browned and tender; add tomatoes, stock, brown sugar, basil and chili powder. Bring to a boil; stir, breaking up tomatoes with back of a spoon. Add browned beef and rice; reduce heat to low. Cook, covered, for 20 minutes or until rice is tender.

8 oz	boneless top sirloin beef steak, cut into 1/2-inch (1 cm) cubes	250 g
3 cups	chopped mushrooms	750 mL
3/4 cup	chopped onions	175 mL
1 1/2 tsp	minced garlic	7 mL
1	can (19 oz [540 mL]) tomatoes, with juice	1
3 1/2 cups	BEEF STOCK *or* CHICKEN STOCK (see recipes, page 50)	875 mL
1 tbsp	packed brown sugar	15 mL
1 tsp	dried basil	5 mL
1 tsp	chili powder	5 mL
1/2 cup	long grain white rice	125 mL

soups

66

essential numbers

PER SERVING	
Calories	170
Protein	13 g
Fat, total	3 g
Fat, saturated	1.3 g
Carbohydrates	23 g
Sodium	187 mg
Cholesterol	29 mg
Fiber	2 g

ask ROSE

The long grain white rice provides a nice light texture. Be careful not to overcook it, though; if you do, all those delicious grains will turn into a sticky mess! For a nuttier flavor — and more fiber — try replacing the white rice with brown rice, and increase cooking time to 45 minutes. Medium grain or converted white rice also work well in this recipe.

cooking 101

Canned tomatoes are available whole (with juice), crushed or puréed. For a soup like this one, where texture is important, I use whole tomatoes, breaking them up slightly with the back of a spoon during cooking. If a recipe calls for crushed tomatoes but you only have whole, just purée them in a food processor.

red lentil soup
with cheese tortellini

1. In a nonstick saucepan sprayed with vegetable spray, cook onions and garlic over medium heat for 5 minutes or until golden. Add stock, sweet potatoes, red peppers, carrots, red lentils and basil; bring to a boil. Reduce heat to low; cook, covered, for 15 minutes or until lentils and vegetables are tender.

2. In a food processor or blender, purée soup in batches. Return to saucepan over medium-high heat; bring to a boil. Add tortellini; reduce heat to simmer. Cook for 5 minutes or until tortellini is tender.

3/4 cup	chopped onions	175 mL
2 tsp	minced garlic	10 mL
4 cups	VEGETABLE STOCK or CHICKEN STOCK (see recipes, pages 51 and 50)	1 L
1 1/2 cups	chopped peeled sweet potatoes	375 mL
1 cup	chopped red bell peppers	250 mL
1/2 cup	chopped carrots	125 mL
1/2 cup	red lentils	125 mL
1 tsp	dried basil	5 mL
4 oz	fresh or frozen cheese tortellini	125 g

soups

67

essential numbers

PER SERVING

Calories	324
Protein	14 g
Fat, total	3 g
Fat, saturated	1.7 g
Carbohydrates	61 g
Sodium	127 mg
Cholesterol	12 mg
Fiber	9 g

ask ROSE

The lentils, red bell peppers and sweet potatoes give this soup a natural sweetness. Lentils come in a wide variety of colors — including the common brown lentil, as well as black, yellow, red and orange. They are an excellent source of folic acid, potassium and a good source of iron. Red lentils are my choice here, since they take only 15 to 20 minutes to cook (compare that to over 1 hour for green lentils). Be careful, though; if overcooked, they will turn to mush!

lifestyle

This soup is perfect for the whole family. It's particularly good to serve to children — because the soup is puréed, they can't identify specific vegetables that they might otherwise object to eating! Cheese tortellini is also a popular favorite.

udon noodle soup
with chicken and dried mushrooms

1. In a bowl cover mushrooms with 1 cup (250 mL) boiling water; let stand for 20 minutes. Drain, reserving liquid. Slice mushroom caps thinly; set aside. Discard stems.

2. In a nonstick wok or large nonstick saucepan sprayed with vegetable spray, cook pork, ginger and garlic over medium-high heat for 2 minutes or until meat is cooked through. Set aside.

3. In a large saucepan over high heat, combine stock, soya sauce and reserved mushroom liquid; bring to a boil. Add udon noodles; return to a boil. Reduce heat to medium-high; cook for 4 minutes or until noodles are tender. Add sliced mushroom caps, bok choy, snow peas and shrimp; cook for 2 minutes or until shrimp are pink and snow peas are tender-crisp.

4. Add pork mixture, bean sprouts and green onions; cook until heated through. Drizzle with sesame oil; serve.

Amount	Ingredient	Metric
1/2 oz	small dried shiitake mushrooms	15 g
4 oz	boneless pork loin, cut into thin strips	125 g
2 tsp	minced ginger root	10 mL
1	clove garlic, minced	1
6 cups	CHICKEN STOCK or BEEF STOCK (see recipes, page 50)	1.5 L
2 tbsp	light soya sauce	25 mL
6 oz	fresh udon noodles	175 g
2 cups	sliced bok choy	500 mL
1/2 cup	sliced snow peas	125 mL
4 oz	raw shrimp, peeled, deveined and chopped	125 g
1 cup	bean sprouts	250 mL
2	large green onions, chopped	2
2 tsp	sesame oil	10 mL

soups

68

essential numbers

PER SERVING

Calories	207
Protein	12 g
Fat, total	7 g
Fat, saturated	2.1 g
Carbohydrates	23 g
Sodium	380 mg
Cholesterol	46 mg
Fiber	1 g

ask ROSE

Udon noodles are used frequently in Japanese cuisine. Long, round and white, they have a wonderfully dense texture and are terrific when added to soups. I usually find them at the supermarket, vacuum-packed, fresh or frozen.

cooking 101

Dried wild mushrooms such as shiitake, chanterelles or morels are less expensive than their fresh counterparts. And they'll keep for a long time in your pantry. To use, just place them in a bowl and cover with boiling water; let sit, covered, for 20 minutes or until tender. Drain and then chop mushrooms. The soaking liquid can be reserved for stock or to enhance the flavor of sauces.

roasted vegetable

minestrone

1 In a bowl combine tomatoes, carrots, red onion, zucchini, sweet potato, red pepper and olive oil; toss well. Arrange in a single layer on baking sheet; add garlic. Roast in preheated oven, turning at halfway point, for 50 minutes or until tender. Set aside to cool.

2 When cool enough to handle, squeeze skins off garlic head. Chop tomatoes, carrots, red onion, zucchini, sweet potato and red pepper; transfer to a large saucepan over medium-high heat. Add stock, basil, bay leaf and black pepper; bring to a boil. Add macaroni; reduce heat to simmer. Cook for 10 minutes or until pasta is tender. Sprinkle with Parmesan cheese. Serve.

PREHEAT OVEN TO 425° F (220° C)
LARGE BAKING SHEET SPRAYED WITH VEGETABLE SPRAY

2	ripe plum tomatoes, quartered	2
2	large carrots, peeled and thinly sliced	2
1	large red onion, cut into wedges	1
1	small zucchini, halved lengthwise	1
1	large sweet potato, peeled and cut into wedges	1
1	large red bell pepper, cored and quartered	1
1 tbsp	olive oil	15 mL
1	large head garlic, top 1/2 inch (1 cm) cut off, wrapped loosely in foil	1
5 cups	VEGETABLE STOCK or CHICKEN STOCK (see recipes, pages 51 and 50)	1.25 L
1 1/2 tsp	dried basil	7 mL
1	bay leaf	1
1/4 tsp	freshly ground black pepper	1 mL
1/2 cup	elbow macaroni	125 mL
2 tbsp	grated low-fat Parmesan cheese	25 mL

soups

69

essential numbers

PER SERVING

Calories	142
Protein	4 g
Fat, total	4 g
Fat, saturated	0.8 g
Carbohydrates	24 g
Sodium	45 mg
Cholesterol	1 mg
Fiber	3 g

ask ROSE

Worried about what eating large amounts of fresh garlic will do to your breath — or stomach lining? Well, here's a solution: just roast that garlic and it will become deliciously sweet and mild. I love to squeeze cloves out of the skin after roasting and spread over fresh bread. So-o-o-o good!

nutrition watch

Garlic may keep the cardiologist at bay
Hailed by the ancient Egyptians for its miraculous healing properties, garlic is now recognized as having a protective effect against heart disease. In fact, studies have found that eating one clove a day can lower elevated cholesterol levels by up to 20%. This is attributed to a sulfur compound found in garlic called S-allyl cysteine, which increases in concentration when garlic is aged. If fresh garlic irritates your stomach, speak to your health practitioner about aged garlic extract.

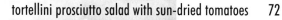

s

tortellini prosciutto salad
with sun-dried tomatoes

1 In a bowl cover sun-dried tomatoes with boiling water. Let sit for 15 minutes; drain and chop.

2 In a large pot of boiling water, cook tortellini according to package directions or until tender; drain.

3 Meanwhile, in a serving bowl, combine red pepper, artichokes, prosciutto, plum tomatoes, green onions, basil, olive oil, balsamic vinegar, garlic, red pepper flakes and sun-dried tomatoes.

4 Add tortellini to salad; toss well. Serve warm or at room temperature.

1/2 cup	dry-packed sun-dried tomatoes	125 mL
1 lb	fresh or frozen cheese tortellini	500 g
1	large roasted red bell pepper, diced or 4 oz (125 g) drained bottled roasted red bell peppers, diced	1
1	can (14 oz [398 mL]) artichokes, drained and chopped	1
2 oz	prosciutto, chopped	50 g
2 cups	diced ripe plum tomatoes	500 mL
1/2 cup	chopped green onions	125 mL
1/2 cup	chopped fresh basil (or 1 tsp [5 mL] dried)	125 mL
2 tbsp	olive oil	25 mL
1 tbsp	balsamic vinegar	15 mL
1 1/2 tsp	minced garlic	7 mL
3/4 tsp	red pepper flakes	4 mL

salads

essential numbers

PER SERVING

Calories	365
Protein	17 g
Fat, total	11 g
Fat, saturated	4.4 g
Carbohydrates	49 g
Sodium	582 mg
Cholesterol	36 mg
Fiber	3 g

ask ROSE

Concentrate the essence of an intensely flavored, sweet, dark red tomato and what have you got? Sun-dried tomatoes — one of my favorite ingredients! Small packages of these tomatoes can be pretty expensive, so I prefer to buy them in bulk and freeze them until needed. Avoid buying those packed in oil. Not only are they very expensive, but they're really high in fat and calories.

for the record

Vitamin C champions

Oranges are an excellent source of vitamin C, but they're not the best. In fact, red bell peppers top the list. Just 1/2 cup (125 mL) packs 95 mg of the vitamin, providing 300% of the daily recommended intake for women (30 mg) and 230% for men (40 mg). Tied for first place is one-half of a papaya. Runners up include strawberries, kiwi fruit, oranges, pink grapefruit, sweet potatoes, green peppers, broccoli and Brussels sprouts.

southwest barley salad

1 In a saucepan over high heat, bring stock to a boil. Add barley; reduce heat to medium-low. Simmer, covered, for 40 minutes or until barley is tender and liquid is absorbed. Transfer to a serving bowl; cool to room temperature. Add corn, black beans, red peppers, green peppers and green onions.

2 In a bowl combine salsa, sour cream, lime juice, coriander and garlic. Pour dressing over salad; toss to coat well.

Salad

3 cups	VEGETABLE STOCK *or* CHICKEN STOCK (see recipes, pages 51 and 50	750 mL
3/4 cup	pearl barley	175 mL
1 cup	canned corn kernels, drained	250 mL
1 cup	canned black beans, rinsed and drained	250 mL
3/4 cup	chopped red bell peppers	175 mL
1/2 cup	chopped green bell peppers	125 mL
1/2 cup	chopped green onions	125 mL

Dressing

1/2 cup	medium salsa	125 mL
3 tbsp	low-fat sour cream	45 mL
2 tbsp	fresh lime or lemon juice	25 mL
1/2 cup	chopped fresh coriander	125 mL
1 tsp	minced garlic	5 mL

salads

73

essential numbers

PER SERVING	
Calories	230
Protein	10 g
Fat, total	2.5 g
Fat, saturated	1.3 g
Carbohydrates	41 g
Sodium	200 mg
Cholesterol	4 mg
Fiber	9 g

ask ROSE

This colorful salad looks great if served in a shaped tortilla shell. Mexican restaurants often use this type of presentation; but because they typically deep-fry the tortilla shell, it adds a lot of fat and calories. Here's my low fat version: Just place a 10-inch (25 cm) flour tortilla (these are available a variety of flavors and colors) in an 8- to 10-inch (20 to 25 cm) fluted baking tin. Bake at 400° F (200° C) for 5 minutes or until slightly browned and the tortilla is holding its shape. Fill with salad — and enjoy!

nutrition watch

Slow-burning carbs keep you going

Carbohydrates provide energy, but not all in the same way. Nutritionists classify them according to a "glycemic index" (GI), which measures how quickly a food will raise your blood sugar. High-GI foods raise blood sugar quickly, giving you a burst of energy; but this also causes your pancreas to release a large amount of insulin, which lowers your blood sugar, so your quick energy boost is followed by a "crash." Low-GI foods take longer to digest; blood sugar rises slowly, without creating a surge of insulin, so the energy lasts longer. Low-GI carbs include oatmeal, bran cereals, rye bread, barley, citrus fruit, yogurt and milk.

penne and mushroom
salad with creamy balsamic dressing

1. In a bowl combine sour cream, mayonnaise, balsamic vinegar, lemon juice, honey, garlic and chili sauce; whisk well. Set aside.

2. In a large nonstick frying pan sprayed with vegetable spray, cook mushrooms over medium-high heat for 5 minutes or until softened and releasing moisture. Drain, discarding liquid. In a serving bowl, combine mushrooms, red peppers, coriander, red onions, black olives and feta cheese. Pour dressing over; toss to coat well.

3. In a large pot of boiling water, cook penne for 8 to 10 minutes or until tender but firm; drain. Rinse under cold running water; drain well. Add to salad; toss well. Serve.

Dressing

1/3 cup	low-fat sour cream	75 mL
2 tbsp	light mayonnaise	25 mL
2 tbsp	balsamic vinegar	25 mL
2 tbsp	fresh lemon juice	25 mL
1 1/2 tbsp	honey	20 mL
1 tsp	minced garlic	5 mL
1 tsp	hot Asian chili sauce (optional)	5 mL

Salad

1 lb	mushrooms, cleaned and quartered	500 g
3/4 cup	chopped red bell peppers	175 mL
1/2 cup	chopped fresh coriander	125 mL
1/2 cup	chopped red onions	125 mL
1/3 cup	sliced black olives	75 mL
2 oz	light feta cheese, crumbled	50 g
12 oz	penne	375 g

salads

74

essential numbers

PER SERVING

Calories	364
Protein	12 g
Fat, total	8.3 g
Fat, saturated	3.6 g
Carbohydrates	62 g
Sodium	252 mg
Cholesterol	18 mg
Fiber	4 g

ask ROSE

OK, so you've just returned from the market with a bag of mushrooms. Kind of dirty aren't they? Maybe you should give them a good wash before putting them in the refrigerator. Don't! Keep them as they are, in a paper bag, refrigerated until ready to use. Then, before cooking, wipe the mushrooms with a damp cloth or, if you must, give them a quick rinse. Otherwise, water will penetrate the mushrooms and change their wonderful texture.

for the record

Deciphering the "% MF" mystery
Look at the label on any dairy product and you'll see a number followed by "% MF." Ever wonder what it means? It's the percentage of milk fat (that's the "MF") present in a given volume of milk or weight of cheese. For example, 31% MF on a package of Cheddar cheese means there are 31 g fat in 100 g cheese, or 9 g fat in a 1 oz (25 g) serving. By comparison, feta cheese, at 22% MF, has only 6.5 g fat per 1 oz (25 g).

Serves 4

kasha with beans

and salsa dressing

1. In a bowl combine coriander, salsa, sour cream, mayonnaise, water and garlic. Set aside.

2. In a saucepan over high heat, bring stock to boil. Meanwhile, in a nonstick saucepan set over medium-high heat, toast kasha for 1 minute. Add hot stock; return to a boil, stirring. Reduce heat to medium-low; cook, covered, for 10 minutes or until kasha is tender and liquid is absorbed. Set aside to cool.

3. In a serving bowl, combine cooled kasha, red kidney beans, chickpeas and red onions. Pour dressing over; toss to coat well. Serve at room temperature or heat in microwave to serve warm.

Dressing

1/2 cup	chopped fresh coriander	125 mL
1/3 cup	medium salsa	75 mL
1/4 cup	low-fat sour cream	50 mL
3 tbsp	light mayonnaise	45 mL
2 tbsp	water	25 mL
1 tsp	minced garlic	5 mL

Salad

1 1/2 cups	VEGETABLE STOCK or CHICKEN STOCK (see recipes, pages 51 and 50)	375 mL
3/4 cup	whole grain kasha	175 mL
1/2 cup	canned red kidney beans, rinsed and drained	125 mL
1/2 cup	canned chickpeas, rinsed and drained	125 mL
1/2 cup	chopped red onions	125 mL

salads

essential numbers

PER SERVING

Calories	167
Protein	7 g
Fat, total	6 g
Fat, saturated	1.3 g
Carbohydrates	23 g
Sodium	200 mg
Cholesterol	5 mg
Fiber	3 g

ask ROSE

Originally from Russia, kasha is the name given to buckwheat seeds that have been hulled and, most often, either finely or coarsely ground. (Despite its name, buckwheat isn't a type of wheat; in fact, it is not a cereal at all.) I prefer to use whole grain kasha. Toasting the kernels enhances their nutty flavor and keeps them from sticking together.

for the record

Lighten up those high-fat recipes
Got an old recipe that you don't use now because it's high in fat? Try replacing some of the ingredients to make a low-fat version. Here are some examples (and the amount of fat and calories you'll save for 1 cup [250 mL]): *for whipping (35%) cream*, use evaporated 2% milk (save 83 g fat, 576 cal) or evaporated skim milk (save 88 g fat, 612 cal); *for regular sour cream*, use light (5%) sour cream (save 34 g fat, 203 cal) or non-fat plain yogurt (save 45 g fat, 350 cal); *for regular mayonnaise*, use light mayonnaise (save 95 g fat, 832 cal).

creamy coleslaw
with peanut butter dressing

1. In a food processor or blender, combine sour cream, water, peanut butter, soya sauce, rice wine vinegar, sesame oil, honey, garlic and ginger; purée until smooth. Set aside.

2. In a large pot of boiling water, cook linguine for 8 to 10 minutes or until tender but firm; drain. Rinse under cold running water; drain.

3. In a serving bowl, combine red cabbage, green cabbage, red pepper, yellow pepper, coriander, carrots, green onions and linguine. Pour dressing over; toss to coat well.

Dressing

1/4 cup	low-fat sour cream	50 mL
1/4 cup	water	50 mL
3 tbsp	smooth peanut butter	45 mL
2 tbsp	light soya sauce	25 mL
2 tbsp	rice wine vinegar	25 mL
1 tbsp	sesame oil	15 mL
1 tbsp	honey	15 mL
1 1/2 tsp	minced garlic	7 mL
3/4 tsp	minced ginger root	4 mL

Salad

8 oz	linguine *or* soba noodles	250 g
1 1/2 cups	thinly sliced red cabbage	375 mL
1 1/2 cups	thinly sliced green cabbage	375 mL
1 cup	red bell pepper strips	250 mL
1 cup	yellow pepper strips	250 mL
3/4 cup	chopped fresh coriander	175 mL
1/2 cup	shredded carrots	125 mL
1/2 cup	chopped green onions	125 mL

salads

essential numbers

PER SERVING

Calories	354
Protein	13 g
Fat, total	11 g
Fat, saturated	2.6 g
Carbohydrates	55 g
Sodium	523 mg
Cholesterol	4 mg
Fiber	6 g

ask ROSE

I would never try making this recipe with regular (14% MF) sour cream. Why? Well, just consider that 1 cup (250 mL) contains 493 calories and 48 g fat. Wow! Compare that to low-fat (1%) sour cream, with only 35 calories and 0 g fat, which we use here. That's a *lot* less fat — but, as you'll see when you try this coleslaw, without any sacrifice in taste!

nutrition watch

High-C for your heart

Amazing! Just one serving of this coleslaw delivers more than four times your daily requirement for vitamin C. And if you're trying to lower your risk of heart disease, you'd be wise to eat up! A Portuguese study of people over the age of 39 found that those with the highest intake of vitamin C from foods had an 80% lower risk of heart attack compared to those with the lowest intake. Good sources include cabbage, bell peppers, broccoli, citrus fruit, strawberries, cantaloupe and tomato juice.

shrimp and macaroni
salad with creamy russian dressing

1 In a pot of boiling water, cook macaroni for 8 to 10 minutes or until tender but firm; drain. Rinse under cold running water; drain.

2 If using large or jumbo shrimp, cut into halves. In a nonstick frying pan sprayed with vegetable spray, cook shrimp over medium-high heat for 2 minutes or until pink. In a bowl combine mayonnaise, sour cream and chili sauce.

3 In a serving bowl, combine green peppers, red peppers, red onions, pasta, shrimp and sauce; toss to coat well. Best served chilled.

8 oz	macaroni or any small shell pasta	250 g
6 oz	raw shrimp, shelled	175 g
1/3 cup	light mayonnaise	75 mL
1/3 cup	low-fat sour cream	75 mL
1/4 cup	sweet tomato chili sauce	50 mL
1/2 cup	minced green bell peppers	125 mL
1/2 cup	minced red bell peppers	125 mL
1/2 cup	minced red onions	125 mL

salads

essential numbers

PER SERVING

Calories	374
Protein	17 g
Fat, total	9 g
Fat, saturated	2.8 g
Carbohydrates	54 g
Sodium	233 mg
Cholesterol	69 mg
Fiber	3 g

ask ROSE

This lively and flavorful salad is a snap to make. Just be sure that you don't mistakenly use hot chili sauce instead of the sweet tomato chili sauce called for in the recipe. (That is, unless you like your salad *really* lively!) Heinz makes the most popular sweet chili sauce, which consists of tomatoes, vinegar, sugar, onions and spices. In many ways, it's like hot sauce, but without the chili peppers.

for the record

The lowdown on deli pasta salads
With only 2 tsp (10 mL) fat per serving, this pasta salad is a great source of low-fat nutrition. But that's not the case with all pasta salads. In fact, the kind typically sold at your local deli can pack as much as 7 tsp (35 mL) of hidden fat (from mayonnaise, cheese and olives) per 1 1/2-cup serving. So stay at home and make this recipe. And if you want to cut even more fat, use fat-free mayonnaise and sour cream.

greek fettuccine

and chicken salad

1 In a food processor or blender, combine olive oil, Parmesan cheese, lemon juice, red wine vinegar, mustard, garlic, anchovies and egg; purée until smooth. Set aside.

2 In a nonstick frying pan sprayed with vegetable spray or on a preheated grill, cook chicken over medium-high heat, turning once, for 12 minutes or until cooked through. Slice thinly crosswise.

3 In a large pot of boiling water, cook fettuccine for 8 to 10 minutes or until tender but firm; drain.

4 In a serving bowl, combine hot pasta, chicken and dressing; toss to coat well. Add tomatoes, cucumber, red peppers, red onions, black olives and feta cheese. Serve immediately.

Dressing

3 tbsp	olive oil	45 mL
2 tbsp	grated low-fat Parmesan cheese	25 mL
1 tbsp	fresh lemon juice	15 mL
1 tbsp	red wine vinegar	15 mL
2 tsp	Dijon mustard	10 mL
1 1/2 tsp	minced garlic	7 mL
3	anchovy fillets, drained and chopped	3
1	large egg	1

Salad

8 oz	skinless boneless chicken breast	250 g
8 oz	fettuccine (regular or whole wheat)	250 g
1 1/2 cups	chopped ripe plum tomatoes	375 mL
1 cup	chopped English cucumber	250 mL
1 cup	chopped red bell peppers	250 mL
3/4 cup	chopped red onions	175 mL
1/3 cup	chopped black olives	75 mL
3 oz	light feta cheese, crumbled	75 g

essential numbers

PER SERVING	
Calories	465
Protein	24 g
Fat, total	18 g
Fat, saturated	5.9 g
Carbohydrates	53 g
Sodium	530 mg
Cholesterol	48 mg
Fiber	4 g

ask ROSE

Order Greek salad at a restaurant and you may think you're about to eat something light and healthy. Well, think again! Most restaurants pile on the olives, oil and cheese — so much so that you could end up consuming 700 calories and 38 g fat. No thanks! If you're eating out and want to order a Greek salad, ask to have the dressing put on the side. Use no more than 2 tbsp (25 mL) of dressing and try to cut back on the cheese and olives.

nutrition watch

Mediterranean health

When Dr. Ancel Keys studied 12,000 healthy, middle-aged men in seven countries (including Greece, Italy, U.S., and Finland) he found that those in Mediterranean regions had the lowest rates of heart disease and the highest life expectancies. Here the diet consists of fresh foods (such as grains, legumes, yogurt, low-fat cheese, fruits and vegetables) that are low in saturated fat and cholesterol, high in monounsaturated fat, high in fiber, and rich in vitamins, minerals and antioxidants.

salmon penne salad

1 In a bowl combine buttermilk, mayonnaise, lemon juice, honey, Dijon mustard, garlic, pepper and salt. Set aside.

2 In a pot of boiling water, cook asparagus for 1 minute or until tender-crisp. Drain; rinse with cold water until cool.

3 In a large pot of boiling water, cook penne for 8 to 10 minutes or until tender but firm; drain. Rinse under cold running water; drain. In a serving bowl, combine pasta, asparagus, red peppers, green onions and dill; toss to combine well.

4 Broil or grill salmon, turning once, for 10 minutes per 1-inch (2.5 cm) thickness or until cooked through; flake with a fork. Add salmon to salad. Pour dressing over; toss to coat well.

PREHEAT BROILER OR SET GRILL TO MEDIUM-HIGH

Dressing

2/3 cup	buttermilk	150 mL
3 tbsp	light mayonnaise	45 mL
1 1/2 tbsp	fresh lemon juice	20 mL
2 tsp	honey	10 mL
1 1/2 tsp	Dijon mustard	7 mL
1 1/2 tsp	minced garlic	7 mL
1/4 tsp	freshly ground black pepper	1 mL
1/4 tsp	salt	1 mL

Salad

8	stalks asparagus, trimmed and cut into 1 1/2-inch (4 cm) lengths	8
8 oz	penne	250 g
3/4 cup	chopped red bell peppers	175 mL
1/2 cup	chopped green onions	125 mL
1/3 cup	chopped fresh dill (or 1 tsp [5 mL] dried)	75 mL
6 oz	salmon fillet	175 g

salads

79

essential numbers

PER SERVING

Calories	389
Protein	19 g
Fat, total	9 g
Fat, saturated	1.8 g
Carbohydrates	58 g
Sodium	318 mg
Cholesterol	29 mg
Fiber	3 g

ask ROSE

Most varieties of salmon come from the Pacific coast. The best is the highly flavored Chinook or King salmon. Although higher in fat, these varieties are also rich in omega-3 fatty acids, which help lower blood cholesterol. For this recipe, use salmon fillets or steaks, whichever you prefer.

for the record

Butterless buttermilk

Despite its rich-sounding name, buttermilk has only 2 g fat for every 1 cup (250 mL). That's the same amount of fat in 1% milk. Buttermilk gets its thick consistency from bacterial cultures added during processing, which convert the sugar in the milk into lactic acid. The result is milk that tastes rich, tart and buttery. It's great in pancakes and muffins, and makes wonderfully creamy salad dressings — without the cream!

chicken bulgur niçoise

1 In a food processor or blender, combine water, lemon juice, vinegar, olive oil, anchovies and garlic; purée until smooth. Set aside.

2 In a saucepan over high heat, bring stock to a boil. Add bulgur; remove from heat. Let stand, covered, for 15 minutes or until tender and liquid is absorbed. Set aside to cool.

3 Meanwhile, in a saucepan over high heat, cover potatoes with cold water. Cover saucepan; bring to a boil. Reduce heat to medium; cook for 15 minutes or until tender when pierced with a knife. Drain; let cool. Cut potatoes into cubes.

4 In a nonstick frying pan sprayed with vegetable spray or on a preheated grill, cook chicken over medium-high heat, turning once, for 12 minutes or until cooked through. Cut chicken into chunks.

5 In a pot of boiling water, cook green beans for 2 minutes or until tender-crisp; drain. Rinse under cold running water; drain.

6 In a serving bowl, combine bulgur, potatoes, chicken, green beans, cherry tomatoes, red onions and black olives. Pour dressing over pasta and vegetables; season to taste with pepper. Toss to coat well. Serve.

Dressing

1/4 cup	water	50 mL
3 tbsp	fresh lemon juice	45 mL
2 tbsp	balsamic or red wine vinegar	25 mL
2 tbsp	olive oil	25 mL
4	anchovy fillets, drained and chopped	4
1 1/2 tsp	minced garlic	7 mL

Salad

1 1/3 cups	CHICKEN STOCK or VEGETABLE STOCK (see recipes, pages 50 and 51)	325 mL
1 cup	bulgur	250 mL
2	medium red potatoes, scrubbed and quartered	2
8 oz	boneless skinless chicken breast	250 g
8 oz	green beans, trimmed and halved	250 g
1 cup	ripe cherry tomatoes, cut into halves	250 mL
1/3 cup	diced red onions	75 mL
1/3 cup	sliced black olives	75 mL
	Freshly ground black pepper	

essential numbers

PER SERVING

Calories	374
Protein	21 g
Fat, total	12 g
Fat, saturated	1.4 g
Carbohydrates	50 g
Sodium	140 mg
Cholesterol	37 mg
Fiber	8 g

ask ROSE

Bulgur is a staple of traditional Middle Eastern cooking, and consists of wheat kernels that have been steamed, dried and crushed. It has a tender, chewy texture and a nutty flavor. I use it in salads, as a pilaf, or as an accompaniment to stews. For an interesting (and healthy!) variation on traditional meatloaf, you can substitute half the meat called for in the recipe with cooked bulgur. It tastes great — and delivers a big boost to your fiber intake.

nutrition watch

Omega who?

Anchovies are a great source of omega-3 fat — a special kind of polyunsaturated fat found in fish oil that may prevent heart attacks. In fact, eating fish three times a week has been associated with a significant reduction in rates of heart disease. How does fish protect your heart? Studies reveal that a diet rich in fish oils can lower blood cholesterol and triglyceride levels and it may increase HDL ("good") cholesterol. More great sources of omega-3 fats include salmon, trout, herring, mackerel and sardines.

two-tomato salad
over penne with basil-parmesan dressing

1 In a bowl cover sun-dried tomatoes with boiling water. Let stand for 15 minutes or until softened; drain. Cut tomatoes into chunks.

2 In a large pot of boiling water, cook penne for 8 to 10 minutes or until tender but firm; drain. Rinse under cold running water; drain. In a serving bowl, combine pasta, sun-dried tomatoes, plum tomatoes and red onions.

3 In a food processor or blender, combine basil, water, sour cream, mayonnaise, Parmesan cheese, olive oil, garlic and pepper; purée until smooth. Pour dressing over salad; toss to coat well. Serve.

1/2 cup	dry-packed sun-dried tomatoes	125 mL
8 oz	penne	250 g
1 cup	chopped ripe plum tomatoes	250 mL
3/4 cup	chopped red onions	175 mL

Dressing

3/4 cup	chopped fresh basil	175 mL
3 tbsp	water	45 mL
2 tbsp	low-fat sour cream	25 mL
2 tbsp	light mayonnaise	25 mL
2 tbsp	grated low-fat Parmesan cheese	25 mL
2 tbsp	olive oil	25 mL
1 tsp	minced garlic	5 mL
1/2 tsp	freshly ground black pepper	2 mL

salads

81

essential numbers

PER SERVING	
Calories	369
Protein	12 g
Fat, total	11 g
Fat, saturated	2.3 g
Carbohydrates	57 g
Sodium	260 mg
Cholesterol	4 mg
Fiber	3 g

ask ROSE

This pesto-like dressing is absolutely delicious — as long as you use fresh basil. (Dried basil is no substitute here!) Large-leaf basil is generally the most widely available, but other varieties are also worth trying if you can find them. Opal basil, for example, has a purple color and can be used in the same way as the green, large-leaf type. You can store basil with stems down in a glass of water, refrigerated, for up to 1 week. Do not wash or chop until ready to use.

variation

If you can't find any fresh basil, or if you want to experiment with different flavors, substitute Italian parsley, dill, spinach or coriander. Each makes a wonderful pesto and lends a distinctive character to this dish.

blue cheese chicken cobb
pasta salad with prosciutto

1. In a food processor or blender, combine lemon juice, olive oil, blue cheese, garlic and pepper; purée until smooth. Set aside.

2. In a large pot of boiling water, cook rotini for 8 to 10 minutes or until tender but firm; drain. Rinse under cold running water; drain.

3. In a nonstick frying pan sprayed with vegetable spray or on a preheated grill, cook chicken over medium-high heat, turning once, for 12 minutes or until cooked through; dice.

4. In a small nonstick frying pan sprayed with vegetable spray, cook egg whites over medium heat for 5 minutes or until set; dice.

5. In a serving bowl, combine pasta, chicken, egg whites, lettuce, tomatoes, green onions and prosciutto. Pour dressing over; toss to coat well. Serve immediately.

salads

82

Dressing

3 tbsp	fresh lemon juice	45 mL
2 tbsp	olive oil	25 mL
2 1/2 oz	blue cheese, crumbled	65 g
1 tsp	minced garlic	5 mL
1/4 tsp	freshly ground black pepper	1 mL

Salad

8 oz	rotini	250 g
4 oz	skinless boneless chicken breast	125 g
2	large egg whites	2
1 1/2 cups	thinly sliced Boston or leaf lettuce	375 mL
1 cup	diced seeded ripe plum tomatoes	250 mL
3/4 cup	chopped green onions	175 mL
1 1/2 oz	prosciutto or ham, diced	40 g

essential numbers

PER SERVING

Calories	399
Protein	22 g
Fat, total	14 g
Fat, saturated	4.9 g
Carbohydrates	47 g
Sodium	432 mg
Cholesterol	37 mg
Fiber	3 g

ask ROSE

Why use whole eggs in a recipe when just the whites will do? Substituting 2 egg whites for 1 whole egg in this recipe saves 5 g fat and 213 mg cholesterol. A big difference! And if it seems wasteful to throw out the yolk, you can always buy pure egg whites (also known by the unappetizing name, "liquid albumen") in the egg section of your grocery store.

variation

If you're cooking vegetarian these days, it's easy to transform this recipe into a meatless dish. Just replace the chicken with firm tofu and the prosciutto with vegetarian salami — a tofu-based product now sold in the vegetable section of many supermarkets.

wheat berry salad
with sesame dressing

1 In a bowl combine honey, rice wine vinegar, sesame oil, sesame seeds, soya sauce, tahini, garlic and ginger; whisk well. Set aside.

2 In a saucepan over high heat, bring stock to a boil. Add wheat berries; reduce heat to low. Cook, covered, for approximately 45 minutes or until berries are tender but chewy. Drain any excess liquid; allow to cool. Add green onions, carrots, green peppers, red peppers and snow peas. Set aside.

3 In a nonstick frying pan sprayed with vegetable spray or on a preheated grill, cook scallops over medium-high heat for 3 minutes or until cooked through. Drain any excess liquid; dice scallops.

4 In a serving bowl, combine wheat berry mixture, scallops and dressing; toss to coat well. Serve.

Dressing

1 tbsp	honey	15 mL
1 tbsp	rice wine vinegar	15 mL
1 tbsp	sesame oil	15 mL
1 tbsp	toasted sesame seeds	15 mL
1 tbsp	light soya sauce	15 mL
1 tbsp	tahini (sesame paste)	15 mL
1 tsp	minced garlic	5 mL
1/2 tsp	minced ginger root	2 mL

Salad

3 1/2 cups	SEAFOOD STOCK or CHICKEN STOCK (see recipes, page 50)	875 mL
1 cup	wheat berries	250 mL
1/2 cup	thinly sliced green onions	125 mL
1/2 cup	diced carrots	125 mL
1/2 cup	diced green bell peppers	125 mL
1/2 cup	diced red bell peppers	125 mL
1/2 cup	diced snow peas	125 mL
8 oz	scallops	250 g

salads

83

essential numbers

PER SERVING

Calories	507
Protein	24 g
Fat, total	12 g
Fat, saturated	1.8 g
Carbohydrates	81 g
Sodium	120 mg
Cholesterol	21 mg
Fiber	9 g

ask ROSE

Wheat berries are unprocessed whole kernels of wheat. They're tender, chewy and crunchy — great for salads and pilafs! Wheat berries are also extremely nutritious, and make a great high-fiber substitute in traditional meat loaf recipes.

for the record

Heart-healthy seafood

Contrary to popular belief, scallops are not high in cholesterol. Not even close! A 3-oz (75 g) serving (about 7 scallops) contains only 48 mg cholesterol and 1 g fat. Compare that to a similar-sized portion of skinless chicken breast, which has 73 mg cholesterol and 3 g fat. Remember, too, that it is the saturated fat in foods that raise your blood cholesterol, not the cholesterol in foods. So enjoy your scallops — just don't dunk them in butter!

millet salad
with dried fruit in an oriental lime dressing

1. In a nonstick skillet over medium-high heat, toast millet for 1 minute.

2. In a saucepan over high heat, bring stock to a boil. Add millet; reduce heat to low. Cook, covered, for 25 minutes or until grain is tender. Drain if any excess liquid. Set aside to cool.

3. In a bowl combine lime zest, lime juice, honey, sesame oil, soya sauce and garlic; whisk well.

4. In a serving bowl, combine millet, apples, apricots, cherries, coriander, green onions and prunes. Pour dressing over salad; toss to coat well. Serve.

1 cup	millet	250 mL
2 cups	VEGETABLE STOCK *or* CHICKEN STOCK (see recipes, pages 51 and 50)	500 mL
1 tsp	grated lime zest	5 mL
2 tbsp	fresh lime juice	25 mL
1 tbsp	honey	15 mL
1 tbsp	sesame oil	15 mL
1 tbsp	light soya sauce	15 mL
1 tsp	minced garlic	5 mL
1/3 cup	diced dried apples	75 mL
1/3 cup	diced dried apricots	75 mL
1/3 cup	dried cherries *or* raisins	75 mL
1/3 cup	chopped fresh coriander	75 mL
1/3 cup	chopped green onions	75 mL
1/3 cup	diced prunes	75 mL

salads

84

essential numbers

PER SERVING

Calories	375
Protein	8 g
Fat, total	6 g
Fat, saturated	0.9 g
Carbohydrates	73 g
Sodium	40 mg
Cholesterol	0 mg
Fiber	8 g

ask ROSE

While North Americans have traditionally used millet for fodder and bird seed, it is a dietary staple for almost one-third of the world's population. Today, you can find millet (with its hull removed) sold in health food stores and oriental markets. This type of millet is easy to digest, cooks quickly and makes a fluffy side dish. It is also rich in protein and has a mild flavor. It's delicious in salads, as a pilaf and as a hot cereal — definitely not for the birds!

nutrition watch

Herbs for health

Can adding herbs to meals reduce your cancer risk? Evidence is sketchy, but it may not hurt to try. Herbs contain a number of phyto (plant) chemicals that interact in the body. Some examples: *coriander* leaves (cilantro) and *parsley*, related to carrot family, have polyacetylenes (immune enhancers) and phthalides (antioxidants); *rosemary, mint, oregano, sage* and *thyme* contain quinones (antioxidants); and, *chives*, a cousin of garlic, are full of the same allyl sulfur compounds (immune enhancers, antioxidants).

pasta and bean salad
with creamy basil dressing

1 In a food processor or blender, combine basil, Parmesan cheese, pine nuts and garlic; process until finely chopped. Add yogurt, lemon juice, mayonnaise, water, olive oil and pepper; purée until smooth. Set aside.

2 In a large pot of boiling water, cook pasta for 8 to 10 minutes or until tender but firm; drain. Rinse under cold running water; drain.

3 In a serving bowl, combine pasta, black beans, chickpeas, kidney beans, red onions, carrots and plum tomatoes. Pour dressing over salad; toss to coat well. Serve immediately.

Dressing

1 1/2 cups	tightly packed fresh basil leaves	375 mL
3 tbsp	grated low-fat Parmesan cheese	45 mL
2 tbsp	toasted pine nuts	25 mL
1 1/2 tsp	minced garlic	7 mL
1/3 cup	low-fat yogurt	75 mL
3 tbsp	fresh lemon juice	45 mL
3 tbsp	light mayonnaise	45 mL
3 tbsp	water	45 mL
1 tbsp	olive oil	15 mL
1/4 tsp	freshly ground black pepper	1 mL

Salad

12 oz	medium shell pasta	375 g
3/4 cup	canned black beans, rinsed and drained	175 mL
3/4 cup	canned chickpeas, rinsed and drained	175 mL
3/4 cup	canned red kidney beans, rinsed and drained	175 mL
3/4 cup	diced red onions	175 mL
1/2 cup	shredded carrots	125 mL
2 cups	diced ripe plum tomatoes	500 mL

salads

85

essential numbers

PER SERVING

Calories	456
Protein	18 g
Fat, total	10 g
Fat, saturated	2.1 g
Carbohydrates	75 g
Sodium	178 mg
Cholesterol	3 mg
Fiber	7 g

ask ROSE

Fresh garlic is one of those ingredients that I almost always have on hand. But every once in a while, I run out — usually when I need it most! For times like these, I like to keep a jar of commercially prepared crushed garlic in the fridge. The garlic is preserved in oil, but the amount of fat added is negligible. Keep in mind that since the garlic has already been crushed, its flavor is less intense. So always add a little more to recipes than you would for fresh garlic.

cooking 101

OK, I'll admit it — I don't always cook my beans from scratch. In fact, I often use canned beans. They're quick, convenient (I can keep a wide variety on hand in my pantry) and, if you rinse them well, are good for most recipes. Of course, freshly prepared beans are still the best. But time is still a problem. That's why, instead of soaking beans overnight, I use the quick-soak method: Cover beans with cold water in a saucepan and bring to a boil; cook for 2 minutes. Remove from heat and let them sit for 1 hour. Drain, replace the water and cook over medium-low heat until beans are tender.

ravioli and mango salad

1. In a food processor or blender, combine mango, stock, lemon juice, olive oil and garlic; purée until smooth. Set aside.

2. In a large pot of boiling water, cook ravioli according to package directions or until tender; drain. Rinse under cold running water; drain.

3. In a serving bowl, combine pasta, coriander, red onions, green peppers and red peppers. Pour dressing over salad; toss to coat well. Serve.

salads

Dressing

2 cups	diced ripe mango	500 mL
1/3 cup	VEGETABLE STOCK *or* CHICKEN STOCK (see recipes, pages 51 and 50)	75 mL
3 tbsp	fresh lemon juice	45 mL
2 tsp	olive oil	10 mL
1 tsp	minced garlic	5 mL

Salad

1 lb	fresh or frozen cheese ravioli	500 g
1/2 cup	chopped fresh coriander	125 mL
1/2 cup	diced red onions	125 mL
1/2 cup	diced green bell peppers	125 mL
1/2 cup	diced red bell peppers	125 mL

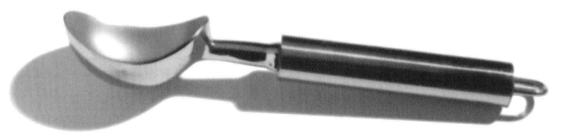

essential numbers

PER SERVING

Calories	211
Protein	5 g
Fat, total	4 g
Fat, saturated	0.9 g
Carbohydrates	42 g
Sodium	478 mg
Cholesterol	1 mg
Fiber	5 g

ask ROSE

A ripe mango is velvety, sweet and juicy. The trick is to find one that's perfectly ripe. Look for fruit that gives slightly when pressed gently with your thumbs. The mango should also be without blemishes, soft areas or shriveled skin. (If it isn't quite ripe, let it sit, uncovered, at room temperature.) To use the mango, cut it with a sharp serrated knife down each side of the pit (like an avocado), then remove the two halves.

for the record

Meganutritious mango

For a blast of beta carotene, it's hard to beat mangoes. One medium-sized fruit contains 5 mg of this potent antioxidant, which appears to offer protection from many types of cancer, especially lung cancer. Studies have found that a diet rich in beta carotene reduces the risk of lung cancer in men and women — both smokers and non-smokers. While there is no official daily recommended intake, most experts agree that 5 mg a day offers protection. Other sources include raw carrots, sweet potatoes, canned pumpkin, cooked spinach and dried apricots.

Serves 6

mango kiwi and apricots
over rotini with raspberry vinaigrette

1 In a large pot of boiling water, cook rotini for 8 to 10 minutes or until tender but firm; drain. Rinse under cold running water; drain. In a serving bowl, combine pasta, mango, kiwi, apricots, dates and almonds.

2 In a bowl combine parsley, raspberry vinegar, green onions, honey, olive oil, orange juice concentrate and garlic; whisk well. Pour dressing over salad; toss to coat well.

8 oz	rotini	250 g
1 cup	diced ripe mango	250 mL
3/4 cup	diced kiwi fruit	175 mL
1/2 cup	diced dried apricots	125 mL
1/2 cup	diced dried dates	125 mL
1/4 cup	toasted sliced almonds	50 mL

Raspberry vinaigrette

1/4 cup	chopped fresh parsley	50 mL
3 tbsp	raspberry vinegar	45 mL
3 tbsp	minced green onions	45 mL
2 tbsp	honey	25 mL
2 tbsp	olive oil	25 mL
2 tbsp	orange juice concentrate	25 mL
1 tsp	minced garlic	5 mL

salads

87

essential numbers

PER SERVING	
Calories	541
Protein	12 g
Fat, total	11 g
Fat, saturated	1.3 g
Carbohydrates	103 g
Sodium	169 mg
Cholesterol	0 mg
Fiber	8 g

ask ROSE

Fresh orange juice tastes great, but for recipes that require an intense orange flavor I like to use orange juice concentrate. I always keep a few cans of unsweetened orange juice concentrate in the freezer. For a different flavor, try pineapple or apple juice concentrate.

cooking 101

To enhance the flavor of nuts, toast them lightly in a skillet over high heat, stirring continuously to prevent them from burning. Another method (although not as easy, I think) is to spread nuts on a baking sheet and toast at 400° F (200° C) for about 5 minutes.

tex-mex rotini salad

1 In a large pot of boiling water, cook rotini for 8 to 10 minutes or until tender but firm; drain. Rinse under cold running water; drain. In a serving bowl combine pasta, tomatoes, kidney beans, corn, coriander and green onions.

2 In a bowl combine barbecue sauce, cider vinegar, molasses and jalapeño pepper; whisk well. Pour dressing over salad; toss to coat well. Garnish with crumbled tortilla chips. Serve.

8 oz	rotini	250 g
1 1/2 cups	diced ripe plum tomatoes	375 mL
1 cup	canned red kidney beans, rinsed and drained	250 mL
1 cup	canned corn kernels, rinsed and drained	250 mL
1/2 cup	chopped fresh coriander	125 mL
1/2 cup	chopped green onions	125 mL

Dressing

1/3 cup	barbecue sauce	75 mL
2 1/2 tbsp	cider vinegar	35 mL
2 tsp	molasses	10 mL
1 tsp	minced jalapeño pepper (optional)	5 mL
1 oz	baked tortilla chips (about 12)	25 g

salads

88

PER SERVING	
Calories	393
Protein	16 g
Fat, total	2 g
Fat, saturated	0.3 g
Carbohydrates	80 g
Sodium	196 mg
Cholesterol	0 mg
Fiber	2 g

essential numbers

ask ROSE

Tortilla chips are a great snack food — but only if they're baked! The traditional deep-fried variety is *much* higher in fat and calories.

For a great snack, melt some light Cheddar cheese over tortillas. Kids love them!

for the record

Salads that sabotage your diet

Feeling virtuous after your trip to the salad bar? Well, don't get too smug just yet! A fat-free salad quickly becomes a high-fat meal when you add generous amounts of dressing. Potato and pasta salads, usually laden with mayonnaise and oil, often pack more than 200 calories per 1/2-cup (125 mL) serving. So here's the plan: First, fill your plate with greens and raw vegetables, then add one or two higher-fat salads in 1-tbsp (15 mL) portions (just enough for a taste!). Finally, add some low-fat dressing or a splash of balsamic vinegar.

quinoa salad
with fennel, red pepper and apricots in an orange dressing

1 In a saucepan over high heat, bring stock to a boil. Meanwhile, in a nonstick skillet over medium-high heat, lightly toast quinoa for 1 minute. Add quinoa to stock; reduce heat to medium-low. Cook, covered, for 15 minutes or until tender and liquid is absorbed. Transfer to a serving bowl.

2 When quinoa has cooled, add fennel, red peppers, snow peas, apricots and dried cranberries.

3 In a bowl combine vinegar, orange juice concentrate, honey, olive oil and garlic; whisk well. Pour dressing over salad; toss to coat well. Serve.

2 cups	VEGETABLE STOCK *or* CHICKEN STOCK (see recipes, pages 51 and 50)	500 mL
1 cup	quinoa, rinsed	250 mL
1 cup	diced fennel	250 mL
1 cup	diced red bell peppers	250 mL
1 cup	diced snow peas	250 mL
1/2 cup	diced dried apricots	125 mL
1/4 cup	dried cranberries *or* dried cherries *or* raisins	50 mL

Dressing

2 tbsp	raspberry vinegar	25 mL
2 tbsp	orange juice concentrate	25 mL
1 tbsp	honey	15 mL
1 tbsp	olive oil	15 mL
1 tsp	minced garlic	5 mL

salads

89

PER SERVING

essential numbers

Calories	339
Protein	9 g
Fat, total	7 g
Fat, saturated	0.9 g
Carbohydrates	64 g
Sodium	188 mg
Cholesterol	0 mg
Fiber	7 g

ask ROSE

Dried fruits offer a concentrated sweetness that is completely different from that of their fresh counterparts. Just compare grapes and raisins, or plums and prunes, and you can imagine the sweet intensity of dried cranberries, cherries, blueberries, pineapple and mangoes. Try them all!

nutrition watch

An iron-rich grain or vegetable?
Although widely considered a grain, quinoa is actually related to the spinach family. And like spinach, quinoa is a good source of iron. (A serving of this quinoa salad gives you 6 mg!) While the iron in grains and vegetables is not as well absorbed as the iron in animal foods, you can enhance the amount of iron your body absorbs from plant foods by eating them with a source of vitamin C. In fact, the orange juice dressing here allows you to absorb up to four times more iron from the quinoa!

grilled fruit salad
over rotini with shrimp

salads

1. In a bowl combine parsley, vinegar, orange juice concentrate, olive oil, honey and garlic; whisk well. Set aside.

2. In a large pot of boiling water, cook rotini for 8 to 10 minutes or until tender but firm; drain. Rinse under cold running water; drain.

3. Meanwhile, in a nonstick frying pan sprayed with vegetable spray or on a preheated grill, cook shrimp over medium-high heat, turning once, for 2 minutes or until pink. Add pears, pineapple rings and peach; cook for 3 minutes per side or until grill-marked and tender. Cut shrimp and fruit into large chunks.

4. In a serving bowl, combine pasta, shrimp mixture and dressing; toss to combine well.

Dressing

1/3 cup	chopped fresh parsley	75 mL
3 tbsp	balsamic vinegar	45 mL
3 tbsp	orange juice concentrate	45 mL
2 tbsp	olive oil	25 mL
1 1/2 tbsp	honey	20 mL
1 tsp	minced garlic	5 mL

Salad

8 oz	rotini	250 g
6 oz	raw shrimp, peeled and deveined	175 g
2	small ripe pears, peeled, cored and cut into quarters	2
2	fresh ripe pineapple rings (1/2 inch [1 cm] thick)	2
1	ripe peach or nectarine, peeled and halved	1

essential numbers

PER SERVING

Calories	452
Protein	18 g
Fat, total	8 g
Fat, saturated	1.1 g
Carbohydrates	78 g
Sodium	76 mg
Cholesterol	67 mg
Fiber	5 g

*ask*ROSE

If grilling works for vegetables, then why not fruit? And work it does — hot, sweet and delicious! Just be sure that the fruit is ripe, then grill it just until slightly tender and grill marks show. Avoid overcooking or the fruit will become mushy. For indoor cooking, invest in an iron-clad grilling skillet; they're inexpensive and last forever.

variation

Not a big fan of seafood? No problem! Just grill some boneless chicken breasts and substitute for the shrimp. Also, try experimenting with other grilled fruit, such as mangoes, apples, papayas — even grapefruit!

potato pasta salad
with creamy parmesan dressing

1 In a bowl cover sun-dried tomatoes with boiling water. Let sit for 15 minutes. Drain; chop tomatoes. Set aside.

2 In a saucepan over high heat, cover potatoes with cold water; bring to a boil. Cook for 10 minutes or until tender; drain. Set aside.

3 In a pot of boiling water, cook pasta for 8 minutes or until tender but firm; drain. Rinse under cold running water; drain.

4 In a food processor or blender, combine milk, ricotta cheese, sour cream, dill, lemon juice, Parmesan cheese, mayonnaise, capers, garlic, pepper and salt; purée until smooth.

5 In a serving bowl, combine pasta, potatoes, sun-dried tomatoes, plum tomatoes, green onions, red onions, red peppers and dressing; toss to coat well. Serve.

1/3 cup	dry-packed sun-dried tomatoes	75 mL
1 lb	potatoes, peeled and cut into 1/2-inch (1 cm) cubes	500 g
8 oz	small shell pasta	250 g
Dressing		
2/3 cup	low-fat milk	150 mL
1/3 cup	5% ricotta cheese or 2% cottage cheese	75 mL
1/3 cup	low-fat sour cream	75 mL
1/3 cup	chopped fresh dill (or 1 1/2 tsp [7 mL] dried)	75 mL
1/4 cup	fresh lemon juice	50 mL
1/4 cup	grated low-fat Parmesan cheese	50 mL
2 tbsp	light mayonnaise	25 mL
1 tbsp	drained capers	15 mL
1 tsp	minced garlic	5 mL
1/4 tsp	freshly ground black pepper	1 mL
1/8 tsp	salt	0.5 mL
1 cup	diced ripe plum tomatoes	250 mL
1/2 cup	chopped green onions	125 mL
1/2 cup	diced red onions	125 mL
1/2 cup	diced red bell peppers	125 mL

salads

91

essential numbers

PER SERVING

Calories	430
Protein	17 g
Fat, total	8 g
Fat, saturated	3.3 g
Carbohydrates	75 g
Sodium	444 mg
Cholesterol	16 mg
Fiber	4 g

ask ROSE

The best potatoes for this salad are medium-sized round white or red potatoes, commonly known as boiling potatoes. This type contains less starch and more moisture than the typical baking potato. If you want to cut potatoes early in the day, be sure to cover with cold water and refrigerate; otherwise they will turn brown.

for the record

A matter of fat

Quickly now, which has more fat — a large Caesar salad (2 cups [500 mL]) with 1 piece garlic bread or macaroni and cheese with a side salad and 1 tbsp (15 mL) dressing? If you guessed the macaroni and cheese, guess again. The Caesar salad meal packs 28 g fat, while the macaroni and cheese plate has only 22 g fat. How to improve the Caesar salad? Ask for plain bread and order the salad with dressing on the side, topped with grilled chicken breast or shrimp.

sweet pepper olive purée
over rotini with chicken

1 Broil or grill red peppers for 20 minutes or until charred; let cool. Peel, stem and seed peppers. In a food processor combine red peppers, basil, black olives, olive oil, balsamic vinegar, garlic and pepper; purée. Set aside.

2 In a nonstick saucepan sprayed with vegetable spray or on a preheated grill, cook chicken over medium-high heat, turning once, for 12 minutes or until cooked through; slice thinly. Meanwhile, in a large pot of boiling water, cook rotini for 8 to 10 minutes or until tender but firm; drain.

3 In a serving bowl combine pasta, chicken, feta cheese and sauce; toss well. Serve immediately.

PREHEAT BROILER OR SET GRILL TO MEDIUM-HIGH

2	large red bell peppers	2
1/2 cup	chopped fresh basil (or 1 tsp [5 mL] dried)	125 mL
1/2 cup	sliced black olives	125 mL
2 tbsp	olive oil	25 mL
2 tsp	balsamic vinegar	10 mL
1 1/2 tsp	minced garlic	7 mL
1/4 tsp	freshly ground black pepper	1 mL
8 oz	skinless boneless chicken breast	250 g
8 oz	rotini	250 g
2 oz	light feta cheese, crumbled	50 g

poultry

94

essential numbers

PER SERVING

Calories	330
Protein	19 g
Fat, total	17 g
Fat, saturated	3.5 g
Carbohydrates	27 g
Sodium	446 mg
Cholesterol	48 mg
Fiber	2 g

ask ROSE

Roasting peppers is easy — it's getting the skins off afterward that's hard! But here's one way to make the job painless: Place the roasted peppers in a paper bag or in a bowl covered with plastic wrap; let them sit for 10 minutes and — *voila!* — the skins slip off. And if the peppers are a little too hot to handle? Just rinse them under cold water.

nutrition watch

The virtues of olive oil

It's good when a recipe is low in fat. It's even better when that relatively small amount of fat is of the "right" type — specifically, monounsaturated fat, which is found in the olive oil, and accounts for 80% of the total fat here. This type of fat can raise HDL cholesterol, which transports cholesterol away from the arteries and out of the body. A Spanish study found a 30% lower risk of breast cancer among women who consumed the most olive oil compared with those who consumed the least. What's more, monounsaturated fat may lower blood sugar in people with diabetes. Time for an oil change?

chicken livers
and rigatoni with prosciutto

1   In a nonstick frying pan sprayed with vegetable spray, cook livers over medium-high heat for 5 minutes or until no longer pink in center; drain liquid. Set aside. In another bowl, combine stock and flour; set aside.

2   In a large pot of boiling water, cook rigatoni for 8 to 10 minutes or until tender but firm; drain.

3   Meanwhile, in a nonstick saucepan sprayed with vegetable spray, cook onions and garlic over medium-high heat for 3 minutes or until softened. Add red peppers and carrots; cook for 2 minutes. Add stock mixture and livers; reduce heat to medium-low. Cook for 2 minutes or until sauce is heated through and thickened.

4   In a serving bowl, combine pasta, sauce and prosciutto; toss well. Sprinkle with Parmesan cheese; serve immediately.

8 oz	chicken livers, cut into quarters, dusted with flour	250 g
1 cup	cold CHICKEN STOCK (see recipe, page 50)	250 mL
2 tsp	all-purpose flour	10 mL
8 oz	rigatoni	250 g
1/2 cup	chopped onions	125 mL
1 1/2 tsp	minced garlic	7 mL
1/2 cup	diced red bell peppers	125 mL
1/2 cup	finely diced carrots	125 mL
2 oz	prosciutto, chopped	50 g
2 tbsp	grated low-fat Parmesan cheese	25 mL

poultry

95

PER SERVING	
Calories	429
Protein	29 g
Fat, total	8 g
Fat, saturated	3.6 g
Carbohydrates	59 g
Sodium	597 mg
Cholesterol	292 mg
Fiber	3 g

essential numbers

ask ROSE

Wondering why we use cold stock here? It's to ensure that the flour dissolves properly. Now, that may not seem right — after all, we're used to thinking that dry ingredients (like sugar) dissolve better in warm liquids. But flour is different. When added to hot liquid it just gets lumpy, and won't thicken your sauce properly. So be sure that your stock is cold — or at least no warmer than room temperature.

for the record

Don't fear the cholesterol

Look at the nutrient analysis here and you might get a shock — 292 mg of cholesterol! Isn't that high? Sure, but keep in mind that for most people, dietary cholesterol has little or no effect on blood cholesterol. And besides, the chicken livers pack a powerful nutrition punch. A 4-oz (125 g) serving (5 livers) provides close to 5 times the recommended intake (RNI) for vitamin A, 2 times the RNI for folate and is an excellent source of niacin and iron. All that for only 5 g fat!

chicken pine nut meatballs
in tomato-grape jelly sauce

1. In a bowl combine chicken, shallot, egg, ketchup, bread crumbs, pine nuts, Parmesan cheese, garlic and basil. Form 2 tbsp (25 mL) mixture into a 1 1/2-inch (4 cm) ball; repeat to make about 24 meatballs. Set aside.

2. In a large saucepan over medium-high heat, combine tomato juice, grape jelly and chili sauce. Bring to a boil; add meatballs. Reduce heat to medium-low; cook, covered, for 20 minutes.

3. Meanwhile, in a large pot of boiling water, cook fettuccine for 8 to 10 minutes or until tender but firm; drain. In a serving bowl, combine pasta and meatball mixture; toss well. Garnish with parsley; serve immediately.

Meatballs

1 lb	ground chicken	500 g
1	large shallot, finely chopped *or* 1/4 cup (50 mL) minced onions	1
1	large egg	1
1/4 cup	ketchup	50 mL
1/3 cup	dry bread crumbs	75 mL
3 tbsp	chopped toasted pine nuts	45 mL
2 tbsp	grated low-fat Parmesan cheese	25 mL
1 1/2 tsp	minced garlic	7 mL
1 tsp	dried basil	5 mL

Sauce

3 cups	tomato juice or V-8 juice	750 mL
2 tbsp	grape jelly	25 mL
2 tbsp	sweet chili sauce	25 mL
12 oz	fettuccine (regular or whole wheat)	375 g
1/4 cup	chopped fresh parsley	50 mL

essential numbers

PER SERVING

Calories	510
Protein	27 g
Fat, total	17 g
Fat, saturated	1.2 g
Carbohydrates	64 g
Sodium	251 mg
Cholesterol	37 mg
Fiber	4 g

ask ROSE

Ever wonder why that small jar of pine nuts is so expensive? Well, just consider that these delicious (but high-fat) nuts must be removed individually from pine cones. A lot of work! To economize, I buy pine nuts in bulk and keep them in the freezer until needed. (This is a good idea in any case, since they will eventually become rancid if left at room temperature.) To enhance their flavor, pine nuts can be lightly toasted in a nonstick skillet over high heat just until browned.

lifestyle

These meatballs are great for the entire family. You can double the recipe and freeze the extra meatballs in their sauce for lunches or dinners. And if your kids are like mine — for reasons I can't figure out, they dislike anything green or chunky in their food — you may want to chop the pine nuts and shallot extra-finely, and omit the parsley garnish.

chicken paella with sausage, shrimp and mussels (page 102)

creamy tomato pesto
and chicken over fettuccine

1 In a bowl cover sun-dried tomatoes with boiling water. Let stand for 15 minutes or until softened; drain.

2 In a food processor or blender, combine sun-dried tomatoes, parsley, 1 tbsp (15 mL) Parmesan cheese, pine nuts and garlic; process until finely chopped. Add stock, evaporated milk and olive oil; purée until smooth. Set aside.

3 In a nonstick skillet sprayed with vegetable spray or on a preheated grill, cook chicken over medium-high heat, turning once, for 12 minutes or until cooked through. Cut into chunks. Meanwhile, in a large pot of boiling water, cook fettuccine for 8 to 10 minutes or until tender but firm; drain.

4 In a serving bowl, combine chicken, pesto, pasta and remaining Parmesan cheese; toss to coat well. Serve immediately.

Sun-dried tomato pesto

1 1/2 oz	dry-packed sun-dried tomatoes	40 g
1/4 cup	chopped fresh parsley	50 mL
2 tbsp	grated low-fat Parmesan cheese	25 mL
1 tbsp	toasted pine nuts	15 mL
1 tsp	minced garlic	5 mL
1/2 cup	CHICKEN STOCK (see recipe, page 50)	125 mL
1/4 cup	low-fat evaporated milk	50 mL
2 tbsp	olive oil	25 mL
8 oz	skinless boneless chicken breast	250 g
12 oz	fettuccine or rice noodles	375 g

poultry

97

PER SERVING

essential numbers

Calories	330
Protein	20 g
Fat, total	4 g
Fat, saturated	1.4 g
Carbohydrates	54 g
Sodium	240 mg
Cholesterol	25 mg
Fiber	2 g

ask ROSE

My favorite parts of chicken are skinless boneless breasts. They're tender, delicious and, best of all, really low in fat! In fact, a 4-oz (125 g) serving contains only 130 calories and only 2.5 g fat. If you're ever tempted to try skin-on chicken breasts, just consider that the skin will add 60 calories and increase the fat by nearly 400% to 12 g. And if you like dark meat? Sorry, but one serving contains a whopping 250 calories and 18 g fat!

nutrition watch

Getting more iron
Calorie for calorie, who would have thought that parsley is one of the best sources of iron? Well, it's true: 1 cup (250 mL) of the green stuff has only 22 calories, yet provides almost 4 mg of iron. (See page 61 for more info on iron.) Unfortunately, much of this iron is unusable because it's chemically bonded to oxalic acid, which carries the iron out of the body with other wastes. To increase iron absorption from plant foods, include a small portion of meat, poultry or fish in the same meal.

curried chicken coconut pasta with apricots and cranberries (page 101)

savory chicken fagioli
over rigatoni

1 In a large nonstick saucepan sprayed with vegetable spray, cook carrots, onions, celery and garlic over medium-high heat for 4 minutes or until softened. Add mashed beans, whole beans, tomatoes, chicken stock, brown sugar, basil, chili powder, oregano and bay leaf. Bring to a boil; reduce heat to medium-low. Cook for 20 minutes or until vegetables are tender, stirring occasionally to break up tomatoes. Add chicken; cook for 3 minutes or until cooked through.

2 Meanwhile, in a large pot of boiling water, cook rigatoni for 10 to 12 minutes or until tender but firm; drain.

3 In a serving bowl, combine pasta and sauce; toss well. Sprinkle with Parmesan cheese and parsley. Serve immediately.

1/2 cup	chopped carrots	125 mL
1/2 cup	chopped onions	125 mL
1/3 cup	chopped celery	75 mL
1 1/2 tsp	minced garlic	7 mL
1	can (19 oz [540 mL]) red kidney beans, rinsed and drained, half the amount mashed	1
1	can (19 oz [540 mL]) tomatoes, with juice	1
2/3 cup	CHICKEN STOCK (see recipe, page 50)	150 mL
2 tsp	packed brown sugar	10 mL
1 1/2 tsp	dried basil	7 mL
1 tsp	chili powder	5 mL
1 tsp	dried oregano	5 mL
1	bay leaf	1
12 oz	skinless boneless chicken breast, diced	375 g
12 oz	rigatoni	375 g
1/4 cup	grated low-fat Parmesan cheese	50 mL
1/4 cup	chopped fresh parsley	50 mL

essential numbers

PER SERVING	
Calories	464
Protein	30 g
Fat, total	4 g
Fat, saturated	1.3 g
Carbohydrates	76 g
Sodium	122 mg
Cholesterol	37 mg
Fiber	12 g

ask ROSE

Ever wonder what goes into chili powder? Well, there's ground chilies (no surprise there), but also a number of other spices common to Southwestern-style cooking. These often include cumin, ginger, cayenne, oregano and dried mustard. But since there is no one formula for chili powder, the actual ingredients vary with different brands. I find that those from the smallest producers are the most flavorful.

for the record

That was then, this is now
Hard to believe, but today's chicken is about 40% leaner than it was as recently as 15 years ago. A 4-oz (125 g) skinless roasted chicken breast now contains a meager 2.1 g fat, down from 3.6 g in the old days. And a serving of chicken leg, with the back attached, has 6.9 g fat, down from almost 11 g.

Serves 6

teriyaki chicken
with sesame seeds over rotini

1. In a bowl combine rice wine vinegar, brown sugar, water, soya sauce, sesame oil, cornstarch, garlic and ginger; set aside.

2. In a nonstick skillet sprayed with vegetable spray or on a preheated grill, cook chicken over medium-high heat, turning once, for 12 minutes or until cooked through. Slice chicken into thin strips; set aside.

3. In a large pot of boiling water, cook rotini for 8 to 10 minutes or until tender but firm; drain.

4. Meanwhile, in a large nonstick frying pan or wok sprayed with vegetable spray, cook red peppers, yellow peppers, snow peas and sesame seeds over medium-high heat for 4 minutes or until tender-crisp. Add sauce; cook for 2 minutes or until thickened and bubbly.

5. In a serving bowl, combine pasta, sauce and chicken strips; toss well. Serve immediately.

Sauce

1/4 cup	rice wine vinegar	50 mL
1/4 cup	packed brown sugar	50 mL
1/4 cup	water	50 mL
1/4 cup	light soya sauce	50 mL
1 tbsp	sesame oil	15 mL
2 1/2 tsp	cornstarch	12 mL
1 1/2 tsp	minced garlic	7 mL
1 1/2 tsp	minced ginger root	7 mL
12 oz	skinless boneless chicken breast	375 g
12 oz	rotini	375 g
1 cup	thinly sliced red bell peppers	250 mL
1 cup	thinly sliced yellow peppers	250 mL
1 cup	snow peas, trimmed and halved	250 mL
2 tsp	sesame seeds	10 mL

poultry

99

essential numbers

PER SERVING	
Calories	371
Protein	22 g
Fat, total	5 g
Fat, saturated	1.0 g
Carbohydrates	59 g
Sodium	396 mg
Cholesterol	34 mg
Fiber	3 g

ask ROSE

Chances are you've heard of (if not actually tasted) Teriyaki chicken, beef or vegetables. But what is it that makes a dish Teriyaki? It's the Japanese technique of marinating and/or cooking food in a mixture of soya sauce, vinegar, sugar, ginger and seasonings. The sugar gives the food its distinctive glazed appearance.

cooking 101

Rice vinegar or rice wine vinegar is made from fermented rice, which gives it a milder flavor than North American vinegars. (These are typically made from grains, wine or cider.) Typically, you'll find two types of rice vinegar — pale yellow or darker brown. Personally, I prefer the lighter variety; it has a smoother flavor. And if you can't find any rice wine vinegar? Just substitute sherry or white wine.

tomato avocado sauce
over chicken fettuccine

1 In a food processor or blender, combine tomatoes, avocado, coriander, green onions, sour cream, water, lime juice, mayonnaise, garlic and chili paste; purée. Set aside.

2 In a nonstick skillet sprayed with vegetable spray or on a preheated grill, cook chicken over medium-high heat, turning once, for 12 minutes or until cooked through. Slice chicken into strips. Meanwhile, in a large pot of boiling water, cook fettuccine for 8 to 10 minutes or until tender but firm; drain.

3 In a serving bowl, combine pasta, chicken and sauce; toss well. Serve immediately.

1 cup	diced peeled plum tomatoes	250 mL
1	medium ripe avocado, peeled, pitted and diced	1
1/3 cup	chopped fresh coriander	75 mL
1/3 cup	chopped green onions	75 mL
1/4 cup	low-fat sour cream	50 mL
1/4 cup	water	50 mL
2 tbsp	fresh lime or lemon juice	25 mL
2 tbsp	light mayonnaise	25 mL
1 tsp	minced garlic	5 mL
1/2 tsp	hot Asian chili paste (optional)	2 mL
12 oz	skinless boneless chicken breast	375 g
12 oz	fettuccine	375 g

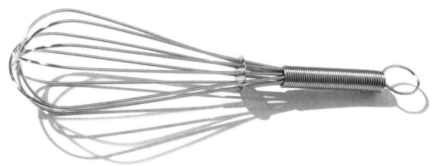

essential numbers

PER SERVING

Calories	422
Protein	28 g
Fat, total	10 g
Fat, saturated	2.0 g
Carbohydrates	53 g
Sodium	78 mg
Cholesterol	53 mg
Fiber	4 g

ask ROSE

Avocados are irresistibly rich and buttery. So naturally they have to be high in fat, right? They sure are — as much as 30 g fat per serving! But at least it's monounsaturated fat, the good kind that actually helps to lower blood cholesterol. Who says life is unfair?

Avocado flesh darkens when exposed to air. And while this doesn't affect the flavor, it's not very attractive. To prevent discoloring, rub cut surfaces with lemon and sprinkle flesh with lemon juice, then cover with plastic wrap.

cooking 101

Light or low-fat mayonnaise is similar to regular mayonnaise, except that it contains fewer eggs and less oil. The result? Less than half the calories and fat! In fact, 1 tbsp (15 mL) of light mayo has only 50 calories and 5 g fat. (OK, so that's still pretty high; but it's still a big improvement.) Use light mayonnaise the same way as you would use the regular variety.

curried chicken coconut
pasta with apricots and cranberries

1. In a bowl coat chicken with 2 tbsp (25 mL) flour; shake off excess. In a large nonstick frying pan sprayed with vegetable spray, cook chicken over medium-high heat for 4 minutes or until cooked through. Remove from pan; set aside.

2. In a bowl combine coconut milk, stock, garlic, curry powder and 2 tsp (10 mL) flour; set aside.

3. In a large pot of boiling water, cook penne for 8 to 10 minutes or until tender but firm; drain. Meanwhile, respray frying pan; return to medium-high heat. Cook red peppers for 2 minutes or until softened. Add apricots, cranberries, coconut milk mixture and chicken; cook for 4 minutes or until thickened and bubbly.

4. In a serving bowl, combine pasta, sauce, green onions and coriander; toss well. Serve immediately.

12 oz	skinless boneless chicken breast, cut into 1/2-inch (1 cm) cubes	375 g
2 tbsp	all-purpose flour	25 mL
1 cup	light coconut milk	250 mL
1/2 cup	CHICKEN STOCK (see recipe, page 50)	125 mL
1 tsp	minced garlic	5 mL
1 tsp	curry powder	5 mL
2 tsp	all-purpose flour	10 mL
12 oz	penne or rotini	375 g
1/2 cup	chopped red bell peppers	125 mL
1/2 cup	chopped dried apricots	125 mL
1/2 cup	dried cranberries *or* raisins	125 mL
1/2 cup	chopped green onions	125 mL
1/3 cup	chopped fresh coriander or parsley	75 mL

poultry

101

essential numbers

PER SERVING

Calories	421
Protein	22 g
Fat, total	3 g
Fat, saturated	0.6 g
Carbohydrates	74 g
Sodium	52 mg
Cholesterol	35 mg
Fiber	4 g

ask ROSE

You can find dried cranberries — as well as dried cherries, blueberries and a whole range of other dried fruits — at bulk food stores, where they are reasonably inexpensive. (But they're not exactly cheap, either.) I buy large quantities and keep them in airtight containers in my freezer until needed. Use them as a delicious alternative to raisins in salads, pastas, rice pilafs and desserts.

nutrition watch

Cranberries and cholesterol

If you're trying to manage your blood cholesterol, consider adding cranberries to your daily menu. It seems these bright red berries are full of antioxidant compounds, called anthocyanins, that may help reduce the risk of heart disease. Researchers at the University of Wisconsin found that cranberry juice was able to inhibit free radicals from oxidizing LDL cholesterol (when oxidized, it sticks more readily to artery walls). Antioxidants, like anthocyanins in cranberries, act to detoxify harmful free radical molecules.

chicken paella
with sausage, shrimp and mussels

1　In a nonstick frying pan sprayed with vegetable spray, cook chicken over medium-high heat, turning occasionally, for 5 minutes or until well browned. Remove from pan; drain off any excess fat. In the same pan, cook sausage for 5 minutes or until cooked through; remove from pan with a slotted spoon. Set aside.

2　In a large nonstick saucepan sprayed with vegetable spray, cook onions and garlic over medium-high heat for 4 minutes or until softened. Add red peppers and green peppers; cook for 3 minutes. Add rice; cook for 1 minute or until heated through. Add chicken, sausage, chicken stock, plum tomatoes, basil, oregano, bay leaf and saffron; bring to a boil.

3　Meanwhile, if using large or jumbo shrimp, cut into halves; add shrimp and mussels to boiling mixture. If pot is ovenproof, cover and put in preheated oven; otherwise transfer mixture to a casserole dish. Bake in preheated oven, stirring halfway through cooking time, for 40 minutes or until rice is tender and chicken and shrimp are cooked through. Discard any mussels that do not open. Remove chicken skin; serve.

PREHEAT OVEN TO 400° F (200° C)

2	chicken legs, separated into thighs and drumsticks	2
6 oz	sweet Italian sausage, cut into 1/2-inch (1 cm) pieces	175 g
1 cup	chopped onions	250 mL
2 tsp	minced garlic	10 mL
1 cup	chopped red bell peppers	250 mL
1 cup	chopped green bell peppers	250 mL
1 cup	Arborio rice (risotto rice)	250 mL
2 cups	CHICKEN STOCK (see recipe, page 50)	500 mL
1 1/2 cups	chopped ripe plum tomatoes	375 mL
2 tsp	dried basil	10 mL
1 tsp	dried oregano	5 mL
1	bay leaf	1
1/2 tsp	crumbled saffron threads (optional)	2 mL
6 oz	raw shrimp, shelled	175 g
12	fresh mussels, scrubbed and beards removed	12

PER SERVING

Calories	547
Protein	38 g
Fat, total	19 g
Fat, saturated	6.2 g
Carbohydrates	56 g
Sodium	632 mg
Cholesterol	161 mg
Fiber	4 g

ask ROSE

Arborio rice is a must-have for risotto dishes. Its kernels are shorter and fatter than other varieties, and its high starch content gives risotto its wonderfully creamy texture. Be sure that you never rinse this rice. You don't want to eliminate any of that starch!

for the record

To skin or not to skin
Whether you remove the skin from chicken parts before or after cooking doesn't affect the fat content. The important thing is that you *do* remove it, however, since the skin accounts for about two-thirds of the fat in chicken. For a small 3-oz (75 g) chicken breast, you'll save 5 g fat by peeling off the crispy stuff!

creamy paprika sauté
with grilled chicken and egg noodles

1 In a nonstick saucepan sprayed with vegetable spray or on a preheated grill, cook chicken over medium-high heat, turning once, for 12 minutes or until cooked through; slice thinly.

2 In a large pot of boiling water, cook noodles for 8 minutes or until tender but firm; drain.

3 Meanwhile, in a nonstick frying pan sprayed with vegetable spray, cook onions and garlic over medium-high heat for 3 minutes or until softened. Add mushrooms; cook for 4 minutes, stirring occasionally. Add flour; cook, stirring, for 1 minute. Add chicken stock and paprika; cook for 2 minutes or until thickened. Remove from heat; add sour cream and dill.

4 In a serving bowl combine sauce, noodles and chicken; toss well. Serve immediately.

8 oz	skinless boneless chicken breast	250 g
8 oz	broad egg noodles	250 g
1/2 cup	chopped red onions	125 mL
1 1/2 tsp	minced garlic	7 mL
1 1/2 cups	chopped oyster mushrooms	375 mL
1 tbsp	all-purpose flour	15 mL
1 1/2 cups	CHICKEN STOCK (see recipe, page 50)	375 mL
2 tsp	paprika	10 mL
1/2 cup	low-fat sour cream	125 mL
1/4 cup	chopped fresh dill (or 1 tsp [5 mL] dried)	50 mL

poultry

103

essential numbers

PER SERVING

Calories	384
Protein	26 g
Fat, total	7 g
Fat, saturated	3.2 g
Carbohydrates	53 g
Sodium	127 mg
Cholesterol	105 mg
Fiber	3 g

ask ROSE

Egg noodles are slightly richer tasting than other noodles — that's because of the eggs — and are therefore somewhat higher in fat and calories. (So live a little!) Egg noodles are available in a variety of widths; the thin variety are commonly used in soups, while broad noodles are used with sauces.

variations

Regular fettuccine can replace the egg noodles. For a change, try seafood or steak instead of chicken; or replace oyster mushrooms with any other wild variety.

maple chicken
with peppers and mustard over rotini

1 In a nonstick saucepan sprayed with vegetable spray or on a preheated grill, cook chicken over medium-high heat, turning once, for 12 minutes or until cooked through. Cut chicken into cubes; set aside.

2 In a large pot of boiling water, cook rotini for 8 to 10 minutes or until tender but firm; drain. Meanwhile, in another saucepan over medium-high heat, combine maple syrup, chicken stock, balsamic vinegar, olive oil, Dijon mustard, cornstarch and garlic; whisk well. Cook, stirring constantly, for 3 minutes or until thickened and bubbly. Add red peppers; reduce heat to medium-low. Cook, covered, for 2 minutes or until peppers are tender.

3 In a large serving bowl, combine pasta, chicken, green onions and sauce; toss to coat well. Serve immediately.

104

6 oz	skinless boneless chicken breast	175 g
8 oz	rotini	250 g
1/3 cup	pure maple syrup	75 mL
1/3 cup	Chicken Stock (see recipe, page 50)	75 mL
3 tbsp	balsamic vinegar	45 mL
2 tbsp	olive oil	25 mL
1 tbsp	Dijon mustard	15 mL
2 tsp	cornstarch	10 mL
1 tsp	minced garlic	5 mL
1 cup	thinly sliced red bell peppers	250 mL
1/3 cup	chopped green onions	75 mL

poultry

essential numbers

PER SERVING	
Calories	396
Protein	17 g
Fat, total	8 g
Fat, saturated	1.3 g
Carbohydrates	64 g
Sodium	116 mg
Cholesterol	24 mg
Fiber	3 g

ask ROSE

Be sure that you buy only pure maple syrup for this recipe. That means 100% maple syrup — not maple *flavored* syrup (funny how "flavored" is so much smaller than "maple" on the label) or the stuff that contains *some* (usually no more than 15%) maple syrup. These artificial syrups contain mostly water, sugar and corn syrup; pure maple syrup is distilled from maple sap, and is twice as sweet as sugar.

nutrition watch

B vitamins and heart disease
Several studies have shown that a diet lacking B vitamins may increase the risk of heart disease by causing a high blood level of homocysteine, an amino acid that we normally convert to other harmless amino acids with the help of three B vitamins: folate, B6 and B12. When homocysteine levels are high, the result can be damaged blood vessel walls and a build-up of cholesterol. Good sources of folate include spinach, lentils, and enriched pasta. One serving of this pasta dish provides 25% of your daily folate needs (0.4 mg).

spaghetti squash
with turkey bolognese and macaroni

1 Microwave squash on High for 15 minutes; let cool. Cut in half lengthwise; discard seeds. Scoop out flesh, leaving shell intact; set aside.

2 In a pot of boiling water, cook macaroni for 8 to 10 minutes or until tender but firm; drain. Rinse under cold running water; drain. Set aside.

3 In a nonstick saucepan sprayed with vegetable spray, cook onions and garlic over medium-high heat for 4 minutes or until softened. Add turkey; cook, stirring to break up meat, for 3 minutes or until no longer pink. Add tomatoes, basil, chili powder, oregano and bay leaves; bring to a boil. Reduce heat to medium-low; cook, uncovered, for 10 minutes or until thickened, breaking up tomatoes with back of a spoon.

4 In a bowl combine squash flesh, macaroni, turkey sauce, feta cheese and half the Parmesan cheese. Spoon into squash shells; sprinkle with mozzarella and remaining Parmesan cheese. Place excess filling in a casserole dish. Place shells on baking sheet; bake with casserole in preheated oven for 25 minutes or until heated through.

PREHEAT OVEN TO 375° F (190° C)
BAKING SHEET

1	2-lb (1 kg) spaghetti squash, pierced with a knife	1
4 oz	elbow macaroni	125 g
1 cup	chopped onions	250 mL
1 tsp	minced garlic	5 mL
12 oz	lean ground turkey or chicken	375 g
1	can (28 oz [796 mL]) tomatoes, with juice	1
1 1/2 tsp	dried basil	7 mL
1 tsp	chili powder	5 mL
1 tsp	dried oregano	5 mL
2	bay leaves	2
2 oz	light feta cheese, crumbled	50 g
1/4 cup	grated low-fat Parmesan cheese	50 mL
1/2 cup	shredded low-fat mozzarella cheese	125 mL

poultry

105

essential numbers

PER SERVING	
Calories	429
Protein	31 g
Fat, total	16 g
Fat, saturated	7.2 g
Carbohydrates	40 g
Sodium	557 mg
Cholesterol	100 mg
Fiber	4 g

ask ROSE

Spaghetti squash — the perfect vegetable for a pasta cookbook! And yes, despite its name, it *is* a vegetable. Also called vegetable spaghetti, this type of squash is notable for its yellow spaghetti-like strands.

For enhanced flavor, roast the squash instead of microwaving it. Just pierce it in several places, and place in a 400° F (200° C) oven for about 45 minutes. Slice, remove seeds and scoop out the flesh.

for the record

Hitting the links

Looking for a healthier hot dog? Then try chicken or turkey franks. While the regular beef and pork variety packs 118 calories and 11 g fat per dog (37 g), a similar-sized chicken or turkey wiener contains 4 g less fat and 30 fewer calories. It's not all good news, however: like all processed meats, these poultry dogs are still high in sodium.

curried vegetable

chicken fettuccine

1. In a nonstick frying pan sprayed with vegetable spray or on a preheated grill, cook chicken over medium-high heat, turning once, for 12 minutes or until cooked through. Cut into thin slices; set aside.

2. In a large pot of boiling water, cook fettuccine for 8 to 10 minutes or until tender but firm; drain. Meanwhile, in a large nonstick frying pan sprayed with vegetable spray, cook onions, green peppers, carrots and garlic over medium-high heat for 5 minutes or until softened. Add flour and curry powder; cook for 30 seconds. Add stock, milk, brown sugar and pepper; reduce heat to medium. Cook for 2 minutes or until thickened.

3. In a serving bowl, combine pasta, sauce and chicken; toss well. Serve immediately.

8 oz	skinless boneless chicken breast	250 g
8 oz	fettuccine	250 g
3/4 cup	chopped onions	175 mL
3/4 cup	chopped green bell peppers	175 mL
1/2 cup	finely chopped carrots	125 mL
1 tsp	minced garlic	5 mL
1 1/2 tbsp	all-purpose flour	20 mL
2 tsp	curry powder	10 mL
1 cup	CHICKEN STOCK (see recipe, page 50)	250 mL
3/4 cup	low-fat milk	175 mL
1 1/2 tsp	packed brown sugar	7 mL
1/4 tsp	freshly ground black pepper	1 mL

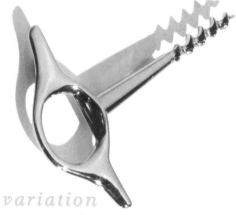

essential numbers

PER SERVING

Calories	369
Protein	23 g
Fat, total	3 g
Fat, saturated	0.9 g
Carbohydrates	60 g
Sodium	102 mg
Cholesterol	37 mg
Fiber	3 g

ask ROSE

When it comes to choosing milk, what's a percentage point here or there? A lot! Just consider that a 1-cup (250 mL) serving of homogenized (3.3%) milk contains 150 calories and 8 g fat, while the same amount of 1% milk has only 102 calories and 2.5 g fat. (As you might expect, 2% milk falls in the middle, with 121 calories and 4.7 g fat.) And the fact is that for many sauces (like the one here), 1% milk delivers all the taste and texture you want. You can substitute low-fat milk in any recipe that calls for homogenized — although, for some sauces, you may need to increase your flour.

variation

It's easy to transform this recipe into a vegetarian or kosher dish: just substitute firm tofu for the chicken (grill or sauté it for 5 minutes or just until lightly browned); use soya milk instead of dairy milk; and, replace chicken stock with vegetable stock.

chicken and sausage
with orzo and tomato sauce

1 In a bowl coat chicken with flour; shake off excess. In a large nonstick frying pan sprayed with vegetable spray, cook chicken over medium-high heat, turning occasionally, for 5 minutes or until browned. Remove to casserole dish.

2 In the same frying pan over medium-high heat, cook sausage, stirring to break up meat, for 4 minutes or until no longer pink. With a slotted spoon, transfer sausage to casserole dish. Wipe frying pan clean with paper towel.

3 Spray frying pan with vegetable spray. Cook onions and garlic over medium-high heat for 3 minutes or until softened. Add green peppers; cook, stirring occasionally, for 3 minutes or until vegetables are golden. Add tomatoes (with juice), stock, orzo, brown sugar, basil and oregano. Bring to a boil, stirring to break up tomatoes. Pour mixture over chicken and sausage.

4 Bake in preheated oven, covered and stirring occasionally, for 30 to 45 minutes or until chicken is cooked through and orzo is tender but firm. Remove chicken skin; serve.

PREHEAT OVEN TO 425° F (220° C)
8-CUP (2 L) CASSEROLE DISH WITH LID

2	chicken legs, separated into thighs and drumsticks	2
2 tbsp	all-purpose flour	25 mL
4 oz	spicy sausage, casings removed	125 g
1 cup	chopped onions	250 mL
1 tsp	minced garlic	5 mL
1 1/2 cups	chopped green bell peppers	375 mL
1	can (19 oz [540 mL]) tomatoes, with juice	1
1 1/2 cups	CHICKEN STOCK (see recipe, page 50)	375 mL
1 cup	orzo or small shaped pasta	250 mL
1 tbsp	packed brown sugar	15 mL
1 tsp	dried basil	5 mL
1 tsp	dried oregano	5 mL

poultry

107

essential numbers

PER SERVING

Calories	585
Protein	30 g
Fat, total	21 g
Fat, saturated	6.0 g
Carbohydrates	69 g
Sodium	510 mg
Cholesterol	108 mg
Fiber	5 g

ask ROSE

For extra flavor — and, yes, just a little extra fat and calories — I like to use chicken legs in this recipe. But you can also use bone-in chicken breasts with the skin on. Keep the skin on during cooking (again, for extra flavor). As long as you don't eat the skin, you needn't worry about fat and calories.

cooking 101

Orzo looks a lot like rice, but is really a pasta. It's usually easy to find in most supermarkets. If you can't find any, however, substitute small-shell pasta or try Arborio (risotto) rice.

chicken with peppers
and chicken livers in orange sauce

1. In a large nonstick frying pan sprayed with vegetable spray, cook red peppers, red onions and garlic over medium-high heat for 3 minutes or until softened. Add chicken livers and ground chicken; cook, stirring to break up meat, for 4 minutes or until no longer pink.

2. Meanwhile, in a bowl combine stock, orange zest, orange juice, flour, brown sugar, salt and pepper. Add to meat mixture; bring to a boil. Reduce heat to medium-low; cook for 2 minutes or until thickened.

3. In a large pot of boiling water, cook fettuccine for 8 to 10 minutes or until tender but firm; drain. In a serving bowl, combine pasta and sauce; toss well. Garnish with green onions; serve.

1 cup	chopped red bell peppers	250 mL
3/4 cup	chopped red onions	175 mL
1 1/2 tsp	minced garlic	7 mL
4 oz	diced chicken livers	125 g
4 oz	lean ground chicken	125 g
1 cup	CHICKEN STOCK (see recipe, page 50)	250 mL
1 tbsp	grated orange zest	15 mL
1/2 cup	orange juice	125 mL
1 1/2 tbsp	all-purpose flour	20 mL
1 tbsp	packed brown sugar	15 mL
Pinch	salt	Pinch
Pinch	freshly ground black pepper	Pinch
8 oz	fettuccine	250 g
1/2 cup	chopped green onions	125 mL

essential numbers

PER SERVING

Calories	405
Protein	21 g
Fat, total	7 g
Fat, saturated	0.7 g
Carbohydrates	64 g
Sodium	140 mg
Cholesterol	137 mg
Fiber	4 g

ask ROSE

When grating oranges or lemons, I like to use a large-hole grater and then finely chop the zest with a chef's knife. A small-hole grater can be frustrating to get large amounts of zest. Be sure not to grate the white pith right under the zest. It has a bitter taste and will spoil the flavor of the dish.

nutrition watch

The power of oranges

Sure, oranges are a good source of vitamin C. But they contain a number of other goodies — such as flavonoids, natural compounds that may help reduce the risk of cancer. Studies indicate that limonene, an essential oil in citrus peel, can be protective against breast, skin, liver, lung and stomach cancers. Grapefruits, tangerines, lemons, limes, tangelos and kumquats all contain citrus flavonoids that may have anti-cancer properties.

chicken and bulgur loaf

1 In a saucepan over medium-high heat, bring stock to a boil. Add bulgur; remove from heat. Let stand, covered, for 20 minutes or until liquid is absorbed and grain is tender. Set aside to cool.

2 In a nonstick frying pan sprayed with vegetable spray, cook red peppers and onions over medium-high heat for 10 minutes or until golden and tender; set aside to cool.

3 In a bowl combine bulgur, ground chicken, egg, egg white, ketchup, bread crumbs, garlic, basil, salt and pepper. On a piece of waxed paper, pat mixture into an 8-inch (20 cm) square. Spread cooled red peppers and onions over surface. Using waxed paper as an aid, roll up mixture from bottom. Lifting waxed paper, gently drop loaf seam-side down into prepared loaf pan. Spread barbecue sauce over top. Bake in preheated oven, uncovered, for 30 minutes.

PREHEAT OVEN TO 375° F (190° C)
8- BY 4-INCH (20 BY 10 CM) LOAF PAN SPRAYED WITH VEGETABLE SPRAY

3/4 cup	CHICKEN STOCK *or* VEGETABLE STOCK (see recipes, pages 50 and 51)	175 mL
1/2 cup	bulgur	125 mL
1 cup	chopped red bell peppers	250 mL
1 cup	chopped onions	250 mL
12 oz	ground chicken	375 g
1	large egg	1
1	large egg white	1
1/4 cup	ketchup	50 mL
1/4 cup	dry seasoned bread crumbs	50 mL
1 1/2 tsp	minced garlic	7 mL
1/2 tsp	dried basil	2 mL
1/8 tsp	salt	0.5 mL
1/8 tsp	freshly ground black pepper	0.5 mL
1/4 cup	barbecue sauce	50 mL

poultry

109

essential numbers

PER SERVING

Calories	226
Protein	15 g
Fat, total	10 g
Fat, saturated	0.4 g
Carbohydrates	20 g
Sodium	307 mg
Cholesterol	36 mg
Fiber	3 g

ask ROSE

Here we use commercially prepared barbecue sauce to add moisture and flavor — and to save time! Feel free to substitute ketchup, sweet chili sauce or any other type of basting sauce.

for the record

Growing feathers yet?

It seems that our appetite for chicken just keeps on growing. In fact, compared to just a decade ago, we now eat an extra 55 lbs (22 kg) of the stuff each year. Chicken now represents 30 % of all meat consumed — equal to pork and second only to beef.

cranberry chicken

over penne

1. In a nonstick saucepan sprayed with vegetable spray, cook onions and red peppers over medium-high heat for 5 minutes or until softened; set aside.

2. In another saucepan combine cranberry sauce, soya sauce, orange juice concentrate, sesame oil, lemon juice, garlic and ginger. Cook over medium heat, stirring, for 4 minutes or until heated through and smooth. Add red pepper mixture.

3. In a nonstick skillet sprayed with vegetable spray, cook chicken over medium-high heat, turning once, for 12 minutes or until cooked through; slice thinly.

4. In a large pot of boiling water, cook penne for 8 to 10 minutes or until tender but firm; drain. In a serving bowl combine pasta, sauce, chicken, dried cranberries and green onions; toss well.

1 cup	chopped onions	250 mL
3/4 cup	chopped red bell peppers	175 mL
1 cup	canned whole cranberry sauce	250 mL
3 tbsp	light soya sauce	45 mL
2 tbsp	orange juice concentrate	25 mL
1 tbsp	sesame oil	15 mL
1 tbsp	fresh lemon juice	15 mL
1 1/2 tsp	minced garlic	7 mL
1 tsp	minced ginger root	5 mL
8 oz	skinless boneless chicken breast	250 g
12 oz	penne	375 g
1/3 cup	dried cranberries *or* dried cherries	75 mL
1/3 cup	chopped green onions	75 mL

poultry

110

essential numbers

PER SERVING	
Calories	423
Protein	18 g
Fat, total	4 g
Fat, saturated	0.8 g
Carbohydrates	78 g
Sodium	563 mg
Cholesterol	23 mg
Fiber	4 g

ask ROSE

When shopping for canned cranberry sauce for this recipe, be sure to get the type that contains whole berries. Avoid jellied cranberry sauce; in this variety, the berries have been puréed.

While commercially prepared cranberry sauce is the most convenient, it's actually quite easy to make your own. Just combine 1 lb (500 g) cranberries, 2 cups (500 mL) sugar and 1 cup (250 mL) water. Cook, uncovered, over medium heat for 10 minutes.

nutrition watch

Liquid plumber

Does a glass of cranberry juice a day keep bladder infections away? There is scientific evidence to suggest that this home remedy is indeed effective in preventing and treating such infections. A Tufts University study found that bacterial urinary tract infections could be reduced by 50% in older women who drank 1 1/4 cups (300 mL) of cranberry juice each day. It seems that cranberries contain a natural antibiotic substance that prevents bacteria from adhering to the bladder wall. Why wait for Thanksgiving? Pass the cranberry sauce, please.

duck with orange
and apricot sauce over fettuccine

1. In a nonstick saucepan sprayed with vegetable spray, cook red peppers, onions and garlic over medium heat for 5 minutes or until onions are lightly browned.

2. In a bowl combine stock, orange zest, orange juice, brown sugar and flour; add to red pepper mixture. Bring to a boil, stirring until thickened slightly. Add dates, apricots and duck; cook for approximately 2 minutes or until heated through.

3. In a large pot of boiling water, cook fettuccine for 8 to 10 minutes or until tender but firm; drain. In a serving bowl, combine pasta and sauce; toss well. Garnish with green onions; serve.

1 cup	chopped red bell peppers	250 mL
1/2 cup	chopped onions	125 mL
2 tsp	minced garlic	10 mL
1 1/2 cups	cold CHICKEN STOCK *or* BEEF STOCK (see recipes, page 50)	375 mL
1 tbsp	grated orange zest	15 mL
1/2 cup	fresh orange juice	125 mL
2 tbsp	packed brown sugar	25 mL
2 tbsp	all-purpose flour	25 mL
1/2 cup	chopped dried dates	125 mL
1/2 cup	chopped dried apricots	125 mL
12 oz	diced cooked duck	375 g
12 oz	fettuccine	375 g
1/2 cup	chopped green onions	125 mL

poultry

essential numbers

PER SERVING

Calories	456
Protein	20 g
Fat, total	6 g
Fat, saturated	2.0 g
Carbohydrates	81 g
Sodium	40 mg
Cholesterol	37 mg
Fiber	4 g

ask ROSE

A recipe for duck? In a *light* cookbook? Absolutely! Sure, duck contains a lot of fat, but it's all in the skin. The meat itself is quite lean — and delicious!

Roast a duck as you would a chicken (on a rack, so fat drips off), at 400° F (200° C) for about 1 1/4 hours. A 4-lb (2 kg) duck will provide the 12 oz (375 g) of meat needed for this recipe. Duck is usually available frozen at most supermarkets; thaw overnight in the refrigerator before cooking.

variation

If you can't find duck, don't worry. This recipe still tastes great if you substitute chicken or turkey.

chicken-fried

vegetable white and wild rice

1 In a nonstick skillet sprayed with vegetable spray or on a preheated grill, cook chicken over medium-high heat, turning once, for 12 minutes or until cooked through; let cool. Chop chicken; set aside.

2 In a small saucepan over medium-high heat, bring 1 cup (250 mL) stock to a boil. Add wild rice; reduce heat to low. Cook, covered, for 45 minutes or until rice is tender and liquid is absorbed.

3 Meanwhile, in another saucepan, bring 1 cup (250 mL) stock to a boil. Add white rice; reduce heat to low. Cook, covered, for 15 minutes. Remove from heat; let stand, covered, for 5 minutes. Transfer wild rice and white rice to a bowl; let cool.

4 In a large nonstick saucepan sprayed with vegetable spray, cook onions, red peppers, carrots and garlic over medium heat, covered, for 8 minutes or until softened. Add cooled rice, chicken and peas; cook, stirring, for 3 minutes or until heated through.

5 In a bowl combine soya sauce, chili sauce, brown sugar, sesame oil and Dijon mustard. Add to rice mixture; mix well. Serve.

8 oz	skinless boneless chicken breast	250 g
1 cup	CHICKEN STOCK (see recipe, page 50)	250 mL
1/2 cup	wild rice	125 mL
1 cup	CHICKEN STOCK	250 mL
1/2 cup	long grain white rice	125 mL
1 cup	chopped onions	250 mL
3/4 cup	chopped red bell peppers	175 mL
1/2 cup	chopped carrots	125 mL
1 1/2 tsp	minced garlic	7 mL
1/2 cup	frozen peas	125 mL
2 tbsp	light soya sauce	25 mL
1 tbsp	sweet chili sauce *or* ketchup	15 mL
1 1/2 tbsp	packed brown sugar	20 mL
2 tsp	sesame oil	10 mL
1 tsp	Dijon mustard	5 mL

essential numbers

PER SERVING	
Calories	325
Protein	20 g
Fat, total	5 g
Fat, saturated	1.0 g
Carbohydrates	51 g
Sodium	350 mg
Cholesterol	35 mg
Fiber	4 g

ask ROSE

When you order fried rice from your local Chinese restaurant, it's tempting to think you're eating healthy food. After all, rice is good for you. So are those vegetables mixed in with it. But what you don't see is the huge amount of lard and oil used to cook the food. In fact, one serving of restaurant-prepared fried rice can have 700 calories and 24 g fat! But not in this recipe. Here we eliminate the need for excess oil by adding lots of vegetables and sweet sauce.

for the record

Build a better BLT

It seems they're making bacon out of all sorts of meat these days. Take "chicken bacon," for example. Is it a better choice than the regular stuff? If you want more meat and less fat, then the answer is yes! On average, 2 slices of uncooked chicken bacon contains 100 calories, 7.5 g fat, and 7.5 g protein; 2 slices of traditional pork side bacon gives you 300 calories, 30 g fat, and 4.6 g protein. Once cooked, of course, both types of bacon lose fat content. But chicken-style bacon still comes out the winner.

chinese ginger chicken
over fettuccine

1 In a saucepan over medium-high heat, cover chicken with cold water; bring to a full boil. Remove saucepan from heat; let stand, covered, for 30 minutes or until chicken is cooked through.

2 Meanwhile, in another saucepan over medium-high heat, combine chicken stock, soya sauce, brown sugar, sesame oil, sesame seeds, cornstarch, ginger and garlic. Bring to a boil, stirring. Reduce heat; simmer for 3 minutes or until thickened.

3 In a large pot of boiling water, cook fettuccine for 8 to 10 minutes or until tender but firm; drain. Meanwhile, remove skin and bones from cooked chicken; slice thinly.

4 In a serving bowl, combine chicken, pasta, sauce and green onions; toss well.

2	chicken legs, separated into thighs and drumsticks	2
3/4 cup	CHICKEN STOCK (see recipe, page 50)	175 mL
3 tbsp	light soya sauce	45 mL
2 tbsp	packed brown sugar	25 mL
1 tbsp	sesame oil	15 mL
1 tbsp	sesame seeds	15 mL
1 tbsp	cornstarch	15 mL
2 tsp	minced ginger root	10 mL
1 1/2 tsp	minced garlic	7 mL
12 oz	fettuccine	375 g
1/2 cup	chopped green onions	125 mL

poultry

113

essential numbers

PER SERVING

Calories	525
Protein	32 g
Fat, total	19 g
Fat, saturated	4.9 g
Carbohydrates	54 g
Sodium	260 mg
Cholesterol	104 mg
Fiber	2 g

ask ROSE

How do you reduce the amount of oil in your stir-fries and salad dressings? Try using sesame oil instead of regular vegetable oil. I love sesame oil for its rich, nutty flavor. And as you'll see in this recipe, 1 tbsp (15 mL) goes a long way. In fact, I would have to use 2 or 3 times as much regular oil to get the same amount of taste! Another benefit of sesame oil is that it has a high smoking point, making it ideal for sautéeing.

nutrition watch

A herbal digestive

For more than 2,500 years, practitioners of traditional Chinese medicine have prescribed ginger as a digestive aid. Its volatile oils contain compounds called gingerols and shogoals, which give the root its characteristic odor and may be responsible for its health benefits. Ginger's active ingredients have been found to improve secretion of digestive compounds that help the body break down dietary fat. Studies have also shown the herb to be effective against motion sickness.

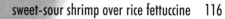

sweet-sour shrimp

over rice fettuccine

1. In a bowl combine stock, brown sugar, chili sauce, orange juice concentrate, soya sauce, rice wine vinegar, cornstarch and sesame oil. Set aside.

2. In a pot of boiling water, cook noodles for 5 minutes or until tender; drain. Meanwhile, in a nonstick wok or large frying pan sprayed with vegetable spray, heat oil over medium-high heat. Add garlic, ginger, broccoli and red peppers; cook for 4 minutes. Add shrimp; cook for 2 minutes or until pink. Add pineapple and sauce; cook for 1 minute or until thickened and bubbly.

3. In a serving bowl combine sauce and noodles; toss to coat well. Serve immediately.

Sauce

3/4 cup	SEAFOOD STOCK *or* CHICKEN STOCK (see recipes, page 50)	175 mL
2 tbsp	packed brown sugar	25 mL
2 tbsp	sweet tomato chili sauce	25 mL
2 tbsp	orange juice concentrate	25 mL
2 tbsp	light soya sauce	25 mL
1 1/2 tbsp	rice wine vinegar	20 mL
1 tbsp	cornstarch	15 mL
2 tsp	sesame oil	10 mL
8 oz	wide rice noodles	250 g
2 tsp	vegetable oil	10 mL
2 tsp	minced garlic	10 mL
1 tsp	minced ginger root	5 mL
3 cups	broccoli florets	750 mL
1 cup	sliced red bell peppers	250 mL
8 oz	medium raw shrimp, peeled	250 g
1	can (14 oz [398 mL]) unsweetened pineapple chunks, drained	1

essential numbers

PER SERVING

Calories	341
Protein	16 g
Fat, total	6 g
Fat, saturated	0.7 g
Carbohydrates	58 g
Sodium	524 mg
Cholesterol	89 mg
Fiber	4 g

ask ROSE

It's no accident that minced fresh ginger root appears in so many of my recipes. After all, there are few ingredients that pack so much flavor. And in my light cooking, flavor is everything! That's why I always try to keep fresh ginger on hand. As a backup, however, or if I'm pressed for time, I also keep a jar of commercially prepared minced or puréed ginger. It's available in the vegetable section of your supermarket alongside the minced garlic. Like prepared garlic, this type of ginger is not as intense as freshly grated; so add a little more than is called for in the recipe.

for the record

Chinese-food lovers beware!

If you love sweet-and-sour dishes, you'll really enjoy this recipe — particularly because it contains only 6 g fat per serving. By comparison, a typical serving of sweet-and-sour pork (batter dipped, deep fried, then stir-fried) has 71 g fat — that's more fat than the average women should consume in an entire day!

creamy spinach sauce
and shrimp over rotini

1. In a nonstick frying pan sprayed with vegetable spray, cook onions and garlic over medium-high heat for 3 minutes or until softened. Add spinach, evaporated milk, stock, olives, 2 oz (50 g) feta cheese, lemon juice and oregano; bring to a boil. Reduce heat to medium-low; simmer for 2 minutes. Transfer mixture to a food processor; process until smooth. Set aside.

2. In a large pot of boiling water, cook rotini for 8 to 10 minutes or until tender but firm; drain. In a large nonstick frying pan sprayed with vegetable spray, cook shrimp over high heat for 2 minutes or until cooked through; drain any excess liquid. In a serving bowl combine pasta, sauce, shrimp and remaining feta cheese; toss well. Serve immediately.

3/4 cup	chopped onions	175 mL
1 tsp	minced garlic	5 mL
1	pkg (10 oz [300g]) frozen spinach, cooked, drained, chopped and squeezed dry	1
3/4 cup	low-fat evaporated milk	175 mL
3/4 cup	SEAFOOD STOCK or CHICKEN STOCK (see recipes, page 50)	175 mL
1/3 cup	chopped black olives	75 mL
3 oz	light feta cheese, crumbled	75 g
1 tbsp	fresh lemon juice	15 mL
1 tsp	dried oregano	5 mL
12 oz	rotini or spinach rotini	375 g
12 oz	medium raw shrimp, shelled	375 g

seafood

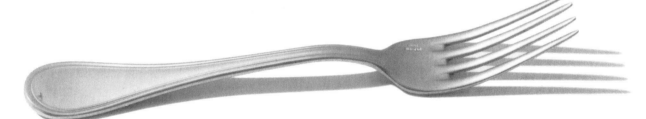

essential numbers

PER SERVING

Calories	364
Protein	23 g
Fat, total	8 g
Fat, saturated	2.9 g
Carbohydrates	51 g
Sodium	396 mg
Cholesterol	105 mg
Fiber	4 g

ask ROSE

While this recipe calls for frozen spinach, you can certainly use the same amount of fresh. Just be sure that you don't boil away those nutrients by cooking the spinach in a big pot of water! All you need to do is quickly rinse the leaves and shake off the excess moisture; place the leaves in a pot, cover and cook over high heat for 3 minutes or until wilted. That's all there is to it!

nutrition watch

Eat your greens

Seems that Popeye had the right idea, because spinach is a powerhouse of nutrients. But it isn't just for cartoon characters: If you're a woman who is (or is planning to be) pregnant, spinach is one vegetable that should be on your dinner plate. One cup (250 mL) of cooked spinach packs 262 micrograms of folate — a B vitamin that's been shown to reduce spinal cord defects in newborns — as well as 1.5 times the recommended intake for vitamin A, 6.5 mg iron, 245 mg calcium, 840 mg potassium and 4 g fiber. All for only 41 calories!

jumbo shells
stuffed with crabmeat, cheese and dill

1. In a large pot of boiling water, cook shells for 14 minutes or until tender; drain. Rinse under cold running water; drain. Set aside.

2. In a bowl combine crabmeat, ricotta cheese, mozzarella cheese, green onions, milk, egg, dill and pepper. Stuff approximately 2 1/2 tbsp (35 mL) mixture into each pasta shell.

3. In a bowl combine tomato sauce and milk; spread half over bottom of baking dish. Add stuffed shells; pour remaining sauce over top. Bake, covered with foil, for 20 minutes or until heated through.

seafood

118

PREHEAT OVEN TO 350° F (180° C)
13- BY 9-INCH (3 L) BAKING DISH

18	jumbo pasta shells	18
6 oz	crabmeat *or* surimi (dried imitation crab)	175 g
1 3/4 cups	5% ricotta cheese	425 mL
2/3 cup	shredded low-fat mozzarella cheese	150 mL
2	green onions, sliced	2
3 tbsp	low-fat milk	45 mL
1	large egg	1
1/4 cup	chopped fresh dill (or 1 tsp [5 mL] dried)	50 mL
1/4 tsp	freshly ground black pepper	1 mL
1 cup	tomato pasta sauce	250 mL
3 tbsp	low-fat milk	45 mL

essential numbers

PER SERVING

Calories	295
Protein	21 g
Fat, total	10 g
Fat, saturated	5.4 g
Carbohydrates	30 g
Sodium	328 mg
Cholesterol	75 mg
Fiber	328 g

ask ROSE

When many of us were growing up, if you'd gone to the store and asked for "tomato pasta sauce" they wouldn't have had a clue what you were talking about. Back then it was just plain old "spaghetti sauce." Well, it's basically the same stuff. Don't use canned tomato sauce, however; it's too salty and has a slightly bitter aftertaste. Better choices for this recipe are commercially prepared sauce in a jar or, if you have the time, your own homemade sauce.

variation

If you don't have jumbo shells you can substitute 12 manicotti or cannelloni pasta shells.

Try replacing the crab meat with diced cooked chicken.

avocado crabmeat
over rice noodles

1 In a serving bowl, combine crabmeat, carrots, red peppers and green onions; set aside.

2 In a food processor combine avocado, mayonnaise, soya sauce, water, honey, sesame oil, garlic, ginger and *wasabi*; process until smooth. Add to crab mixture.

3 In a large pot of boiling water, cook rice noodles for 5 minutes or until tender; drain well. Add to crab mixture; toss well. Garnish with 2 thin slices avocado. Serve immediately.

8 oz	crabmeat *or* surimi (imitation crab), diced	250 g
1 cup	julienned carrots	250 mL
1 cup	julienned red bell peppers	250 mL
1/3 cup	sliced green onions	75 mL
1/2 cup	diced ripe avocado	125 mL
1/4 cup	light mayonnaise	50 mL
3 tbsp	light soya sauce	45 mL
2 tbsp	water	25 mL
2 tbsp	honey	25 mL
1 tbsp	sesame oil	15 mL
1 1/2 tsp	minced garlic	7 mL
1 1/2 tsp	minced ginger root	7 mL
1/2 tsp	*wasabi* (Japanese horseradish), optional	2 mL
8 oz	wide rice noodles	250 g

seafood

119

essential numbers

PER SERVING

Calories	355
Protein	13 g
Fat, total	12 g
Fat, saturated	2.0 g
Carbohydrates	50 g
Sodium	631 mg
Cholesterol	19 mg
Fiber	3 g

ask ROSE

Sure, it would be nice to prepare this recipe with fresh crab. But I'll be the first to admit that it's hard to find — and even when you do, it's expensive and a real pain to extract from the shell. Yes, you can use canned crabmeat, but personally I don't care for its taste. A better substitute, I think, is "surimi," an imitation crab that is processed from white fish fillets, usually Pacific pollock. It looks — and tastes! — a lot like crab.

for the record

A high-fat fruit?

If you've heard that avocados are high in fat, you've heard right. In fact, one medium California avocado has 30 g of the stuff. The good news is that most of the fat is monounsaturated and does not raise blood cholesterol levels. If you want less fat, try a Florida avocado, which contains only 20 g fat per fruit.

orange black bean sauce
with mussels over chow mein noodles

1 In a bowl cover noodles with boiling water; soak for 5 minutes or until soft. Drain; set aside.

2 In a nonstick wok or large saucepan sprayed with vegetable spray, heat oil over medium-high heat. Add onions; cook for 3 minutes or until lightly browned. Add red peppers, green peppers, garlic and ginger; cook for 3 minutes. Add water; bring to a boil. Add mussels; cook, covered, for 2 minutes or until mussels begin to open.

3 Meanwhile, in a bowl combine orange juice, honey, black bean sauce and cornstarch; add to wok. Cook, covered, for 2 minutes or until mussels are open. (Discard any that do not open.)

4 On a serving platter, arrange noodles; pour mussel mixture over top. Garnish with coriander; serve immediately.

8 oz	fresh chow mein noodles	250 g
2 tsp	vegetable oil	10 mL
1 cup	sliced onions	250 mL
1 1/2 cup	thinly sliced red bell peppers	375 mL
1 cup	thinly sliced green bell peppers	250 mL
1 1/2 tsp	minced garlic	7 mL
1 tsp	minced ginger root	5 mL
1/4 cup	water	50 mL
2 lbs	fresh mussels, cleaned	1 kg
1 cup	orange juice	250 mL
3 tbsp	honey	45 mL
3 tbsp	black bean sauce	45 mL
1 1/2 tbsp	cornstarch	22 mL
1/2 cup	chopped fresh coriander or parsley	125 mL

seafood

120

essential numbers

PER SERVING

Calories	717
Protein	38 g
Fat, total	28 g
Fat, saturated	4.5 g
Carbohydrates	81 g
Sodium	900 mg
Cholesterol	70 mg
Fiber	5 g

ask ROSE

The most common type of mussels sold today — known as "blue mussels" — are cultivated, rather than harvested from the open sea. The result is that they're much cleaner (not as much grit and other stuff from the ocean bed); to prepare they need only be rinsed and trimmed ("beards" removed). Before using, check mussels carefully; discard any with broken shells or that won't close when tapped gently. Store mussels in a bowl or mesh bag in the refrigerator for up to 2 days.

nutrition watch

Mussel power

Mussels are a great-tasting protein food with very little fat. They're also a rich source of minerals — including calcium, phosphorus, magnesium, iron and zinc. Studies have shown that zinc is extremely important for a healthy immune system. But be careful before you run out to buy zinc supplements: While this mineral is beneficial at specific levels (the daily recommended intake is 9 mg for women and 12 mg for men) excess zinc (50 mg) actually *suppresses* the immune system. So stick with natural sources of zinc, such as mussels, oysters, lean beef, baked beans and ricotta cheese.

coconut seafood fettuccine
in a creamy sauce

1. In a nonstick wok or large frying pan sprayed with vegetable spray, cook shrimp over medium-high heat for 2 minutes or just until pink. Place shrimp on a plate; respray wok. Add peppers, carrots, garlic and curry; cook for 3 minutes or until vegetables are tender-crisp. Add coconut milk and soya sauce; reduce heat to medium-low. Cook for 4 minutes or until carrots are tender. Add shrimp, coriander and green onions; reduce heat to low.

2. In a large pot of boiling water, cook pasta for 8 to 10 minutes or until tender but firm; drain. In a serving bowl, combine pasta and sauce; toss well. Serve immediately.

6 oz	raw shrimp, shelled (if very large, cut into halves)	175 g
1 cup	thinly sliced red bell peppers	250 mL
3/4 cup	thinly sliced carrots	175 mL
1 1/2 tsp	minced garlic	7 mL
1 tsp	curry powder	5 mL
2/3 cup	light coconut milk	150 mL
2 tbsp	light soya sauce	25 mL
1/2 cup	chopped fresh coriander	125 mL
1/2 cup	chopped green onions	125 mL
8 oz	fettuccine	250 g

seafood

121

PER SERVING

essential numbers

Calories	304
Protein	15 g
Fat, total	2 g
Fat, saturated	0.2 g
Carbohydrates	55 g
Sodium	544 mg
Cholesterol	62 mg
Fiber	3 g

ask ROSE

Coconut milk is a traditional ingredient in many Thai dishes. It's wonderfully rich and fragrant, but it's also packed with saturated fat. In fact, 1/4 cup (50 mL) has 153 calories and 15 g fat. Not exactly the healthiest choice! Thankfully, there is an alternative — light coconut milk, which has 66% less fat and only one-third of the calories. Yet it's still creamy and delicious!

cooking 101

Curry powder isn't a spice in itself, but a blend of up to 20 spices and herbs — typically including cardamom, chilies, cinnamon, cloves, coriander, cumin, fennel seed, saffron, tamarind and turmeric. Depending on the balance of ingredients, curry powder can be mild or mouth-scorching! So be sure to adjust the amount you use according to your taste.

For maximum freshness and flavor, store curry powder in airtight containers for no more than 2 months.

scallops and spinach
with yellow peppers over linguine

1. Under the broiler or on a grill over medium-high heat, cook peppers, turning occasionally, for 15 minutes or until charred; let cool. Peel, remove stems and seeds; cut into strips. Set aside.

2. In a nonstick frying pan sprayed with vegetable spray, cook onions and garlic over medium-high heat for 4 minutes or until softened. Add peppers, stock, evaporated milk and pepper; cook for 2 minutes or until vegetables are tender. Set aside.

3. In a large saucepan over high heat, cook spinach, covered, for 1 minute; stir. Cook uncovered, stirring occasionally, just until spinach wilts. Add to sauce.

4. In a large pot of boiling water, cook linguine for 8 to 10 minutes or until tender but firm; drain. Meanwhile, in a large nonstick frying pan sprayed with vegetable spray, cook scallops over medium-high heat, stirring occasionally, for 2 minutes or until golden and cooked through. Drain any excess liquid.

5. In a serving bowl, combine pasta, sauce and scallops; toss well. Sprinkle with Parmesan cheese; serve immediately.

seafood

122

PREHEAT BROILER

2	medium yellow bell peppers	2
1/2 cup	chopped onions	125 mL
1 tsp	minced garlic	5 mL
1/2 cup	SEAFOOD STOCK *or* CHICKEN STOCK (see recipes, page 50)	125 mL
1/4 cup	low-fat evaporated milk	50 mL
1/4 tsp	freshly ground black pepper	1 mL
6 cups	packed fresh spinach leaves, rinsed and drained	1.5 L
8 oz	linguine	250 g
8 oz	scallops (if large, cut into quarters)	250 g
3 tbsp	grated low-fat Parmesan cheese	45 mL

essential numbers

PER SERVING

Calories	315
Protein	24 g
Fat, total	4 g
Fat, saturated	1.2 g
Carbohydrates	49 g
Sodium	400 mg
Cholesterol	26 mg
Fiber	5 g

ask ROSE

What's the difference between green and red bell peppers? Apart from their color — and price! — they're exactly the same; it's just that red peppers are left to ripen longer on the plant (which also makes them more expensive). Today, bell peppers come in a variety of other shades — including yellow, orange, brown and purple. Use them interchangeably to add a rainbow of colors to your recipes!.

variation

Try replacing the scallops in this recipe with shrimp or boneless chicken breast — or, to make this a vegetarian dish, with 8 oz (250 g) sautéed cubes of firm tofu.

lobster alfredo
over smoked salmon fettuccine

1. In a large pot of boiling water, blanch sugar snap peas for 2 minutes or until tender-crisp. Remove with slotted spoon to a bowl of cold water; drain.

2. In the same pot of boiling water, cook fettuccine for 8 to 10 minutes or until tender but firm; drain. Meanwhile, in a nonstick saucepan, heat margarine over medium heat. Add flour; cook, stirring, for 1 minute. Gradually whisk in seafood stock, milk and pepper; cook, stirring constantly, for 4 minutes or until thickened and bubbly. Add peas, Parmesan cheese and lobster meat; cook for 3 minutes or until heated through.

3. In a serving bowl, combine pasta, sauce, dill and smoked salmon; toss well. Serve immediately.

8 oz	sugar snap peas *or* snow peas	250 g
8 oz	fettuccine	250 g
2 tsp	margarine *or* butter	10 mL
1 tbsp	all-purpose flour	15 mL
1 cup	SEAFOOD STOCK (see recipe, page 50) *or* clam juice	250 mL
3/4 cup	low-fat milk	175 mL
1/8 tsp	freshly ground black pepper	0.5 mL
2 tbsp	grated low-fat Parmesan cheese	25 mL
8 oz	chopped cooked lobster *or* crabmeat *or* shrimp	250 g
1/3 cup	chopped fresh dill (or 1 tsp [5 mL] dried)	75 mL
2 oz	smoked salmon, shredded	50 g

seafood

123

essential numbers

PER SERVING

Calories	408
Protein	26 g
Fat, total	6 g
Fat, saturated	2.0 g
Carbohydrates	60 g
Sodium	384 mg
Cholesterol	28 mg
Fiber	3 g

ask ROSE

Sugar snap peas are a cross between the common green pea and the snow pea. And as the name suggests, they are wonderfully sweet! Unfortunately, they are only available at certain times of the year (usually spring and fall), and when you do find them, they are almost always expensive. But if you ask me, they're worth it! Be sure you don't overcook these little treasures or they'll lose their crunch. If you can't find any sugar snap peas for this recipe, substitute snow peas.

for the record

The fattest fettuccine

There are high-fat dishes — and then there's fettuccine Alfredo. Prepared in the traditional manner — with liberal amounts of whipping (35% M.F.) cream, butter, Parmesan cheese and sometimes even eggs — a plate of this pasta and sauce contains as much as 97 g fat (58% calories from fat). Yikes! That's a whole day's worth for a healthy male. So be kind to your arteries — try this skinny version of fettuccine Alfredo, which cuts the fat by a whopping 90%.

shrimp macaroni

and cheese casserole

1. In a saucepan over medium-high heat, bring 1/2 cup (125 mL) water to a boil; add mussels. Cook, covered and shaking pot occasionally, for 3 minutes or until mussels open. Discard liquid and any unopened mussels. Shell mussels; set aside.

2. In a nonstick saucepan sprayed with vegetable spray, cook red peppers, onions and garlic over medium heat for 5 minutes or until softened. Add flour; cook, stirring, for 1 minute. Add stock, milk and Dijon mustard; bring to a boil, stirring. Add shelled mussels, shrimp and scallops; reduce heat to medium. Cook, stirring occasionally, for 2 minutes or until shrimp turn pink and scallops are cooked through. Add Cheddar cheese, Swiss cheese, Parmesan cheese and dill; cook, stirring, for 1 minute or until cheese melts. Season to taste with pepper; set aside.

3. In a large pot of boiling water, cook macaroni for 6 to 8 minutes or until tender but firm; drain. Add pasta to seafood sauce; pour into baking dish.

4. In a bowl combine bread crumbs, parsley, garlic and oil; sprinkle over mixture in baking dish. Broil in preheated oven for 3 minutes or until golden.

seafood

124

PREHEAT BROILER
9-INCH (2.5 L) SQUARE BAKING DISH

Sauce

12	mussels, scrubbed	12
1 cup	diced red bell peppers	250 mL
1/2 cup	chopped onions	125 mL
1 1/2 tsp	minced garlic	7 mL
2 tbsp	all-purpose flour	25 mL
3/4 cup	SEAFOOD STOCK or CHICKEN STOCK (see recipes, page 50)	175 mL
3/4 cup	low-fat milk	175 mL
1 tsp	Dijon mustard	5 mL
4 oz	raw shrimp, shelled and chopped	125 g
4 oz	scallops, chopped	125 g
1/2 cup	shredded low-fat Cheddar cheese	125 mL
1/2 cup	shredded low-fat Swiss cheese	125 mL
2 tbsp	grated low-fat Parmesan cheese	25 mL
1/4 cup	chopped fresh dill (or 1/2 tsp [2 mL] dried)	50 mL
	Freshly ground black pepper	
8 oz	macaroni	250 g

Topping

1/4 cup	dried bread crumbs	50 mL
2 tbsp	chopped fresh parsley	25 mL
1/2 tsp	minced garlic	2 mL
1/2 tsp	olive oil	2 mL

essential numbers

PER SERVING

Calories	537
Protein	36 g
Fat, total	14 g
Fat, saturated	7.5 g
Carbohydrates	65 g
Sodium	545 mg
Cholesterol	103 mg
Fiber	3 g

ask ROSE

You can use commercially prepared bread crumbs for this recipe, but you'll get better flavor if you make your own. Just take some 2-day-old bread — such as whole wheat, rye, pumpernickel or challah — and bake in a 300° F (150° C) oven for about 30 minutes or until completely dry and lightly browned. Let bread cool and then process in a food processor. Store crumbs in an airtight container. If you wish, you can vary the flavor of the crumbs by mixing in dried spices such as garlic, chili powder or onion powder.

nutrition watch

Calcium and blood pressure

If you have high blood pressure, this recipe may be just what the doctor ordered. Why? Because it's high in calcium — the bone building mineral that studies have shown also helps to lower blood pressure. And with 400 mg calcium per serving, this dish meets one-third to one-half your daily calcium requirement (depending on your age; see page 134). According to the famous DASH study, the best diet for blood pressure is low in fat, with 2 servings of dairy products and 8 to 10 servings of fruits and vegetables each day.

squid with couscous
and oyster mushroom stuffing

1 In a saucepan over medium-high heat, bring stock to a boil. Add couscous; remove from heat. Let stand, covered, for 5 minutes.

2 In a large nonstick frying pan sprayed with vegetable spray, cook mushrooms, onions, garlic, basil and pepper over medium-high heat for 5 minutes or until softened. Remove from heat; add feta cheese, parsley and couscous.

3 Stuff each squid tube with mushroom mixture. Spread half tomato sauce over bottom of baking dish; add stuffed squid. Top with remaining tomato sauce; sprinkle with Parmesan cheese. Bake in preheated oven, covered, for 25 minutes.

PREHEAT OVEN TO 425° F (220° C)
13- BY 9-INCH (3 L) BAKING DISH

1 1/4 cups	SEAFOOD STOCK or CHICKEN STOCK (see recipes, page 50)	300 mL
3/4 cups	couscous	175 mL
1 1/2 cups	finely chopped oyster mushrooms	375 mL
1 cup	finely chopped onions	250 mL
1 tsp	minced garlic	5 mL
1 tsp	dried basil	5 mL
1/8 tsp	freshly ground black pepper	0.5 mL
2 oz	light feta cheese, crumbled	50 g
1/4 cup	chopped fresh parsley	50 mL
6	medium squid tubes, cleaned (about 1 1/2 lbs [750 g])	6
3/4 cup	tomato pasta sauce	175 mL
2 tbsp	grated low-fat Parmesan cheese	25 mL

essential numbers

PER SERVING

Calories	301
Protein	30 g
Fat, total	5 g
Fat, saturated	2.4 g
Carbohydrates	33 g
Sodium	208 mg
Cholesterol	302 mg
Fiber	3 g

ask ROSE

A relative of the octopus (but with 10 arms instead of 8), squid is something you'll usually either love or hate. For those who love it, squid (also served up in restaurants as *calamari*) is deliciously mild and chewy. (Squid-haters, which include most kids, it seems, respond with a simple "yuck!") Still, I like squid — and it's remarkably inexpensive. I prefer to buy "cleaned" squid (with the ink sac and "quill" removed). Cook squid over high heat; avoid overcooking, however, or its chewy texture will become like rubber.

cooking 101

For the best flavor, use homemade seafood stock for this dish (see recipe, page 50). But if you haven't got the time — and with 4 kids, believe me, I know what that's about — you can always use seafood bouillon cubes or powder. These alternatives are convenient (if high in sodium), and you can usually find them at your supermarket in the same section where chicken stock and beef stock are sold.

seafood and fennel chili
over fettuccine

1 In a nonstick saucepan sprayed with vegetable spray, cook fennel, red peppers, onions and garlic over medium-high heat, stirring occasionally, for 5 minutes or until softened. Add tomatoes, kidney beans, stock, brown sugar, fennel seeds, basil, chili powder, oregano and pepper; bring to a boil. Reduce heat to medium-low; cook, covered, for 15 minutes or until vegetables are tender, breaking tomatoes with back of a spoon.

2 Meanwhile, in a large pot of boiling water, cook fettuccine for 8 to 10 minutes or until tender but firm; drain.

3 Add mussels, shrimp and scallops to tomato mixture; cook, covered, over medium-high heat for 4 minutes or until mussels are open (discard unopened ones). In a serving bowl combine chili and pasta; toss well. Serve.

1 1/2 cups	chopped fennel	375 mL
1 cup	chopped red bell peppers	250 mL
3/4 cup	chopped onions	175 mL
2 tsp	minced garlic	10 mL
1	can (19 oz [540 mL]) tomatoes, with juice	1
1 cup	canned cooked white kidney beans, rinsed and drained	250 mL
1/2 cup	SEAFOOD STOCK or CHICKEN STOCK (see recipes, page 50)	125 mL
2 tsp	packed brown sugar	10 mL
1 1/2 tsp	fennel seeds	7 mL
1 tsp	dried basil	5 mL
1 tsp	chili powder	5 mL
1/2 tsp	dried oregano	2 mL
1/4 tsp	freshly ground black pepper	1 mL
12 oz	fettuccine	375 g
24	mussels, cleaned	24
6 oz	raw shrimp, shelled and chopped	175 g
6 oz	scallops (if large, cut in half)	175 g
1/2 cup	chopped parsley	125 mL

seafood

127

essential numbers

PER SERVING

Calories	428
Protein	24 g
Fat, total	3 g
Fat, saturated	0.5 g
Carbohydrates	77 g
Sodium	282 mg
Cholesterol	46 mg
Fiber	4 g

ask ROSE

Fennel, also called "finocchio," has a broad, bulbous base which can be eaten raw or cooked. (The stems are also edible.) This vegetable has a sweet taste that's a bit like anise — but not so much that it will put off licorice-haters! — and works beautifully with the flavors of fish, tomatoes and dill. When shopping for fennel, choose plants with rounder (instead of flatter) bulbs; they're more tender.

lifestyle

I love to serve this dish at informal dinner gatherings. The various shellfish cook beautifully and the aroma of fennel is wonderful. Be sure to give everyone small bowls in which to place empty mussel shells.

shrimp tomato salsa
over rice fettuccine

1 In a large nonstick frying pan sprayed with vegetable spray, cook shrimp over medium-high heat for 2 minutes or until cooked through; remove from pan. Set aside.

2 In a large pot of boiling water, cook rice noodles for 5 minutes or until tender; drain. Rinse under cold running water; drain. Set aside.

3 In a serving bowl combine shrimp, tomatoes, red peppers, red onions, coriander, garlic, lemon juice, olive oil, chili sauce and pasta; toss well. Serve.

8 oz	raw shrimp, peeled, deveined and cut in half	250 g
8 oz	wide rice noodles	250 g
3 cups	diced ripe plum tomatoes	750 mL
3/4 cup	diced red bell peppers	175 mL
1/2 cup	diced red onions	125 mL
1/2 cup	chopped fresh coriander	125 mL
1 1/2 tsp	minced garlic	7 mL
3 1/2 tbsp	fresh lemon juice	55 mL
2 1/2 tbsp	olive oil	35 mL
2 tsp	hot Asian chili sauce (optional)	10 mL

seafood

128

essential numbers

PER SERVING

Calories	273
Protein	13 g
Fat, total	7 g
Fat, saturated	1.0 g
Carbohydrates	40 g
Sodium	121 mg
Cholesterol	89 mg
Fiber	3 g

ask ROSE

Asian chili sauce is a fiery concoction of chili peppers, garlic, sugar and rice vinegar. Believe me, it's really hot! So if you've got a sensitive palate, use it sparingly. This sauce also makes a good substitute in recipes that call for hot chili peppers.

nutrition watch

Watch those fast-food sandwiches!
Looking for a quick sandwich when you're on the road? Keep in mind that a typical fast-food fillet of fish packs 23 g fat. You can improve on this by holding the tartar sauce and look for fish that's breaded, not deep-fried. Also, some deli tuna sandwiches can come to 600 calories and 40 g fat. Look for outlets that use low-fat dressings or ask for plain tuna and spread each slice of bread with only a little mayonnaise.

avocado crabmeat over rice noodles (page 119)

overleaf: orange black bean sauce with mussels over chow mein noodles (page 120)

mussel mushroom
linguine

1. In a large saucepan over medium-high heat, bring water to a boil; add mussels. Cook, covered, for 3 minutes or until mussels are opened (discard unopened ones); drain, reserving liquid. Remove mussels from shells; set aside.

2. Meanwhile, in a large nonstick frying pan sprayed with vegetable spray, cook onions and garlic over medium-high heat for 3 minutes or until softened. Add mushrooms; cook for 8 minutes or until browned. Add 1 cup (250 mL) reserved mussel cooking liquid; cook for 2 minutes.

3. In a bowl combine milk and flour; whisk well. Add flour mixture and mussels to sauce; cook for 3 minutes or until heated through and slightly thickened.

4. Meanwhile, in a large pot of boiling water, cook linguine for 8 to 10 minutes or until tender but firm; drain. In a serving bowl combine pasta, sauce and dill; toss well. Serve immediately.

3/4 cup	water *or* SEAFOOD STOCK (see recipe, page 50)	175 mL
2 lbs	mussels, scrubbed and beards removed	1 kg
1 cup	chopped onions	250 mL
1 1/2 tsp	minced garlic	7 mL
3 cups	coarsely chopped mushrooms (preferably oyster mushrooms)	750 mL
3/4 cup	low-fat evaporated milk	175 mL
2 tsp	all-purpose flour	10 mL
8 oz	linguine	250 g
1/3 cup	chopped fresh dill (or 1 tsp [5 mL] dried)	75 mL

seafood

129

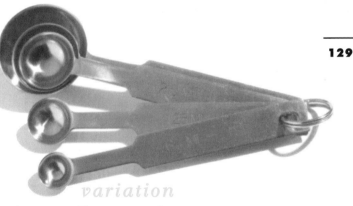

essential numbers

PER SERVING

Calories	461
Protein	41 g
Fat, total	8 g
Fat, saturated	2.1 g
Carbohydrates	56 g
Sodium	775 mg
Cholesterol	74 mg
Fiber	3 g

ask ROSE

Mussels are sensational with mushrooms, but this dish also works well with clams. Buy the freshest clams you can find (Littleneck or Cherrystone are the most common varieties) and check the shells — unlike mussels, they should be almost impossible to pry open. Cook clams as you would mussels, for at least 5 minutes or until the shells open; discard any that do not.

variation

This recipe provides a great opportunity to experiment with different types of linguine. Try the tomato, spinach or whole wheat varieties. Keep in mind that whole wheat linguine requires a few extra minutes of cooking time.

grilled salmon fillet with creamy basil-tomato sauce (page 137)

fish

tuna and cucumber

over penne

1. In a food processor or blender combine 1/2 cup (125 mL) cucumber, red peppers, dill, olives, mayonnaise, sour cream, capers, Dijon mustard and garlic; process until smooth. Set aside.

2. In a large pot of boiling water, cook penne for 8 to 10 minutes or until tender but firm; drain. Meanwhile, in a nonstick skillet sprayed with vegetable spray or on a preheated grill, cook tuna for 3 minutes per side or according to taste; slice thinly.

3. In a serving bowl combine penne, dressing and tuna; toss well. Season to taste with pepper; garnish with remaining cucumber. Serve immediately.

1 cup	diced English cucumber	250 mL
1/2 cup	diced red bell peppers	125 mL
1/3 cup	chopped fresh dill (or 1 tsp [5 mL] dried)	75 mL
1/3 cup	pimento-stuffed green olives	75 mL
1/4 cup	light mayonnaise	50 mL
1/4 cup	low-fat sour cream	50 mL
1 tbsp	drained capers	15 mL
1 tsp	Dijon mustard	5 mL
1 tsp	minced garlic	5 mL
8 oz	penne	250 g
8 oz	skinless boneless tuna steak	250 g
	Freshly ground black pepper	

fish

essential numbers

PER SERVING

Calories	400
Protein	27 g
Fat, total	9 g
Fat, saturated	1.8 g
Carbohydrates	51 g
Sodium	627 mg
Cholesterol	42 mg
Fiber	3 g

ask ROSE

Canned tuna is fine for a lot of things — but fresh tuna (or frozen) is another fish entirely! The key to enjoying fresh tuna is to make sure that you don't overcook it, which makes the flesh dry and unappetizing. My favorite method is to sear the outside and leave the inside rare. Varieties of tuna include albacore, bluefin, yellowfin and bonito. The flesh is moderately fatty, firmly textured and tender. In a pinch, you use canned tuna for this recipe; buy solid white albacore, packed in water.

nutrition watch

Fish oils and health

Fish contains two important fatty acids that belong to the omega-3 family: eicosapentanoic acid (EPA) and docosahexaenoic acid (DHA). Our bodies use omega-3 fats to manufacture prostaglandins, chemicals that regulate our blood, antibodies, hormones and skin. Some of the richest sources of omega-3 fats (EPA, DHA) include fresh tuna, salmon, trout, mackerel, sardines and herring. Cod, sole and canned tuna contain very little.

portobello mushrooms
and sea bass fettuccine alfredo

1. In a large nonstick frying pan sprayed with vegetable spray, cook onions and garlic over medium-high heat for 3 minutes or until softened. Add mushrooms; cook, stirring often, for 5 minutes or until tender and browned. Add evaporated milk, stock, Parmesan cheese, Dijon mustard and thyme; cook for 2 minutes. Set aside.

2. In a nonstick frying pan sprayed with vegetable spray or on a preheated grill, cook sea bass over medium-high heat, turning once, for 10 minutes per 1-inch (2.5 cm) thickness or until just cooked through. Flake fish with a fork. Meanwhile, in a large pot of boiling water, cook fettuccine for 8 to 10 minutes or until tender but firm; drain.

3. In a serving bowl, combine fish, sauce and pasta; toss well. Garnish with green onions; serve immediately.

1/2 cup	chopped onions	125 mL
1 1/2 tsp	minced garlic	7 mL
4 cups	coarsely chopped portobello mushrooms	1 L
3/4 cup	low-fat evaporated milk	175 mL
1/2 cup	SEAFOOD STOCK or CHICKEN STOCK (see recipes, page 50)	125 mL
1/4 cup	grated low-fat Parmesan cheese	50 mL
1 tsp	Dijon mustard	5 mL
1/4 tsp	dried thyme leaves	1 mL
12 oz	sea bass or other firm white fish	375 g
12 oz	fettuccine or soba noodles	375 g
1/4 cup	chopped green onions	50 mL

fish

133

essential numbers

PER SERVING

Calories	359
Protein	25 g
Fat, total	4 g
Fat, saturated	1.6 g
Carbohydrates	54 g
Sodium	157 mg
Cholesterol	31 mg
Fiber	2 g

ask ROSE

The portobello mushroom belongs to the same family as the common mushroom — it's just a lot bigger. Darker and stronger tasting than their pint-sized cousins, portobellos have a distinctively meaty texture and are wonderful sautéed, broiled or grilled. I love to grill them whole and stuff them in a pita bread with veggies and a light dressing. A meal in itself!

cooking 101

Sea bass is moist, flaky, delicious — and quite fatty. Keep in mind, however, that the fat consists of omega 3-fatty acids, which help lower blood cholesterol. Sea bass isn't always readily available, so feel free to replace it in this recipe with another firm white fish, such as halibut, haddock, grouper or swordfish.

As an alternative to fettuccine, try using soba noodles. Made from buckwheat and wheat flour, these noodles have a chewy texture and nutty flavor. Cook in boiling water until tender.

salmon in phyllo
with fettuccine and dill sauce

1. In a large pot of boiling water, cook fettuccine for 8 to 10 minutes or until tender but firm; drain. Meanwhile, in a saucepan over medium-high heat, combine evaporated milk, stock, Parmesan cheese, flour, Dijon mustard, garlic, pepper and salt; bring to a boil. Reduce heat to medium-low; simmer for 2 minutes or until thickened. In a bowl combine pasta and sauce; let stand for 5 minutes. Add salmon and dill.

2. Lay 1 phyllo sheet on top of another; spray with vegetable spray. Lay 2 more sheets on top; spray. Lay remaining 2 phyllo sheets on top. Pour salmon filling in center; spread to within 1 inch (2.5 cm) of edges. Fold one long end over filling; tuck in short ends and carefully roll up. Transfer to prepared baking sheet; brush with melted margarine. Bake in preheated oven for 20 minutes or until golden; slice.

3. Meanwhile in a bowl combine sour cream, dill and lemon juice. Serve salmon slices warm with a dollop of sauce on side.

PREHEAT OVEN TO 400° F (200° C)
LARGE BAKING SHEET SPRAYED WITH VEGETABLE SPRAY

4 oz	fettuccine	125 g
2/3 cup	low-fat evaporated milk	150 mL
1/4 cup	SEAFOOD STOCK or CHICKEN STOCK (see recipes, page 50)	50 mL
3 tbsp	grated low-fat Parmesan cheese	45 mL
2 tsp	all-purpose flour	10 mL
1/2 tsp	Dijon mustard	2 mL
1/2 tsp	minced garlic	2 mL
1/4 tsp	freshly ground black pepper	1 mL
1/8 tsp	salt	0.5 mL
8 oz	skinless boneless salmon fillet, cut into 1/2-inch (1 cm) cubes	250 g
2 tbsp	chopped fresh dill (or 1/4 tsp [1 mL] dried)	25 mL
6	sheets phyllo pastry	6
1 tsp	melted margarine or butter	5 mL
1/2 cup	low-fat sour cream	125 mL
2 tbsp	finely chopped fresh dill (or 1/4 tsp [1 mL] dried)	25 mL
1 tbsp	fresh lemon juice	15 mL

fish

134

essential numbers

PER SERVING

Calories	333
Protein	24 g
Fat, total	8 g
Fat, saturated	3.5 g
Carbohydrates	39 g
Sodium	480 mg
Cholesterol	52 mg
Fiber	1 g

ask ROSE

Phyllo dough creates wonderful, tissue-thin layers of pastry. It's traditionally used in Greek cuisine, but I find that it works with just about any style of cooking. And for light cooking, it's the perfect replacement for butter-laden puff pastry. Just spray every other piece with vegetable spray and it stays crisp.

Remember to work fast with phyllo pastry, since it dries quickly when exposed to air. (To keep phyllo pliable, I often cover it with a damp tea towel.) Rewrap extra dough and keep it in the freezer.

for the record

Bone up with salmon
Canned salmon is a great source of calcium — but only if you don't throw away the bones. One-half can of salmon with the bones has 225 mg calcium. That's almost 25% of the recommended daily intake for this bone-building mineral.

Here's how much calcium you need each day:

Children	800 mg
Teenagers	1300 mg
Adults, 19 to 50 years	1000 mg
Adults, 50+	1200 mg
During pregnancy	1000 mg

caesar tortellini

with smoked salmon

1. In a large pot of boiling water, cook tortellini according to package directions or until tender; drain. Meanwhile, in a food processor or blender combine sour cream, Parmesan cheese, mayonnaise, lemon juice, garlic, Dijon mustard, egg yolk and anchovies; process until smooth.

2. In a serving bowl, combine tortellini and dressing. Add smoked salmon; toss well. Serve immediately.

1 lb	fresh or frozen cheese tortellini	500 g
3 tbsp	low-fat sour cream	45 mL
2 tbsp	grated low-fat Parmesan cheese	25 mL
2 tbsp	light mayonnaise	25 mL
2 tsp	fresh lemon juice	10 mL
1 tsp	minced garlic	5 mL
1/2 tsp	Dijon mustard	2 mL
1	large egg yolk	1
2	anchovy fillets, drained and chopped	2
3 oz	smoked salmon, cut into shreds	75 g

fish

135

essential numbers

PER SERVING

Calories	495
Protein	26 g
Fat, total	15 g
Fat, saturated	7.5 g
Carbohydrates	59 g
Sodium	647 mg
Cholesterol	112 mg
Fiber	2 g

ask ROSE

Caesar salads are delicious, but the dressing is a killer — 200 calories and 15 g fat per 2 tbsp (25 mL). Talk about heart-attack-on-a-plate! But that doesn't mean giving up the great taste of Caesar salad. The dressing here uses light sour cream, low-fat mayonnaise and no oil, bringing the calories down by over half. Add the exquisite flavors of smoked salmon and tortellini, and you've got a divinely light dish!

nutrition watch

Easing joint pain with fish

Can regular consumption of fish help reduce joint soreness and inflammation caused by rheumatoid arthritis? Scientists believe that the body uses omega-3 fats found in oily fish to make the kind of immune compounds that cause less inflammation. In fact, studies suggest that as little as 1.6 g omega-3 fat each day might be helpful. Prime sources of this fat include Atlantic salmon, anchovies, Atlantic herring, whitefish, canned salmon, rainbow trout and sardines.

black bean and mango
salsa over swordfish and rotini

1 Sauce: In a bowl combine black bean sauce, water, lemon juice, barbecue sauce, olive oil, brown sugar and garlic; set aside.

2 Salsa: In a bowl combine green onions, mango, black beans, red peppers, red onions and coriander; set aside.

3 In a large pot of boiling water, cook rotini for 8 to 10 minutes or until tender but firm; drain. Meanwhile, broil or grill fish for 10 minutes per 1-inch (2.5 cm) thickness or until cooked through; cut into cubes.

4 In a serving bowl, combine pasta, sauce, salsa and fish; toss well. Serve immediately.

fish

136

PREHEAT BROILER OR SET GRILL TO MEDIUM-HIGH

Sauce

2 tbsp	black bean sauce	25 mL
1 1/2 tbsp	water	20 mL
1 1/2 tbsp	fresh lemon juice	20 mL
1 1/2 tbsp	barbecue sauce	20 mL
1 tbsp	olive oil	15 mL
1 1/2 tbsp	packed brown sugar	20 mL
1 tsp	minced garlic	5 mL

Salsa

2	green onions, chopped	2
1	large ripe mango, peeled and chopped	1
1 cup	canned cooked black beans, rinsed and drained	250 mL
1 cup	chopped red bell peppers	250 mL
1/2 cup	chopped red onions	125 mL
1/2 cup	chopped fresh coriander	125 mL
8 oz	rotini	250 g
6 oz	swordfish	175 g

essential numbers

PER SERVING

Calories	432
Protein	21 g
Fat, total	7 g
Fat, saturated	1.3 g
Carbohydrates	71 g
Sodium	169 mg
Cholesterol	17 mg
Fiber	8 g

ask ROSE

Black bean sauce is made from fermented soybeans and a lot of salt. Doesn't sound too appetizing, does it? And it isn't — at least, not on its own. But put it together with a liquid and sweetener, and this sauce is outstanding! Try it with vegetables, fish, chicken and meat. You can find bottled black bean sauce in the Asian section of your supermarket.

for the record

Hold the tartar please!

Yikes! Bet you didn't realize that a small 2-tbsp (25 mL) portion of tartar sauce packs 170 calories and 18 g fat! But when you consider its mayonnaise base (consisting of vegetable oil and egg yolks) these numbers are no surprise. Want a better alternative? Try the fat-free Black Bean Mango Salsa in this recipe.

grilled salmon fillet
with creamy basil-tomato sauce

1. In a nonstick saucepan sprayed with vegetable spray, cook onions, carrots and garlic over medium heat for 3 minutes or until softened. Add tomatoes, stock, evaporated milk, tomato paste, basil, oregano and bay leaf; bring to a boil. Reduce heat to medium-low; cook, stirring occasionally, for 10 minutes.

2. Meanwhile, in a large pot of boiling water, cook pasta for 8 to 10 minutes or until tender but firm; drain. Broil or grill salmon, turning once, for 10 minutes per 1-inch (2.5 cm) thickness or until cooked through.

3. In a bowl combine pasta and sauce; toss well. Divide among 4 plates; top each serving with salmon. Sprinkle with cheese and fresh basil.

PREHEAT BROILER OR SET GRILL TO MEDIUM-HIGH

1 cup	finely chopped onions	250 mL
1/3 cup	finely chopped carrots	75 mL
1 tsp	minced garlic	5 mL
1	can (19 oz [540 mL]) tomatoes, crushed	1
1/3 cup	SEAFOOD STOCK or CHICKEN STOCK (see recipes, page 50) or water	75 mL
1/4 cup	low-fat evaporated milk	50 mL
1 tbsp	tomato paste	15 mL
1 1/2 tsp	dried basil	7 mL
1 tsp	dried oregano	5 mL
1	bay leaf	1
8 oz	spaghetti	250 g
8 oz	salmon fillets, cut into 4 pieces	250 g
1/4 cup	grated Asiago or low-fat Parmesan cheese	50 mL
	Chopped fresh basil (optional)	

fish

137

essential numbers

PER SERVING

Calories	415
Protein	23 g
Fat, total	8 g
Fat, saturated	2.5 g
Carbohydrates	59 g
Sodium	90 mg
Cholesterol	49 mg
Fiber	4 g

ask ROSE

Once opened, a can of tomato paste will keep in the refrigerator for only about a week. But here's a way to make it last a whole lot longer: Just spoon leftover tomato paste into ice cube trays and freeze; then transfer the cubes to freezer bags and keep frozen until needed.

nutrition watch

Fish and bone health

Just about everyone knows that calcium is important for strong bones. But calcium itself isn't enough. You also need vitamin D which, among other important things, helps to maintain your blood calcium in the normal range. It does this by ensuring your intestine absorbs more calcium from the foods you eat. (If you're not getting enough calcium, vitamin D removes it from your bones to keep blood levels constant.) Adults need 200 to 600 I.U. (international units) of vitamin D each day. Next to fortified milk, oily fish is one of the best sources.

halibut with cornmeal
crust and creamy vegetable sauce

1 Dressing: In a bowl combine sour cream, stock, lemon juice, mayonnaise, honey and garlic; set aside.

2 In a large pot of boiling water, cook penne for 8 to 10 minutes or until tender but firm; drain.

3 Meanwhile, in a bowl, beat together egg white and milk. Pour cornmeal onto a plate. Dip halibut cubes into milk mixture; coat with cornmeal. In a large nonstick skillet sprayed with vegetable spray, heat oil over medium-high heat. Add fish; cook for 5 minutes or until golden and cooked through.

4 In a serving bowl, combine pasta, fish, dressing, celery, red peppers, green onions and dill; toss well. Serve immediately.

fish

138

Dressing

1/2 cup	low-fat sour cream	125 mL
1/3 cup	SEAFOOD STOCK or CHICKEN STOCK (see recipes, page 50)	75 mL
3 tbsp	fresh lemon juice	45 mL
3 tbsp	light mayonnaise	45 mL
2 tbsp	honey	25 mL
1 tsp	minced garlic	5 mL
8 oz	penne	250 g
1	large egg white	1
2 tbsp	low-fat milk	25 mL
3/4 cup	cornmeal	175 mL
1 tbsp	vegetable oil	15 mL
12 oz	skinless boneless halibut fillet, cut into 1-inch (2.5 cm) cubes	375 g
1/2 cup	chopped celery	125 mL
1/2 cup	chopped red bell peppers	125 mL
1/3 cup	chopped green onions	75 mL
1/3 cup	chopped fresh dill (or 1 tsp [5 mL] dried)	75 mL

essential numbers

PER SERVING	
Calories	556
Protein	33 g
Fat, total	14 g
Fat, saturated	4.0 g
Carbohydrates	74 g
Sodium	180 mg
Cholesterol	41 mg
Fiber	4 g

ask ROSE

Halibut is a sensational fish — white in color, mild in taste and low in fat. It also has a wonderfully firm texture that makes it ideal for baking, sautéeing, grilling or braising. Here we put the mildness of halibut together with a crunchy cornmeal crust and tasty sauce. A super combination!

Fresh halibut is available throughout the year, but most widely between March and September.

cooking 101

When purchasing light sour cream, look for 1% M.F. or less. (Some supermarkets carry a "no-fat" version which also works well in recipes.) You can substitute low-fat yogurt for the light sour cream, although your sauce won't be as thick.

smoked salmon
and plum sauce over rice noodles

1 In a large pot of boiling water, cook noodles for 5 minutes or until soft; drain. Rinse under cold running water; drain well.

2 In a bowl combine plum sauce, water, rice wine vinegar, sesame oil, garlic, ginger and chili oil.

3 In a serving bowl, combine noodles, sauce, smoked salmon, napa cabbage, red onions and coriander; toss well. Garnish with peanuts; serve immediately.

6 oz	wide rice noodles	175 g
1/3 cup	Asian plum sauce	75 mL
1/4 cup	water	50 mL
3 tbsp	rice wine vinegar	45 mL
2 tsp	sesame oil	10 mL
1 tsp	minced garlic	5 mL
1 tsp	minced ginger root	5 mL
1/2 tsp	hot Asian chili oil or paste (optional)	2 mL
4 oz	smoked salmon, shredded	125 g
1 1/2 cups	thinly sliced napa cabbage	375 mL
1/2 cup	diced red onions	125 mL
1/3 cup	chopped fresh coriander	75 mL
3 tbsp	chopped peanuts	45 mL

fish

139

essential numbers

PER SERVING

Calories	245
Protein	10 g
Fat, total	8 g
Fat, saturated	1.2 g
Carbohydrates	35 g
Sodium	444 mg
Cholesterol	7 mg
Fiber	2 g

ask ROSE

Napa cabbage is often called "Chinese cabbage" — although this name is also applied (often mistakenly) to a number of related varieties, including bok choy. In any case, it's quite different from your everyday round cabbage. The head is roughly heart shaped, and has tender, juicy, flavorful leaves. The trick is to make sure that you don't overcook them, or they'll become limp and tasteless. For best results, add napa cabbage at the end of cooking time.

for the record

Watch the fat in those fish sticks
Sure they're convenient, but some brands of breaded frozen fish contain a surprising amount of fat, ranging from 8 g to as much as 16 g fat per 100 g serving. Your best strategy: buy plain frozen fish, dip in egg whites and add your own breading!

tuna and eggplant
ratatouille over rigatoni

1 In a large nonstick saucepan sprayed with vegetable spray, heat oil over medium-high heat. Add onions and garlic; cook for 3 minutes or until softened. Add eggplant and green peppers; cook for 5 minutes or until vegetables are tender and golden. Add tomatoes, stock, tomato paste, balsamic vinegar, capers, basil and pepper; bring to a boil. Reduce heat to low; cook, covered, for 5 minutes or until tomatoes break down and sauce thickens. Add tuna, stirring to break up.

2 Meanwhile, in a large pot of boiling water, cook rigatoni for 8 to 10 minutes or until tender but firm; drain. In a serving bowl, combine pasta, sauce and parsley; toss well. Serve immediately.

2 tsp	vegetable oil	10 mL
1 cup	chopped onions	250 mL
2 tsp	minced garlic	10 mL
2 cups	chopped eggplant (not peeled)	500 mL
1 cup	chopped green peppers	250 mL
1 1/2 cups	chopped ripe plum tomatoes	375 mL
1/2 cup	Seafood Stock or Vegetable Stock (see recipes, page 50 and 51)	125 mL
2 tbsp	tomato paste	25 mL
2 tbsp	balsamic vinegar	25 mL
2 tsp	drained capers	10 mL
1 1/2 tsp	dried basil	7 mL
1/4 tsp	freshly ground black pepper	1 mL
1	can (6 oz [175 g]) water-packed tuna, drained	1
8 oz	rigatoni	250 g
1/2 cup	chopped fresh parsley	125 mL

essential numbers

PER SERVING

Calories	428
Protein	23 g
Fat, total	6 g
Fat, saturated	0.8 g
Carbohydrates	74 g
Sodium	530 mg
Cholesterol	18 mg
Fiber	9 g

ask ROSE

Canned tuna isn't expensive, so don't try to save money by purchasing anything other than white, water-packed tuna. Cheaper varieties of "light" tuna don't taste as good and, when packed in oil, they certainly aren't light! In fact, oil-packed tuna contains double the calories and 6 times the fat.

nutrition watch

Getting more omega-3s
Eating fish is a good way to add omega-3 fatty acids to your diet. But what if you don't eat a lot of fish? Try increasing your intake of alpha linolenic acid (ALA) from sources such as flaxseed, walnut and canola oil, soybeans, green leafy vegetables and omega-3 eggs. ALA is the primary member of the omega-3 family and it's called an essential fatty acid. That means it cannot be made by the body and must be supplied from food. Omega-3s are needed for proper growth and brain development during fetal life and infancy.

black olive-anchovy
tapenade over gnocchi

1. In a food processor or blender, combine olives, olive oil, water, balsamic vinegar, garlic and anchovies; process until smooth. Set aside.

2. In a large pot of boiling water, cook gnocchi according to package directions or until tender; drain. Meanwhile, in a large nonstick skillet sprayed with vegetable spray, cook zucchini over medium-high heat, stirring occasionally, for 5 minutes or until tender and browned. Add plum tomatoes and basil; cook, stirring occasionally, for 2 minutes or until tomatoes break down.

3. In a serving bowl combine gnocchi and tapenade; toss to coat well. Add vegetable mixture; toss well. Serve immediately.

Olive-anchovy tapenade

1/2 cup	sliced black olives	125 mL
2 tbsp	olive oil	25 mL
2 tbsp	water	25 mL
2 tsp	balsamic vinegar	10 mL
1 tsp	minced garlic	5 mL
2	anchovy fillets, drained	2
1 lb	fresh or frozen potato gnocchi	500 g
1 1/2 cups	thinly sliced zucchini	375 mL
2	ripe plum tomatoes, diced	2
1 tsp	dried basil	5 mL

fish

141

essential numbers

PER SERVING

Calories	308
Protein	5 g
Fat, total	21 g
Fat, saturated	6.3 g
Carbohydrates	28 g
Sodium	347 mg
Cholesterol	26 mg
Fiber	2 g

ask ROSE

Gnocchi sounds pretty exotic, but is really just the Italian word for "dumpling." Usually made from potatoes and flour, plain gnocchi are just that — plain. But add other ingredients, and these dumplings come to life. Try my SWEET POTATO GNOCCHI (page 199) or my SPINACH GNOCCHI (page 200) and you'll see what I mean! You won't need to eat much — a small amount is quite filling. Try gnocchi as an appetizer or side dish.

cooking 101

Originally from from the French region of Provence, tapenade is a thick paste made from olives, olive oil, capers, anchovies, lemon juice and seasonings. In its traditional form, which is heavy on the oil and olives, tapenade is often very high in calories and fat. This version is substantially lighter. Yet all the great flavor remains!

mango-leek sauce
over halibut and spaghettini

1 In a nonstick saucepan sprayed with vegetable spray, cook leeks over medium-high heat for 3 minutes or until softened. Add mango, garlic and stock; bring mixture to a boil. Reduce heat to medium-low; cook, covered, for 5 minutes or until leeks are tender. Transfer to a food processor. Add lemon juice, sour cream and Dijon mustard; process until smooth.

2 Broil or grill halibut, turning once, for 10 minutes per 1-inch (2.5 cm) thickness or until cooked through. Flake fish with a fork. Meanwhile, in a large pot of boiling water, cook spaghettini for 8 to 10 minutes or until tender but firm; drain.

3 In a large serving bowl, combine spaghettini, fish, red peppers, green onions, dill and dressing; toss to coat well.

PREHEAT BROILER OR SET GRILL TO MEDIUM-HIGH

1 cup	chopped leeks	250 mL
1	ripe mango, peeled and chopped	1
1 tsp	minced garlic	5 mL
3/4 cup	SEAFOOD STOCK or CHICKEN STOCK (see recipes, page 50)	175 mL
3 tbsp	fresh lemon juice	45 mL
2 tbsp	low-fat sour cream	25 mL
1 tsp	Dijon mustard	5 mL
8 oz	halibut	250 g
8 oz	spaghettini or bean noodles	250 g
1 cup	thinly sliced red bell peppers	250 mL
1/2 cup	chopped green onions	125 mL
1/3 cup	chopped fresh dill (or 1 tsp [5 mL] dried)	75 mL

fish

142

PER SERVING

essential numbers

Calories	381
Protein	23 g
Fat, total	3 g
Fat, saturated	0.8 g
Carbohydrates	65 g
Sodium	37 mg
Cholesterol	22 mg
Fiber	4 g

ask ROSE

Imagine a green onion on steroids, and you've got the basic picture of a leek. And while it's related to the garlic and onion families, the leek's flavor is milder and more complex. When buying leeks, look for smaller ones; they're more tender.

The only real downside to leeks is that dirt gets trapped between their tightly packed leaves. A simple rinse won't help much. Your best bet is to slit them from top to bottom and wash thoroughly.

nutrition watch

Fish in a capsule
Thinking about fish oil capsules as an alternative to fish? Cod liver, halibut and salmon oils do provide omega-3 fats, along with vitamins A and D. A word of caution, though: Because vitamins A and D are fat-soluble, they remain in the body. And fish oil supplements, when taken in large doses over a period time, can lead to vitamin A and D toxicity. Too much vitamin A can cause blurred vision, appetite loss, diarrhea and skin rashes. Excess vitamin D can lead to kidney stones. So before you rush out to the health food store, consult your health care practitioner.

peppers with barley
stuffing and tuna-caper dressing

1. In a saucepan over medium-high heat, bring stock to a boil. Add barley; reduce heat to medium-low. Cook, covered, for 45 minutes or until barley is tender; drain any excess liquid.

2. In a large pot of boiling water, cook peppers for 5 minutes; drain. Set aside to cool.

3. In a food processor or blender, combine tuna, water, mayonnaise, olive oil, lemon juice, capers and garlic; purée.

4. In a bowl combine barley, tomatoes, red onions, green onions and black olives. Pour dressing over; toss to coat well. Spoon mixture into peppers; top with reserved pepper tops. Serve.

3 cups	VEGETABLE STOCK *or* CHICKEN STOCK (see recipes, pages 51 and 50)	750 mL
3/4 cup	pearl barley	175 mL
4	medium red, yellow or green bell peppers, top 1 inch (2.5 cm) cut off, ribs and seeds removed	4

Dressing

Half	can (6 oz [175 g]) water-packed tuna, drained	Half
1/4 cup	water	50 mL
1 tbsp	light mayonnaise	15 mL
1 tbsp	olive oil	15 mL
2 tsp	fresh lemon juice	10 mL
2 tsp	drained capers	10 mL
1 tsp	minced garlic	5 mL
1/2 cup	diced ripe plum tomatoes	125 mL
1/3 cup	diced red onions	75 mL
1/4 cup	chopped green onions	50 mL
3 tbsp	diced black olives	45 mL

fish

143

essential numbers

PER SERVING

Calories	307
Protein	17 g
Fat, total	10 g
Fat, saturated	1.3 g
Carbohydrates	41 g
Sodium	445 mg
Cholesterol	19 mg
Fiber	8 g

ask ROSE

This tuna dressing makes a wonderful sauce over cooked beef, especially steak. I also use it for a dip with vegetables or as a sauce over pasta. It will keep in the refrigerator for up to 5 days.

lifestyle

This is a perfect dish for entertaining, either as an appetizer or as a side dish. Use a variety of colored bell peppers and be sure to save the lids of the peppers for a dramatic garnish. Also garnish with sliced basil.

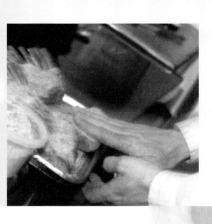

phyllo meatloaf
rolled with couscous and mushrooms

1. In a bowl combine ground beef, green onions, bread crumbs, egg, egg white, ketchup, garlic and basil; set aside.

2. In a saucepan over medium-high heat, bring stock to a boil. Add couscous and garlic; turn off heat. Let stand, covered, for 5 minutes or until stock is absorbed.

3. In a nonstick frying pan sprayed with vegetable spray, cook mushrooms, onions and chili powder over medium-high heat for 4 minutes or until tender. Add to couscous.

4. On a work surface lay 1 phyllo sheet on top of another; spray with vegetable spray. Lay 2 more sheets on top; spray. Lay remaining 2 phyllo sheets on top. Pat out meat mixture, leaving a 1-inch (2.5 cm) border all around. Spread couscous mixture over meat mixture. Starting from long end, roll up tightly; tuck ends under. Transfer to prepared baking sheet; brush with melted margarine. Bake in preheated oven for 25 to 30 minutes or until golden.

meat

146

PREHEAT OVEN TO 400° F (200° C)
BAKING SHEET SPRAYED WITH VEGETABLE SPRAY

Meatloaf

1 lb	lean ground beef	500 g
1/3 cup	chopped green onions	75 mL
1/4 cup	plain dry bread crumbs	50 mL
1	large egg	1
1	large egg white	1
1/3 cup	ketchup or barbecue sauce	75 mL
1 1/2 tsp	minced garlic	7 mL
1 tsp	dried basil	5 mL

Couscous

1 cup	BEEF STOCK or CHICKEN STOCK (see recipes, page 50)	250 mL
1/2 cup	couscous	125 mL
1/2 tsp	minced garlic	2 mL
1 cup	chopped mushrooms	250 mL
1/2 cup	chopped onions	125 mL
1/2 tsp	chili powder	2 mL
6	sheets phyllo pastry	6
2 tsp	melted margarine or butter	10 mL

essential numbers

PER SERVING

Calories	368
Protein	22 g
Fat, total	16 g
Fat, saturated	5.8 g
Carbohydrates	32 g
Sodium	343 mg
Cholesterol	83 mg
Fiber	2 g

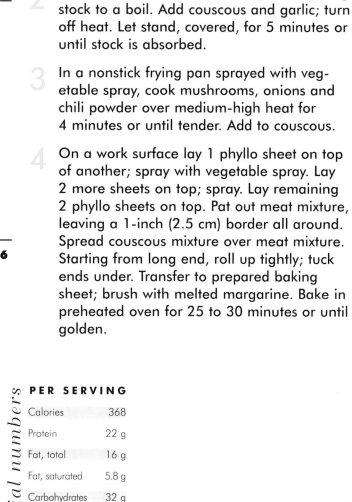

ask ROSE

Your mother's meatloaf never looked like this! Here we combine ground beef with savory couscous, all wrapped elegantly in phyllo pastry. A delight to serve at any gathering — yet so easy to make!

Here's a great way to reduce the fat in any meatloaf. Just buy a loaf pan with an insert that has holes in it, which allows excess fat to drip off and prevents it from cooking into the loaf.

for the record

Grading ground beef

What's the difference between regular, lean and extra lean? Here's a look at how they compare:

Type...	Fat content...	What that really means...
Regular	Maximum 23%	5 3/4 tsp (29 mL) hidden fat in 100 g
Lean	Maximum 17%	4 1/4 tsp (21 mL) hidden fat in 100 g
Extra Lean	Maximum 10%	2 1/2 tsp (12 mL) hidden fat in 100 g

How you cook ground meat will also make a difference. When you brown or fry meat in a nonstick pan, you'll lose some fat. For dishes like this meatloaf, use lean or extra lean since the fat can't drip away when cooking — at least, not unless you have a special pan insert (see "Ask Rose", at left).

calves' liver
with caramelized onions over linguine

1 In a large nonstick frying pan sprayed with vegetable spray, cook onions, garlic and brown sugar over medium heat, stirring occasionally, for 20 minutes or until soft and golden. Remove from pan; set aside.

2 In a bowl whisk together stock and flour; set aside.

3 In a large pot of boiling water, cook linguine for 8 to 10 minutes or until tender but firm; drain. Meanwhile, in the same frying pan used in Step 1 (wiped clean and sprayed with vegetable spray), cook liver over medium-high heat, stirring, for 1 minute or until just pink inside. Add stock and flour mixture; cook, stirring, for 2 minutes or until bubbly and slightly thickened.

4 In a serving bowl, combine sauce, caramelized onions and pasta; toss well. Season to taste with pepper. Serve immediately.

4 cups	thinly sliced sweet white onions (Spanish, Bermuda or Vidalia)	1 L
2 tsp	minced garlic	10 mL
2 tbsp	packed brown sugar	25 mL
1 1/2 cups	cold BEEF STOCK *or* CHICKEN STOCK (see recipes, page 50)	375 mL
1 tbsp	all-purpose flour	15 mL
8 oz	linguine (regular or whole wheat)	250 g
8 oz	calves' liver, cut into 1/4-inch (5 mm) strips	250 g
	Freshly ground black pepper	

meat

148

essential numbers

PER SERVING

Calories	327
Protein	21 g
Fat, total	4 g
Fat, saturated	0.1 g
Carbohydrates	54 g
Sodium	330 mg
Cholesterol	226 mg
Fiber	4 g

ask ROSE

Yes, it's more expensive, but calves' liver really is the best choice for this recipe. Not only is it more delicately flavored and tender than beef liver, but it's higher in nutrients — a good source of protein, iron and vitamin A. You *can* use beef liver in this recipe (and save a few dollars), but it will have a stronger taste and odor, and will be less tender. Of course, no matter what type of liver you use, be sure you don't overcook it — otherwise you'll end up with something resembling shoe leather!

variation

For a change of pace, try this recipe with chicken livers. They're very economical and provide a mild (yet distinctive) taste. The key to success here is in cooking the livers — cut them into quarters and cook in small batches in a hot pan.

beef manicotti
with wild mushrooms and three cheeses

1 In a large pot of boiling water, cook manicotti shells for 14 minutes or until tender; drain. Rinse under cold running water; drain. Set aside.

2 In a large nonstick frying pan sprayed with vegetable spray, cook mushrooms, leeks and garlic over medium-high heat for 8 minutes or until softened. Add beef; cook, stirring to break up beef, for 3 minutes or until no longer pink. Add stock, tomato paste and thyme; cook for 2 minutes. Remove from heat.

3 In a food processor combine beef mixture, ricotta cheese, mozzarella cheese, 2 tbsp (25 mL) Parmesan cheese, egg, salt and pepper; pulse on and off until well-mixed. Set aside.

4 In a bowl combine tomato sauce and milk. Spread half of sauce over bottom of baking dish. Stuff each manicotti shell with about 3 tbsp (45 mL) filling; place stuffed shells in baking dish. Cover with remaining sauce; sprinkle with remaining Parmesan cheese. Cover dish with foil; bake in preheated oven for 20 minutes or until heated through.

PREHEAT OVEN TO 375° F (190° C)
13- BY 9-INCH (3 L) BAKING DISH

12	manicotti shells	12
Filling		
3 cups	chopped wild mushrooms	750 mL
2 cups	chopped leeks, white and pale green parts only	500 mL
1 1/2 tsp	minced garlic	7 mL
4 oz	lean ground beef	125 g
1/4 cup	BEEF STOCK *or* CHICKEN STOCK (see recipes, page 50)	50 mL
2 tbsp	tomato paste	25 mL
3/4 tsp	dried thyme leaves	4 mL
1/2 cup	5% ricotta cheese	125 mL
1/3 cup	shredded low-fat mozzarella cheese	75 mL
3 tbsp	grated low-fat Parmesan cheese	45 mL
1	large egg	1
1/8 tsp	salt	0.5 mL
1/8 tsp	freshly ground black pepper	0.5 mL
Sauce		
1 cup	tomato pasta sauce	250 mL
3 tbsp	low-fat milk	45 mL

meat

149

essential numbers

PER SERVING

Calories	285
Protein	17 g
Fat, total	9 g
Fat, saturated	4.0 g
Carbohydrates	35 g
Sodium	300 mg
Cholesterol	61 mg
Fiber	3 g

ask ROSE

I prefer the soft, creamy type of ricotta cheese that is sold in tubs and contains 5% M.F. (Higher-fat 10% ricotta is also sold this way.) If you like the firmer, drier type of ricotta cheese, add 2 tbsp (25 mL) milk or water to make it smoother for this recipe.

I prefer oyster mushrooms for this recipe, but feel free to substitute your favorite.

for the record

Leaner than ever
Today's beef is 50% leaner than it was 20 years ago. In fact, all cuts of beef now sold (except short ribs) qualify as "lean" — meaning they contain no more than 10% fat when trimmed of all visible fat. The leanest cuts of beef include inside round steak, sirloin steak, rump roast, and eye of round. To ensure meat is as lean as possible, trim visible fat before cooking and then broil, grill, roast or stir-fry in a nonstick pan.

beef cabbage rolls

with orzo in tomato sauce

1. In a large pot of boiling water, cook whole cabbage for 20 to 25 minutes; drain. When cool enough to handle, separate leaves carefully. Set aside.

2. In a pot of boiling water, cook orzo for 8 to 10 minutes or until tender but firm; drain. Rinse under cold running water; drain. Set aside.

3. In a nonstick frying pan sprayed with vegetable spray, cook mushrooms, onions and garlic over medium-high heat for 7 minutes or until slightly browned; transfer to a bowl. Add orzo, ground beef, barbecue sauce, basil and egg white; mix well.

4. Place about 1/3 cup (75 mL) beef-orzo mixture in center of 1 cabbage leaf. Fold in sides; roll up. Repeat with remaining filling.

5. In a food processor, combine tomatoes, brown sugar, basil, water and lemon juice; purée. Add raisins; pour mixture into a large nonstick saucepan over medium-high heat. Bring to a boil; reduce heat to low. Add cabbage rolls; cook, covered, for 1 hour 15 minutes, turning rolls over at halfway point.

1	head green savoy cabbage, core removed	1
1/2 cup	orzo or any small shaped pasta	125 mL
1 cup	chopped mushrooms	250 mL
1/3 cup	chopped onions	75 mL
1 tsp	minced garlic	5 mL
8 oz	lean ground beef	250 g
3 tbsp	barbecue sauce	45 mL
1/2 tsp	dried basil	2 mL
1	large egg white	1

Sauce

1	can (28 oz [796 mL]) tomatoes, with juice	1
3 tbsp	packed brown sugar	45 mL
1 tsp	dried basil	5 mL
1/2 cup	water	125 mL
1 tbsp	lemon juice	15 mL
1/3 cup	raisins	75 mL

essential numbers

PER SERVING	
Calories	395
Protein	22 g
Fat, total	10 g
Fat, saturated	3.9 g
Carbohydrates	53 g
Sodium	331 mg
Cholesterol	35 mg
Fiber	9 g

ask ROSE

For my money, nothing cooks up better than savoy cabbage. This variety has a distinctively loose, full head of crinkled leaves; it's mild in flavor and doesn't lose its color or texture after being simmered. It's not always available, however, so you may have to make do with ordinary green cabbage.

nutrition watch

Cruciferous crunch

Studies suggest that eating more cabbage — as well as other cruciferous vegetables (cauliflower, broccoli, Brussels sprouts) — can decrease the risk of colon cancer. It may also protect from stomach, lung and breast cancer. Why? Well, for one thing they're loaded with fiber and vitamin C. (In fact, one serving of these cabbage rolls gives you 3 1/2 times the daily requirement for vitamin C.) Cabbage is also full of natural compounds called indoles and monoterpenes. These phytochemicals inhibit tumor growth and help the body detoxify cancer-causing substances.

pesto and cheese
manicotti with beef tomato sauce

1. In a large pot of boiling water, cook manicotti for 14 minutes or until tender; drain. Rinse under cold running water; drain. Set aside.

2. In a bowl combine ricotta cheese, pesto, Parmesan cheese and egg white; mix well. Set aside.

3. In a nonstick saucepan sprayed with vegetable spray, cook onions and garlic over medium-high heat for 3 minutes or until softened. Add beef; cook, stirring to break up beef, for 2 minutes or until no longer pink. Add tomatoes, tomato paste, brown sugar and basil; bring to a boil. Reduce heat to medium-low; cook for 15 minutes.

4. Spread half of the sauce over bottom of baking dish. Stuff each manicotti shell with about 3 tbsp (45 mL) filling; arrange in baking dish. Cover with remaining sauce; sprinkle with mozzarella cheese. Cover dish with foil; bake in preheated oven for 20 minutes or until heated through.

PREHEAT OVEN TO 375° F (190° C)
13- BY 9- INCH (3 L) BAKING DISH

12	manicotti shells	12
2 cups	5 % ricotta cheese	500 mL
1/4 cup	pesto (see recipe, page 204)	50 mL
3 tbsp	grated low-fat Parmesan cheese	45 mL
1	large egg white	1
Sauce		
1/2 cup	chopped onions	250 mL
1 tsp	minced garlic	5 mL
4 oz	lean ground beef	125 g
1	can (19 oz [540 mL]) tomatoes, crushed	1
2 tbsp	tomato paste	25 mL
1 tbsp	packed brown sugar	15 mL
1 tsp	dried basil	5 mL
1/3 cup	shredded low-fat mozzarella cheese	75 mL

meat

151

PER SERVING

essential numbers

Calories	389
Protein	24 g
Fat, total	17 g
Fat, saturated	7.9 g
Carbohydrates	36 g
Sodium	330 mg
Cholesterol	47 mg
Fiber	2 g

ask ROSE

For me, lean ground beef provides a nice compromise between reducing fat and maximizing flavor. But if you really want to cut down on the fat, use extra-lean ground beef for this recipe. (It contains about 30% less fat than regular ground beef.) Even-lower-fat alternatives include ground chicken or turkey, which have about 40% less fat than extra lean beef. Whatever works for you!

variation

Try cannelloni shells or jumbo pasta shells instead of manicotti. You'll need about 15 cannelloni shells or 18 jumbo shells.

As noted at left, you can reduce the fat in this dish by replacing the ground beef with ground chicken or turkey. Ground veal is also good.

rose's hearty pasta sauce
with beef and sausage

1. In a nonstick saucepan sprayed with vegetable spray, cook onions, carrots and garlic over medium-high heat for 3 minutes or until onions are softened. Add beef and sausage; cook, stirring to break up meat, for 4 minutes or until no longer pink. Add tomatoes, tomato paste, bay leaf, basil and chili powder. Season to taste with salt and pepper. Reduce heat to medium; cook, covered, for 20 minutes or until thickened.

2. Meanwhile, in a large pot of boiling water, cook rigatoni for 8 to 10 minutes or until tender but firm; drain. In a serving bowl combine pasta and sauce; sprinkle with Parmesan cheese. Serve immediately.

1/2 cup	chopped onions	125 mL
1/4 cup	finely chopped carrots	50 mL
1 tsp	minced garlic	5 mL
6 oz	lean ground beef	175 g
4 oz	Italian sausage, casings removed	125 g
1 1/2 lbs	ripe plum tomatoes, chopped	750 g
2 tbsp	tomato paste	25 mL
1	bay leaf	1
1 1/2 tsp	dried basil	7 mL
1 tsp	chili powder	5 mL
1/4 tsp	salt	1 mL
1/4 tsp	freshly ground black pepper	1 mL
1 lb	rigatoni	500 g
1/4 cup	grated low-fat Parmesan cheese	50 mL

meat

essential numbers

PER SERVING

Calories	319
Protein	14 g
Fat, total	5 g
Fat, saturated	2.0 g
Carbohydrates	53 g
Sodium	135 mg
Cholesterol	14 mg
Fiber	3 g

ask ROSE

Sweet and mild or spicy and hot, sausages add a wonderful flavor to meat dishes. Although traditionally made from beef and/or pork, they're now made with other (often leaner) meats, including chicken and turkey. So experiment — and use whatever type of sausage you prefer. Just remember that all sausages have extra fat added, so use them in moderate quantities and be sure to drain the fat after sautéeing.

lifestyle

This tomato sauce is so good that I keep it on hand for all kinds of dishes. I'll usually make up a large batch in the late summer, when plum tomatoes are their peak, and preserve it in sterilized jars. Alternatively, you can freeze the sauce in airtight containers and defrost as needed. If the defrosted sauce appears too watery, add 1 to 2 tbsp (15 to 25 mL) tomato paste and simmer for 10 minutes.

hoisin lamb stew
with tomato over rotini

1. In a bowl dust lamb with flour; coat well. In a large nonstick saucepan sprayed with vegetable spray, cook lamb over medium-high heat, stirring occasionally, for 5 minutes or until browned on all sides. Remove lamb from pan; set aside.

2. Respray saucepan; cook mushrooms and garlic over medium-high heat for 5 minutes or until browned. Add carrots, onions, stock, tomatoes, hoisin sauce, oyster sauce and lamb; bring to a boil. Reduce heat to low; cook, covered, for 45 minutes or until lamb and vegetables are tender, breaking tomatoes with back of a spoon. Season to taste with pepper.

3. In a large pot of boiling water, cook rotini for 8 to 10 minutes or until tender but firm; drain. Pour stew over pasta; garnish with parsley. Serve immediately.

12 oz	boneless stewing lamb, cut into 3/4-inch (4 cm) cubes	375 g
3 tbsp	all-purpose flour	45 mL
3 cups	coarsely chopped oyster mushrooms or regular mushrooms	750 mL
2 tsp	minced garlic	10 mL
20	baby carrots	20
16	pearl onions, peeled	16
2/3 cup	BEEF STOCK or CHICKEN STOCK (see recipes, page 50)	150 mL
1	can (19 oz [540 mL]) tomatoes, with juice	1
3 tbsp	hoisin sauce	45 mL
3 tbsp	oyster sauce	45 mL
	Freshly ground black pepper	
1 lb	rotini	500 g
1/2 cup	chopped fresh parsley	125 mL

meat

153

essential numbers

PER SERVING

Calories	437
Protein	26 g
Fat, total	5 g
Fat, saturated	1.5 g
Carbohydrates	70 g
Sodium	307 mg
Cholesterol	41 mg
Fiber	4 g

ask ROSE

Stewing lamb usually comes from the shoulder, neck, breast, shanks or leg. And while the best-tasting meat comes from the shoulder and neck, I often find that I prefer the milder flavor that you get with leg of lamb. The only disadvantage of leg meat is that it dries out easily while cooking. Remember that stewing lamb is different from beef: You need to cook it on a lower heat in a lot of liquid; the longer you cook it, the more tender it will become.

for the record

Lighter lamb

Think lamb contains more fat than beef? Wrong! When it comes to fat and calories, lamb and beef are almost identical. Just compare a 3-oz (75 g) serving of leg of lamb (lean only) with the same amount of lean-only sirloin steak. The lamb contains 162 calories and 6 g fat, compared to 163 calories and 6 g fat for the beef. In fact, lamb wins — by 1 calorie!

veal scaloppini
with red peppers and lime sauce over penne

1. In a bowl combine stock, pineapple juice concentrate, lime zest, lime juice, brown sugar and cornstarch. Set aside.

2. In a nonstick frying pan sprayed with vegetable spray, cook red peppers, green peppers and garlic over medium-high heat for 6 minutes or until tender. Add pineapple mixture; cook, stirring, for 1 minute or until thickened. Remove from heat; add green onions and coriander.

3. In a large pot of boiling water, cook rotini for 8 to 10 minutes or until tender but firm; drain. Meanwhile, in a nonstick frying pan sprayed with vegetable spray or on a preheated grill, cook scallopini over medium-high heat, turning once, for 4 minutes or until cooked through; remove from heat. Slice scallopini into thin strips.

4. In a serving bowl, combine pasta, sauce and veal; toss well. Serve immediately.

1/2 cup	BEEF STOCK or CHICKEN STOCK (see recipes, page 50)	125 mL
1/4 cup	pineapple juice concentrate	50 mL
	Finely grated zest of 1 lime	
1 tbsp	fresh lime juice	15 mL
2 tbsp	packed brown sugar	25 mL
1 tsp	cornstarch	5 mL
1 1/2 cups	thinly sliced red bell peppers	375 mL
3/4 cup	thinly sliced green bell peppers	175 mL
1 tsp	minced garlic	5 mL
1/2 cup	chopped green onions	125 mL
1/3 cup	chopped fresh coriander	75 mL
8 oz	rotini	250 g
8 oz	veal scallopini	250 g

meat

154

PER SERVING

essential numbers

Calories	440
Protein	20 g
Fat, total	14 g
Fat, saturated	3.8 g
Carbohydrates	58 g
Sodium	307 mg
Cholesterol	41 mg
Fiber	3 g

ask ROSE

Scallopini is the Italian term for a thin cut (or scallop) of meat, usually veal. It's the same type of cut that, when breaded and fried, gives you a cutlet or schnitzel. (Not to mention lots of calories and fat!) Typically, the meat is taken from the leg, although top- or bottom-round cuts are also used. Avoid buying paper-thin scallopini; it overcooks quickly and will dry out. Also, look for a smooth surface; if it's bumpy, chances are the meat was cut with (not against) the grain, making it tough.

nutrition watch

Red meat report

How much red meat should you eat? According to *Food, Nutrition and the Prevention of Cancer*, a report that sets out a number of dietary recommendations based on our current scientific knowledge, diets containing substantial amounts of red meat probably increase the risk of colon cancer and possibly increase the risk of breast, prostate and kidney cancers. If eaten at all, red meat consumption should be kept to less than 3 oz (75 g) a day. (It helps to remember that this amount is about the size of a deck of cards.) All of the recipes in this chapter provide 2 to 3 oz (50 to 75 g) per serving.

pork tenderloin
with apricots and bok choy over fettuccine

1. In a bowl combine stock, plum sauce, chili sauce, soya sauce and cornstarch. Set aside.

2. In a nonstick frying pan sprayed with vegetable spray or on a preheated grill, cook pork tenderloin over medium-high heat, turning once, for 15 minutes or until cooked through.

3. Meanwhile, in a large nonstick frying pan sprayed with vegetable spray, cook onions, garlic and ginger over medium-high heat for 5 minutes or until softened. Add bok choy and apricots; cook for 3 minutes or until bok choy wilts. Add sauce; reduce heat to medium-low. Cook for 2 minutes or until thickened; remove from heat.

4. In a large pot of boiling water, cook fettuccine for 8 to 10 minutes or until tender but firm; drain. Slice pork tenderloin thinly crosswise. In a large serving bowl, combine pasta, sauce and pork; toss well. Serve immediately.

Sauce

1 cup	BEEF STOCK or CHICKEN STOCK (see recipes, page 50)	250 mL
1/4 cup	Asian plum sauce	50 mL
3 tbsp	sweet tomato chili sauce	45 mL
1 1/2 tbsp	light soya sauce	20 mL
2 tsp	cornstarch	10 mL
8 oz	pork tenderloin	250 g
1 cup	chopped onions	250 mL
1 1/2 tsp	minced garlic	7 mL
1 tsp	minced ginger root	5 mL
5 cups	sliced bok choy	1.25 L
3/4 cup	chopped dried apricots	175 mL
12 oz	fettuccine	375 g

meat

155

essential numbers

PER SERVING

Calories	379
Protein	21 g
Fat, total	2 g
Fat, saturated	0.6 g
Carbohydrates	68 g
Sodium	246 mg
Cholesterol	25 mg
Fiber	4 g

ask ROSE

The good news about pork tenderloin is that it's very low in fat. The bad news is that its low fat content makes it susceptible to drying out when cooked. That's why you should always cook tenderloin quickly over high heat. Use it whole, sliced into medallions and pounded for scallopini, or cut into strips or cubes for stir-fries or kebabs. Keep in mind when shopping that the smaller the tenderloin, the more tender the meat.

for the record

Another white meat?

Looking for a low-fat alternative to chicken breast? Think pork! Here's a comparison chart for a 3 1/2 oz (90 g) serving of cooked meat:

Chicken breast	2.1 g fat	159 calories
Pork tenderloin	3.6 g fat	162 calories
Pork leg, inside round	4.0 g fat	161 calories
Pork loin, center-cut chop	6.2 g fat	186 calories
Chicken leg, with back	6.9 g fat	170 calories
Chicken drumstick	6.9 g fat	170 calories

grilled flank steak
with asian fruit sauce over fettuccine

1. In baking dish, combine apricot jam, stock, orange juice concentrate, soya sauce, vinegar, sesame oil, garlic and ginger. Place steak in marinade, turning to coat well. Let stand, covered, for 1 hour at room temperature or overnight in refrigerator, turning occasionally. Bring to room temperature before cooking.

2. Remove steak from marinade, reserving liquid. On preheated grill or in grill pan, cook flank steak for 5 to 7 minutes per side or according to taste. Meanwhile, in a saucepan over medium-high heat, bring marinade to a boil. Reduce heat to medium; simmer for 5 minutes. In a bowl combine cornstarch and 1 tbsp (15 mL) cold water; add to simmering marinade. Cook for 1 minute or until thickened. Add apricots and pineapple; cook for 2 minutes or until heated through. Remove from heat.

3. In a large pot of boiling water, cook fettuccine for 8 to 10 minutes or until tender but firm; drain. Meanwhile, let flank steak rest, covered with foil, for 5 minutes; slice thinly across grain. In a bowl combine sauce and pasta; toss well. Spoon onto a serving platter; arrange flank steak over pasta. Sprinkle with green onions; serve immediately.

meat

156

PREHEAT GRILL *OR* CAST-IRON GRILL PAN, GREASED, TO MEDIUM-HIGH HEAT
SHALLOW GLASS BAKING DISH

Marinade

1/2 cup	apricot jam	125 mL
1/2 cup	BEEF STOCK *or* CHICKEN STOCK (see recipes, page 50)	125 mL
3 tbsp	orange juice concentrate	45 mL
2 tbsp	light soya sauce	25 mL
1 1/2 tbsp	rice wine vinegar	20 mL
2 tsp	sesame oil	10 mL
2 tsp	minced garlic	10 mL
1 1/2 tsp	minced ginger root	7 mL
12 oz	flank steak	375 g
1 tbsp	cornstarch	15 mL
3/4 cup	diced dried apricots	175 mL
3/4 cup	diced canned pineapple, drained	175 mL
1 lb	fettuccine	500 g
1 cup	sliced green onions	250 mL

essential numbers	PER SERVING	
	Calories	544
	Protein	27 g
	Fat, total	8 g
	Fat, saturated	2.3 g
	Carbohydrates	89 g
	Sodium	180 mg
	Cholesterol	29 mg
	Fiber	3 g

ask ROSE

Flank steak is a boneless cut of beef that comes from — you guessed it! — the cow's flank, or lower hind quarters. It's very lean and, left on its own, pretty tough. But once marinated, flank steak is wonderful! Like all lean meat, it must be cooked quickly at a high temperature to keep it from drying out. And for maximum tenderness, be sure to cut thinly across the grain.

nutrition watch

Where there's smoke...

When you cook meat on an outdoor grill — whether charcoal, gas or electric — fat drips onto the coals and creates smoke. And while that smoke provides the grilled flavor, it also contains potentially cancer-causing substances called benzopyrenes which are deposited on the surface of the meat. A University of Chicago study found that a well-done charcoal-broiled steak contained as many benzopyrenes as the smoke from several hundred cigarettes. Until more is known about grilled food and cancer, North American cancer societies recommend eating barbecued foods in moderation. As well, here's what you can do to reduce the amount of smoke and benzopyrenes in barbecued food:

Grill lean cuts of meat, such as flank steak, sirloin, pork tenderloin, center-cut pork chops, poultry breast.

Trim visible fat before cooking.

Don't char meat; keep a water bottle handy for coals that flare up.

Baste foods frequently during grilling (with a low-fat marinade!).

quick sloppy joes

over rigatoni

meat

1. In a nonstick saucepan sprayed with vegetable spray, cook onions and garlic over medium-high heat for 3 minutes or until softened. Add sausage and chicken; cook, stirring to break up, for 5 minutes or until no longer pink. Drain off excess fat. Add tomatoes, basil and chili powder; bring to a boil. Reduce heat to medium-low; cook, covered, for 20 minutes or until thickened.

2. Meanwhile, in a pot of boiling water, cook rigatoni for 8 to 10 minutes or until tender but firm; drain.

3. In a food processor, purée sauce, pulsing on and off several times. (Sauce should be slightly chunky.) In a serving bowl combine pasta and sauce; toss well. Serve immediately.

1 cup	chopped onions	250 mL
2 tsp	minced garlic	10 mL
6 oz	medium-spicy Italian sausage, casings removed	175 g
8 oz	lean ground chicken	250 g
1	can (28 oz [796 mL]) tomatoes, crushed	1
1 1/2 tsp	dried basil	7 mL
1 tsp	chili powder	5 mL
12 oz	rigatoni	375 g

essential numbers

PER SERVING

Calories	460
Protein	20 g
Fat, total	16 g
Fat, saturated	3.5 g
Carbohydrates	55 g
Sodium	350 mg
Cholesterol	32 mg
Fiber	4 g

ask ROSE

Once served up under the not-so-appetizing name of "loosemeat," the origins of today's Sloppy Joe date back to the 1950s. No one knows where "Joe" came from, but once you make this dish, you'll understand why it's called "sloppy"!

lifestyle

Here's a dish that has instant appeal for younger children and teenagers alike. After all, it's messy — that alone is enough to guarantee its popularity with kids! — and tastes like a crumbly burger over top thick pasta. For my family, I like to store portions of this dish in small containers and freeze until needed for lunches or dinners. The sauce is also delicious served over a large Italian bun.

Serves 4

baked beans
with molasses and ham over small shell pasta

1 If using cooked beans, proceed to step 2. Otherwise, in a saucepan over medium-high heat, cover uncooked beans with cold water; bring to a boil. Reduce heat; simmer for 5 minutes. Remove from heat; let stand, covered, for 1 hour. Drain beans. Return to saucepan; cover with cold water. Bring to a boil; reduce heat to medium. Cook, covered, for 1 hour or until tender; drain.

2 In a nonstick saucepan sprayed with vegetable spray, cook onions and garlic over medium-high heat for 3 minutes or until softened. Add ham, stock, pasta sauce, ketchup, molasses and brown sugar; bring to a boil. Pour ham mixture and beans into baking dish; bake, covered, in preheated oven for 20 minutes.

3 Meanwhile, in a large pot of boiling water, cook pasta for 8 to 10 minutes or until tender but firm; drain. In a serving bowl combine pasta and bean mixture; toss well. Serve immediately.

PREHEAT OVEN TO 400° F (200° C)
SMALL BAKING DISH

1 cup	dried navy or pea beans, rinsed and drained *or* 2 3/4 cups [675 mL] canned cooked beans, drained	250 mL
1 cup	chopped onions	250 mL
1 1/2 tsp	minced garlic	7 mL
4 oz	cooked ham, chopped	125 g
1 1/4 cups	BEEF STOCK *or* CHICKEN STOCK (see recipes, page 50)	300 mL
1/2 cup	tomato pasta sauce	125 mL
1/4 cup	ketchup	50 mL
1/3 cup	molasses	75 mL
1/4 cup	packed brown sugar	50 mL
8 oz	small shell pasta	250 g

meat

159

essential numbers

PER SERVING

Calories	440
Protein	20 g
Fat, total	3 g
Fat, saturated	0.7 g
Carbohydrates	88 g
Sodium	375 mg
Cholesterol	12 mg
Fiber	10 g

ask ROSE

If you've got 2 or 3 hours to spare, you can make a tasty pot of old-fashioned baked beans. Or you can take a few shortcuts — as I've done here — and still end up with a great result! Store-bought cooked ham gives this dish a smoky-salty flavor that's delicious with the beans-and-molasses combination. Who needs all the fatty bacon that comes with traditional baked beans?

nutrition watch

Iron and brain power
Did you know that iron deficiency can affect attention span, learning ability and intellectual performance in adolescents and children? Well, according to a number of studies, it's true. With less iron available to transport oxygen to body cells, less energy is produced for concentration, thinking and learning. Iron is also used to make brain compounds called neurotransmitters, in particular the ones that regulate the ability to pay attention. So focus on this recipe for baked beans — it'll give you 5 mg iron per serving!

braised veal shanks

over orzo

1 In a bowl, dust veal with flour. In a large frying pan sprayed with vegetable spray, cook meat over medium-high heat, turning occasionally, for 8 minutes or until browned on all sides. Set aside.

2 In a large nonstick saucepan sprayed with vegetable spray, cook mushrooms, onions and garlic over medium-high heat for 8 minutes or until mushrooms are slightly browned. Add tomatoes, stock, tomato pasta sauce, carrots, potatoes, olives, tomato paste, brown sugar, basil, oregano and rosemary. Bring to a boil, stirring to crush tomatoes with back of spoon. Reduce heat to simmer; add meat. Cook, covered, for 1 1/2 hours or until meat is tender.

3 Meanwhile, in a pot of boiling water, cook orzo for 8 minutes or until tender but firm; drain. In a serving bowl pour sauce over orzo; top with meat. Serve immediately.

meat

160

1 1/2 lbs	veal shanks	750 g
2 tbsp	all-purpose flour	25 mL
2 cups	sliced mushrooms	500 mL
1 cup	chopped onions	250 mL
1 1/2 tsp	minced garlic	7 mL
1	can (19 oz [540 mL]) tomatoes, drained	1
1 cup	BEEF STOCK or CHICKEN STOCK (see recipes, page 50)	250 mL
2/3 cup	tomato pasta sauce	150 mL
1 cup	chopped carrots	250 mL
1 cup	diced potatoes	250 mL
1/3 cup	sliced black olives	75 mL
2 tbsp	tomato paste	25 mL
2 tbsp	packed brown sugar	25 mL
1 tsp	dried basil	5 mL
1/2 tsp	dried oregano	2 mL
1 tsp	dried rosemary leaves	5 mL
8 oz	orzo	250 g

essential numbers

PER SERVING

Calories	591
Protein	51 g
Fat, total	9 g
Fat, saturated	1.5 g
Carbohydrates	76 g
Sodium	714 mg
Cholesterol	156 mg
Fiber	6 g

ask ROSE

Here's my take on the traditional Italian osso buco — a delectable stew made from veal shanks, where flavorful meat surrounds bone and marrow. The meat, like a stewing veal, must be cooked over a low heat in its sauce for a long period of time. The result is a tender, melt-in-your-mouth delight!

for the record

Oily olives

The next time you reach for the antipasto tray, go easy on the olives. Remember, it's from these tasty little fruit that we get olive oil. In fact, 8 large black olives (or 8 medium-sized green) are equivalent to 1 tsp (5 mL) of oil — a quick way to munch down 41 calories and 4.6 g fat. So if you're tempted to eat more, then at least skip the oil on your salad!

beef cabbage rolls with orzo in tomato sauce (page 150)

polenta with veal stew

1 In a bowl coat veal with flour. In a nonstick saucepan sprayed with vegetable spray, cook veal over medium-high heat, stirring occasionally, for 5 minutes or until browned on all sides. Remove from pan.

2 Respray saucepan; cook onions and garlic over medium-high heat for 3 minutes or until browned; add mushrooms. Cook for 3 minutes or until tender. Add potatoes, carrots, bay leaves, basil, pepper, salt, stock and pasta sauce; bring to a boil. Add meat; reduce heat to low. Cook for 40 minutes or until meat is tender.

3 In a nonstick saucepan over medium-high heat, bring stock to a boil. Reduce heat to low; gradually whisk in cornmeal. Cook, stirring constantly, for 5 minutes. Pour polenta onto a serving platter; pour stew over top. Serve.

12 oz	boneless stewing veal, cut into 1-inch (2.5 cm) cubes	375 g
2 tbsp	all-purpose flour	25 mL
1 cup	diced onions	250 mL
2 tsp	minced garlic	10 mL
1 1/2 cups	chopped mushrooms	375 mL
2 cups	diced peeled potatoes	500 mL
1 cup	diced carrots	250 mL
2	bay leaves	2
1 1/2 tsp	dried basil	7 mL
1/4 tsp	freshly ground black pepper	1 mL
1/4 tsp	salt	1 mL
2 cups	BEEF STOCK *or* CHICKEN STOCK (see recipes, page 50)	500 mL
1 cup	tomato pasta sauce	250 mL

Polenta

| 3 cups | CHICKEN STOCK *or* VEGETABLE STOCK (see recipes, pages 50 and 51) | 750 mL |
| 1 cup | cornmeal | 250 mL |

meat

161

essential numbers

PER SERVING	
Calories	253
Protein	18 g
Fat, total	5 g
Fat, saturated	1.0 g
Carbohydrates	36 g
Sodium	400 mg
Cholesterol	53 mg
Fiber	5 g

ask ROSE

Ever wonder why we dust the veal with flour before we sauté it? Simple: the flour, when browned, forms a coating that seals in the juices; without it, the lean meat would dry out. This method doesn't require a lot of oil — as this delicious stew will prove!

for the record

Bugs Bunny quiz

While there's no official recommended intake for beta carotene, most experts feel we should be aiming for 5 mg of this antioxidant each day. How many carrots do you think it takes to get this daily dose?

a) one   b) two or three   c) four or five
d) more than five

Give yourself a pat on the back if you picked a). Just one medium carrot has 11 mg of beta carotene. Th-th-that's all, folks!

grilled flank steak with asian fruit sauce over fettuccine (page 156)

rice noodle basket
with hoisin beef and vegetables

1. In a pot of boiling water, cook rice noodles for 5 minutes or until tender; drain. In a bowl combine rice noodles, sesame oil and egg white; pour into prepared springform pan. Bake in preheated oven for 10 minutes. Increase oven heat to broil. Cook for 5 to 8 minutes or until top is golden; set aside.

2. In a bowl combine hoisin sauce, soya sauce, rice wine vinegar, honey, sesame oil, garlic, ginger and cornstarch. Set aside.

3. In a large nonstick frying pan sprayed with vegetable spray or on a preheated grill, cook beef over high heat, stirring, for 5 minutes or according to taste; remove from pan. Slice thinly; set aside. Respray pan; cook red peppers, snow peas and corn cobs over medium-high heat, stirring, for 5 minutes or until tender-crisp. Add sauce and beef; cook for 1 minute or until heated through. Pour over crust; sprinkle with green onions. Serve immediately.

PREHEAT OVEN TO 450° F (220° C)
9-INCH (2.5 L) SPRINGFORM PAN SPRAYED WITH VEGETABLE SPRAY

6 oz	wide rice noodles	175 g
2 tsp	sesame oil	10 mL
1	large egg white, beaten	1

Sauce

3 tbsp	hoisin sauce	45 mL
1 tbsp	light soya sauce	15 mL
1 tbsp	rice wine vinegar	15 mL
2 tsp	honey	10 mL
1 tsp	sesame oil	5 mL
1 tsp	minced garlic	5 mL
1/2 tsp	minced ginger root	2 mL
1/2 tsp	cornstarch	2 mL
8 oz	boneless grilling steak, such as striploin	250 g
1 1/2 cups	julienned red bell peppers	375 mL
1 cup	sliced snow peas	250 mL
1/2 cup	canned baby corn cobs, cut into chunks	125 mL
3 tbsp	chopped green onions	45 mL

meat

162

essential numbers

PER SERVING

Calories	248
Protein	11 g
Fat, total	10 g
Fat, saturated	3.8 g
Carbohydrates	28 g
Sodium	350 mg
Cholesterol	28 mg
Fiber	2 g

ask ROSE

When a recipe calls for baby corn cobs, it's not talking about corn that was picked too early! This type of corn is a special miniature variety that originates from China. These tender cobs are great added to salads or eaten on their own. They're sold in cans, and can be found in the Asian section of your supermarket. If you can't find them, substitute corn kernels.

for the record

Gluten-free grains

If you know someone who has Celiac Disease, then chances are you know they are unable to tolerate gluten, a naturally occurring protein in wheat, barley, rye or oats. For people with this disease, gluten causes intestinal damage and results in the inability to digest and absorb nutrients. The only treatment is a lifelong gluten-free diet. What's left to eat? Rice, rice noodles, rice pasta, potatoes, corn, buckwheat, quinoa, gluten-free breads and legumes — any of these provide gluten-free starches, and can be found in health food stores, specialty food shops and some supermarkets.

pasta casserole
with mini meatballs and tomato cheese sauce

1. In a bowl combine ground beef, egg white, onions, bread crumbs, barbecue sauce and garlic. Form 1 1/2 tsp (7 mL) of mixture into a round meatball. Repeat to make about 36 balls; set aside.

2. In a nonstick saucepan over medium-high heat, combine salsa, tomato sauce and water. Bring to a boil; add meatballs. Reduce heat to low; cook, covered, for 20 minutes, gently stirring occasionally. Set aside.

3. Meanwhile, in a saucepan over medium-high heat, whisk together milk, stock and flour. Bring to a boil, stirring constantly; reduce heat to low. Cook for 4 minutes or until thickened and bubbly. Add Cheddar cheese and 2 tbsp (25 mL) Parmesan cheese; set aside.

4. In a pot of boiling water, cook pasta for 8 to 10 minutes or until tender but firm; drain. In a bowl combine pasta and cheese sauce; pour into casserole dish. Top with meatball mixture; sprinkle with remaining 1 tbsp (15 mL) Parmesan cheese. Bake, covered, for 20 minutes or until heated through.

meat

164

PREHEAT OVEN TO 350° F (180° C)
9-INCH (2.5 L) BAKING DISH

Meatballs

8 oz	lean ground beef	250 g
1	large egg white	1
3 tbsp	minced onions	45 mL
3 tbsp	plain dry bread crumbs	45 mL
1 tbsp	barbecue sauce	15 mL
1 tsp	minced garlic	5 mL

Sauce

1/3 cup	mild salsa	75 mL
1/4 cup	tomato pasta sauce	50 mL
1/4 cup	water	50 mL

Cheese Sauce

1 cup	low-fat milk	250 mL
1 cup	BEEF STOCK or CHICKEN STOCK (see recipes, page 50)	250 mL
2 1/2 tbsp	all-purpose flour	35 mL
1/2 cup	shredded low-fat Cheddar cheese	125 mL
3 tbsp	grated low-fat Parmesan cheese	45 mL
8 oz	small shell pasta	250 g

essential numbers

PER SERVING

Calories	575
Protein	32 g
Fat, total	19 g
Fat, saturated	8.6 g
Carbohydrates	69 g
Sodium	600 mg
Cholesterol	57 mg
Fiber	4 g

ask ROSE

This recipe is a sure-fire hit with kids of all ages. And why not? It combines macaroni and cheese, "beefa-roni" and pasta and meatballs — all into one dish! The mini-meatballs are also unusual, appetizing, and just plain fun.

for the record

It's usable iron that counts

Although many foods contain iron, the type found in grains and vegetables is not as available to the body as the iron found in meat, poultry and fish. In fact, a 3-oz (75 g) serving of lean beef provides as much useable iron as 4 cups (1 L) raw spinach.

polenta lasagna
with meat tomato sauce

1 In a saucepan over medium-high heat, bring stock to a boil. Reduce heat to low; gradually whisk in cornmeal and garlic. Cook, stirring constantly, for 5 minutes. Spread mixture into baking dish; chill for 15 minutes.

2 Meanwhile, in a bowl combine ricotta cheese, mozzarella cheese, 2 tbsp (25 mL) Parmesan cheese, milk, egg and pepper. Set aside.

3 In a nonstick saucepan over medium-high heat, cook ground beef, stirring, for 4 minutes or until no longer pink. Add tomato pasta sauce; reduce heat to medium-low. Cook for 5 minutes or until thickened.

4 Turn polenta out onto a cutting board; cut into 3 equal strips. Carefully slice each strip horizontally into half, creating 6 long thin strips. Spread one-third meat sauce over bottom of baking dish. Lay 3 polenta strips on top; spread with half of cheese mixture, then another one-third meat sauce. Repeat layers; sprinkle with remaining Parmesan cheese. Cover with foil; bake in preheated oven for 30 minutes or until heated through.

PREHEAT OVEN TO 400° F (200° C)
9-INCH (2.5 L) SQUARE BAKING DISH

Polenta

3 cups	CHICKEN STOCK (see recipe, page 50)	750 mL
1 cup	cornmeal	250 mL
1 tsp	minced garlic	5 mL
1 1/2 cups	5% ricotta cheese	375 mL
1 cup	shredded low-fat mozzarella cheese	250 mL
3 tbsp	grated low-fat Parmesan cheese	45 mL
1/4 cup	low-fat milk	50 mL
1	large egg	1
1/4 tsp	freshly ground black pepper	1 mL

Sauce

4 oz	lean ground beef	125 g
2 cups	tomato pasta sauce	500 mL

meat

166

PER SERVING

Calories	397
Protein	22 g
Fat, total	19 g
Fat, saturated	8.2 g
Carbohydrates	36 g
Sodium	500 mg
Cholesterol	82 mg
Fiber	4 g

essential numbers

ask ROSE

What makes traditional lasagna such a high-fat dish? It's all that meat, cheese and white cream sauce, of course! But then, those big sheets of pasta need *something*. So here's my solution: Just replace the lasagna noodles with thick layers of creamy polenta — delicious and satisfying! And by using a greater proportion of ricotta cheese, we reduce the amount of high-fat cheese needed in the recipe.

cooking 101

If you prepare the polenta in advance (before you've had a chance to place it in the baking dish), you'll notice that it soon hardens to a firm consistency. Don't worry, it's easy to restore that creamy texture — just add some hot water; then cook the polenta, stirring, until smooth again.

sausage bolognese
over egg noodles

1 In a large nonstick saucepan sprayed with vegetable spray, cook sausage over medium-high heat, stirring to break up the meat, for 4 minutes or until no longer pink; drain excess fat. Add onions, carrots and garlic; cook, stirring, for 3 minutes or until vegetables are soft and starting to brown. Add tomatoes, red peppers, stock, wine, basil, chili powder and pepper; bring to a boil. Reduce heat to medium-low; cook, uncovered, for 20 minutes or until thickened. Add evaporated milk; cook for 2 minutes or until heated through.

2 In a large pot of boiling water, cook egg noodles for 8 minutes or until tender but firm; drain. In a serving bowl, combine noodles and sauce; toss well. Sprinkle with Parmesan cheese; serve immediately.

4 oz	Italian sausage, casings removed	125 g
1 cup	chopped onions	250 mL
1/2 cup	chopped carrots	125 mL
2 tsp	minced garlic	10 mL
1	can (19 oz [540 mL]) tomatoes, crushed	1
1/2 cup	chopped roasted red bell peppers	125 mL
1/2 cup	BEEF STOCK *or* CHICKEN STOCK (see recipes, page 50)	125 mL
1/4 cup	red wine	50 mL
1 tsp	dried basil	5 mL
1 tsp	chili powder	5 mL
1/4 tsp	freshly ground black pepper	1 mL
1/2 cup	low-fat evaporated milk	125 mL
12 oz	medium egg noodles	375 g
3 tbsp	grated low-fat Parmesan cheese	45 mL

meat

167

essential numbers

PER SERVING	
Calories	361
Protein	15 g
Fat, total	10 g
Fat, saturated	3.6 g
Carbohydrates	52 g
Sodium	287 mg
Cholesterol	73 mg
Fiber	3 g

ask ROSE

Traditional Bolognese sauce is heavy on the beef, with tomato playing a supporting role and cream providing the big finale. Well, I took some liberties with tradition and here's the result — a light-yet-delicious remake, with the meat replaced by a small amount of flavorful sausage, plus a big blast of tomatoes and roasted red bell peppers for sweetness. Finally, by using evaporated milk instead of cream, I've retained the original character of the dish, but without all the fat!

Roast your own red peppers or use commercially prepared roasted red peppers packed in water.

for the record

Calcium in a can

Evaporated milk can do a whole lot more than replace high-fat cream in your recipes. It can also help ward off osteoporosis. No kidding — 1 cup (250 mL) evaporated 2% milk packs 740 mg calcium; the same amount of evaporated skim has 780 mg. That's more than double the amount of calcium in a glass of regular milk. Okay, so chances are you won't be pouring the canned stuff over your breakfast cereal, but with 92 mg calcium in 2 tbsp (25 mL), why not use it to whiten your coffee?

meatloaf-polenta
roulade with tomato sauce

1. In a bowl combine ground beef, garlic, egg, bread crumbs, green onions, chili sauce, basil and pepper. Set aside.

2. In a saucepan over medium-high heat, bring stock to a boil. Reduce heat to low; gradually whisk in cornmeal, Parmesan cheese and garlic. Cook, stirring, for 5 minutes. Set aside.

3. In a small nonstick skillet sprayed with vegetable spray, cook red peppers for 3 minutes or until soft; add to polenta.

4. On a piece of waxed paper, form meat mixture into an 8-inch (20 cm) square; spread with polenta. Using waxed paper to help, roll mixture from one end to the other. Pick up by waxed paper; gently drop into loaf pan. Spread with barbecue sauce; cover pan with foil. Bake in preheated oven for 40 minutes.

PREHEAT OVEN TO 350° F (180° C)
8- BY 4-INCH (20 BY 10 CM) LOAF PAN

12 oz	lean ground beef	375 g
1 1/2 tsp	minced garlic	7 mL
1	large egg	1
1/3 cup	seasoned bread crumbs	75 mL
1/4 cup	chopped green onions	50 mL
3 tbsp	sweet tomato chili sauce *or* ketchup	45 mL
1 tsp	dried basil	5 mL
1/4 tsp	freshly ground black pepper	1 mL
Polenta		
1 cup	CHICKEN STOCK *or* BEEF STOCK (see recipes, page 50)	250 mL
1/4 cup	cornmeal	50 mL
1 tbsp	grated low-fat Parmesan cheese	15 mL
1/2 tsp	minced garlic	2 mL
1/2 cup	diced red bell peppers	125 mL
1/4 cup	barbecue sauce *or* tomato pasta sauce	50 mL

meat

168

PER SERVING

Calories	223
Protein	15 g
Fat, total	11 g
Fat, saturated	4.4 g
Carbohydrates	14 g
Sodium	498 mg
Cholesterol	72 mg
Fiber	1 g

essential numbers

ask ROSE

Tired of boring, same-old meatloaf? Then try this one. Polenta is the surprise ingredient here, and it gives this loaf a sophisticated turn — as well as a big nutritional boost. It also reduces the amount of beef needed, which means a lot less fat and calories.

variation

There's no rule here that says you have to use beef — so try this recipe with ground chicken, veal or turkey.

nutrition watch

Hamburger 101
Do you like your burgers pink in the middle? Well, you might want to develop a taste for well-done. Why? Hamburger can contain an especially nasty bug called E. coli 0157, which causes severe food poisoning. The so-called "hamburger disease" causes nausea, vomiting, fever — even death. The bacteria are present on the surface of meat and are killed by cooking to a high temperature. So while a medium-rare steak is safe, ground beef may not be, since the bacteria are dispersed within the meat. So play it safe and leave your burgers on the grill for a few minutes more.

savory cabbage
with steak over rigatoni

1. In a large nonstick saucepan sprayed with vegetable spray, cook onions, red peppers, carrots and garlic over medium heat, stirring occasionally, for 5 minutes or until softened. Add cabbage; cook for 3 minutes. Add tomatoes, stock, potatoes, lemon juice, caraway seeds, salt and pepper; bring to a boil. Reduce heat to low; cook, covered, for 25 minutes, breaking up tomatoes occasionally with the back of a spoon.

2. Meanwhile, in a nonstick frying pan sprayed with vegetable spray or on a preheated grill, cook steak, turning once, over medium-high heat for 5 minutes or until medium-rare; slice thinly. Set aside.

3. In a large pot of boiling water, cook rigatoni for 8 to 10 minutes or until tender but firm; drain. In a serving bowl combine pasta, sauce and beef; toss well. Serve.

1 cup	chopped onions	250 mL
2/3 cup	chopped red bell peppers	150 mL
1/2 cup	chopped carrots	125 mL
2 tsp	minced garlic	10 mL
3 cups	shredded green cabbage	750 mL
1	can (19 oz [540 mL]) tomatoes, with juice	1
1 cup	BEEF STOCK or CHICKEN STOCK (see recipes, page 50)	250 mL
2/3 cup	diced peeled potatoes	150 mL
2 tsp	fresh lemon juice	10 mL
1 1/2 tsp	caraway seeds	7 mL
1/4 tsp	salt	1 mL
1/4 tsp	freshly ground black pepper	1 mL
8 oz	boneless beef steak, such as top sirloin	250 g
12 oz	rigatoni	375 g

meat

169

essential numbers

PER SERVING

Calories	345
Protein	19 g
Fat, total	3 g
Fat, saturated	0.8 g
Carbohydrates	60 g
Sodium	182 mg
Cholesterol	20 mg
Fiber	5 g

ask ROSE

I've always loved the sweet-and-sour cabbage flavor of European borscht. But as a pasta sauce? Well, why not! Here we combine it with strips of lean beef — and I urge you to use the best (which is to say, most tender) steak you can afford. If using sirloin or rib-eye, be sure to cut away the visible fat.

cooking 101

Traditionally, this type of dish calls for regular green cabbage. But frankly, I think it's even better with savoy cabbage, which has a milder flavor, and retains its texture and color better than regular cabbage. Definitely worth a try!

spicy beef polenta

layered casserole

1 In a nonstick saucepan sprayed with vegetable spray, cook beef over medium-high heat, stirring, for 3 minutes or until no longer pink. Add onions and garlic; cook for 3 minutes or until softened. Add green peppers, carrots and jalapeño peppers; cook for 2 minutes. Add tomatoes, corn, black olives, bay leaf, chili powder and Italian seasoning; bring to a boil. Reduce heat to low; cook, covered, for 20 minutes or until thickened and vegetables are tender.

2 In a nonstick saucepan over medium-high heat, bring stock to a boil. Reduce heat to low; gradually whisk in cornmeal. Cook, stirring, for 5 minutes. Spread half of meat sauce over bottom of prepared baking dish; top with half of polenta. Repeat layers; sprinkle with mozzarella cheese and Parmesan cheese. Cover pan with foil. Bake in preheated oven for 15 minutes or until heated through; let stand for 5 minutes before serving.

PREHEAT OVEN TO 425° F (220° C)
13- BY 9-INCH (3 L) BAKING DISH SPRAYED WITH VEGETABLE SPRAY

8 oz	lean ground beef	250 g
3/4 cup	diced onions	175 mL
2 tsp	minced garlic	10 mL
3/4 cup	diced green bell peppers	175 mL
3/4 cup	diced carrots	175 mL
2 tsp	minced jalapeño peppers (optional) or 1/2 tsp (2 mL) dried chili flakes	10 mL
1	can (19 oz [540 mL]) tomatoes, crushed	1
3/4 cup	canned or frozen corn kernels	175 mL
1/3 cup	sliced black olives	75 mL
1	bay leaf	1
1 tbsp	chili powder	15 mL
1 1/2 tsp	Italian seasoning	7 mL
6 cups	CHICKEN STOCK or BEEF STOCK (see recipes, page 50)	1.5 L
1 1/2 cup	cornmeal	375 mL
1 cup	shredded low-fat mozzarella cheese	250 mL
2 tbsp	grated low-fat Parmesan cheese	25 mL

meat

170

essential numbers

PER SERVING

Calories	270
Protein	13 g
Fat, total	10 g
Fat, saturated	3.5 g
Carbohydrates	30 g
Sodium	130 mg
Cholesterol	27 mg
Fiber	5 g

ask ROSE

Ever heard of pepper spray — you know, the kind used to subdue attackers? Well, if you ever want to find out why it's so effective, just brush your fingers against your eyes or nose after handling minced hot peppers. Talk about pain! That searing heat comes from an oil found in the pepper's seeds and membrane. So protect yourself — use rubber gloves when chopping hot peppers, and always wash your utensils with hot soapy water immediately afterwards. (Water alone will not wash away the irritating oil.) If you're still concerned about using fresh hot peppers in this recipe, use dried chili flakes or hot chili sauce.

nutrition watch

Feel the heat

The jalapeños in this recipe pack a lot of heat. But if you have a chronic pain disorder, that may not be such a bad thing. Hot green and red peppers contain capsaicin, a natural compound that gives your salsa its kick. And the hotter the chili, the more capsaicin it contains. Today this pungent ingredient is being used in creams to treat painful conditions such as rheumatoid arthritis and diabetic neuropathy. Scientists are also studying its ability to reduce pain in cancer patients undergoing chemotherapy. It seems that adding a few chilies to that cure-all bowl of chicken soup may be just what the doctor ordered.

layered tortilla cheese
and pasta pie

1. In a nonstick saucepan sprayed with vegetable spray, cook onions, carrots and garlic over medium-high heat for 4 minutes or until softened. Add ground beef; cook, stirring to break up, for 3 minutes or until no longer pink. Add tomato sauce, kidney beans and basil. Reduce heat to low; cook, covered, for 10 minutes.

2. Meanwhile, in a pot of boiling water, cook shell pasta for 8 minutes or until tender but firm; drain. Add to meat sauce, stirring well. Set aside.

3. In a bowl combine ricotta cheese, 1/2 cup (125 mL) Cheddar cheese, sour cream, Parmesan cheese, egg and black pepper. Add to tomato mixture.

4. Place one tortilla in bottom of prepared springform pan; top with one-third meat and cheese mixture. Repeat layers twice. Top with remaining tortilla; sprinkle with 2 tbsp (25 mL) Cheddar cheese. Cover pan with foil; bake in preheated oven for 20 minutes or until heated through. Cut into wedges; serve.

PREHEAT OVEN TO 350° F (180° C)
8-INCH (2 L) SPRINGFORM PAN SPRAYED WITH VEGETABLE SPRAY

2/3 cup	finely chopped onions	150 mL
1/3 cup	finely chopped carrots	75 mL
1 1/2 tsp	minced garlic	7 mL
8 oz	lean ground beef	250 g
1 1/4 cups	tomato pasta sauce	300 mL
3/4 cup	canned cooked red kidney beans, rinsed and drained	175 mL
3/4 tsp	dried basil	4 mL
4 oz	small shell pasta	125 g
1 cup	5% ricotta cheese	250 mL
1/2 cup	shredded low-fat Cheddar cheese	125 mL
1/4 cup	low-fat sour cream	50 mL
2 tbsp	grated low-fat Parmesan cheese	25 mL
1	large egg	1
1/4 tsp	freshly ground black pepper	1 mL
4	8-inch (20 cm) flour tortillas	4
2 tbsp	shredded low-fat Cheddar cheese	25 mL

meat

172

essential numbers

PER SERVING

Calories	440
Protein	27 g
Fat, total	17 g
Fat, saturated	6.0 g
Carbohydrates	54 g
Sodium	626 mg
Cholesterol	89 mg
Fiber	3 g

ask ROSE

It used to be that flour tortillas came in just one color — sandy beige. But now you can find them in a wide variety of colors and flavors. These include green (spinach), red (tomato or bell pepper), brown (whole wheat), as well as many others. Sizes vary, too, ranging from 6 inches (15 cm) to 10 inches (25 cm). To economize, I buy tortillas in bulk and freeze them until needed.

for the record

Mexican meltdown

So you figured the taco salad at your local Mexican fast food joint was a healthier choice than the beef burrito. Salad certainly sounds healthier, right? Not in this case!. A typical taco salad can run you 905 calories and 61 g fat. Ouch! This so-called salad gets its calories from the deep-fried shell, cheese and sour cream. The beef burrito, however, contains about half the calories and one-third the fat. This recipe scores even better — with 85% less fat!

beef pad thai
with bell peppers and snow peas

1. In a bowl cover rice noodles with boiling water; let stand for 15 minutes. Drain.

2. Meanwhile, in a bowl combine stock, oyster sauce, ketchup, lime juice, brown sugar, cornstarch, garlic and ginger. Set aside.

3. In a large nonstick frying pan sprayed with vegetable spray or on a preheated grill, cook beef over high heat for 6 minutes or until medium-rare; remove from pan. Slice thinly; set aside. Respray pan; cook green peppers and red peppers over medium-high heat, stirring, for 3 minutes. Add snow peas; cook, stirring, for 1 minute. Add sauce, beef and rice noodles; cook for 1 minute or until noodles are tender. Add green onions, coriander and cashews; serve immediately.

8 oz	wide rice noodles	250 g
Sauce		
1/2 cup	BEEF STOCK or CHICKEN STOCK (see recipes, page 50)	125 mL
1/4 cup	oyster sauce or fish sauce	50 mL
3 tbsp	ketchup	45 mL
2 tbsp	fresh lime or lemon juice	25 mL
2 tsp	packed brown sugar	10 mL
1 1/2 tsp	cornstarch	7 mL
1 1/2 tsp	minced garlic	7 mL
1 tsp	minced ginger root	5 mL
12 oz	boneless beef sirloin	375 g
1 cup	sliced green bell peppers	250 mL
1 cup	sliced red bell peppers	250 mL
1 cup	halved snow peas	250 mL
1/2 cup	chopped green onions	125 mL
1/3 cup	chopped fresh coriander	75 mL
3 tbsp	chopped cashews	45 mL

meat

173

essential numbers

PER SERVING

Calories	350
Protein	25 g
Fat, total	7 g
Fat, saturated	1.9 g
Carbohydrates	46 g
Sodium	345 mg
Cholesterol	45 mg
Fiber	3 g

ask ROSE

Perhaps the best known (and loved) of Thai dishes, pad thai is typically made with rice noodles and a combination of ingredients that can include seafood, tofu, eggs, chicken, pork, beef — plus a mixture of vegetables flavored with fish sauce. In this low-fat version, I've eliminated the eggs, increased the amount of vegetables and given you the choice of fish sauce or oyster sauce. This is a wonderful dish — best prepared just before serving.

cooking 101

If you have an intolerance to the gluten contained in wheat-based pasta, then rice noodles are an ideal substitute. You can either soak them in boiling water (about 15 minutes), or boil them until tender (about 8 minutes). Avoid excessive rinsing, or the noodles will become starchy.

beefaroni wraps

with two cheeses

1 In a pot of boiling water, cook pasta for 8 to 10 minutes or until tender but firm; drain. Set aside.

2 In a nonstick saucepan sprayed with vegetable spray, cook onions, green peppers and garlic over medium heat for 4 minutes or until softened. Add ground beef; cook, stirring to break up, for 5 minutes or until no longer pink. Add tomato sauce; cook, covered, for 5 minutes or until thickened. Remove from heat.

3 Wrap tortillas in foil. Bake in preheated oven for 5 minutes or until heated through.

4 In a small nonstick saucepan over medium-high heat, bring evaporated milk to a boil. Add Cheddar cheese and Parmesan cheese; reduce heat to low. Cook, stirring, for 2 minutes or until melted.

5 In a bowl combine pasta, meat sauce and cheese sauce. Place about 3/4 cup (175 mL) mixture in center of each tortilla. Fold bottom one-third up over filling; roll from left to right. Serve.

PREHEAT OVEN TO 425° F (220° C)

6 oz	small shell pasta	175 g
1 cup	chopped onions	250 mL
1/2 cup	chopped green bell peppers	125 mL
1 1/2 tsp	minced garlic	7 mL
8 oz	lean ground beef	250 g
1 cup	tomato pasta sauce	250 mL
6	10-inch (25 cm) flour tortillas	6
1/2 cup	low-fat evaporated milk	125 mL
1/2 cup	shredded low-fat Cheddar cheese	125 mL
2 tbsp	grated low-fat Parmesan cheese	25 mL

meat

174

PER SERVING

essential numbers

Calories	498
Protein	23 g
Fat, total	15 g
Fat, saturated	6 g
Carbohydrates	66 g
Sodium	547 mg
Cholesterol	37 mg
Fiber	4 g

ask ROSE

There isn't a child or teenager who doesn't love the taste of a beefaroni-type dish. But commercially prepared versions typically contain a lot of fatty beef, salt and cheese. Well, my kids don't need all that — and neither do yours! So here's my light version, with lean ground beef, low-fat cheese and tomato sauce, all wrapped in a tortilla. For extra fun, try using colored/ flavored tortillas. These wraps are also easy to make in advance; just heat them for 10 minutes in a 400° F (200° C) oven before serving.

for the record

Guilt-free burgers
Looking for the healthiest choice on fast-food row? Surprisingly, the much-maligned burger may be your best bet. The average single-patty hamburger has 12 g fat. Compare that to a fish sandwich at 23 g, half a dozen chicken nuggets at 18 g, and a piece of fried chicken breast at 14 g fat.

beef-pepper wraps
with rice vermicelli

1 In a pot of boiling water, cook rice noodles for 5 minutes or until tender; drain. Rinse under cold running water. Set aside.

2 In a nonstick frying pan sprayed with vegetable spray, cook beef over medium-high heat, turning once, for 3 to 5 minutes or until medium-rare. Slice thinly; set aside. Respray frying pan; cook red peppers and snow peas over medium-high heat, stirring, for 4 minutes or until tender-crisp.

3 In a bowl combine stock, brown sugar, soya sauce, rice vinegar, orange juice concentrate, cornstarch, sesame oil, garlic and ginger. Add to vegetables along with beef. Simmer for 1 minute or until thickened.

4 Place about 1/2 cup (125 mL) filling in center of each tortilla. Fold bottom end up over filling; tuck sides in. Roll up tightly. Serve.

3 oz	wide rice noodles	75 g
8 oz	boneless steak (such as striploin)	250 g
1 cup	julienned red bell peppers	250 mL
1 cup	julienned snow peas	250 mL
1/3 cup	Beef Stock or Chicken Stock (see recipes, page 50)	75 mL
2 tbsp	packed brown sugar	25 mL
1 1/2 tbsp	light soya sauce	22 mL
1 tbsp	rice wine vinegar	15 mL
1 tbsp	orange juice concentrate	15 mL
2 1/2 tsp	cornstarch	12 mL
2 tsp	sesame oil	10 mL
1 1/2 tsp	minced garlic	7 mL
1 1/2 tsp	minced ginger root	7 mL
6	8-inch (20 cm) flour tortillas	6

meat

175

essential numbers

PER SERVING

Calories	274
Protein	14 g
Fat, total	7 g
Fat, saturated	1.9 g
Carbohydrates	37 g
Sodium	350 mg
Cholesterol	28 mg
Fiber	2 g

ask ROSE

Move over sandwiches — here comes the wrap! This innovation in portable eating is wonderfully versatile. Basically, it's just a flour tortilla (plain or colored and flavored) wrapped around any combination of vegetable, chicken, fish or meat and a tasty sauce. Try these wraps for lunch, or a light, nutritious snack.

nutrition watch

Vitamin C and the common cold
As you might expect, these wraps are low in fat. But thanks to the red peppers, snow peas and orange juice, they're also high in vitamin C, providing 125% of your daily requirement. An important nutrient for immunity, vitamin C is able to reduce the severity and duration of cold symptoms. It does this, in part, by enhancing the body's production of interferon, a natural antiviral agent. While supplements are handy, you can get all the vitamin C you need through your diet. See page 72 for top food sources.

lamb chili with leeks
and sweet potatoes over rigatoni

1   In a bowl coat lamb with flour; shake off excess. In a large nonstick saucepan, heat oil over medium-high heat; add lamb. Cook, turning occasionally, for 5 minutes or until browned on all sides; remove from pan.

2   Respray saucepan; cook leeks, mushrooms, zucchini, red peppers and garlic over medium-high heat, stirring occasionally, for 5 minutes or until vegetables are softened. Add lamb, tomatoes, stock, sweet potatoes, kidney beans, chili powder, basil, oregano and salt. Bring to a boil, stirring to break up tomatoes. Reduce heat to low; cook, covered, for 30 minutes or until lamb and vegetables are tender.

3   Meanwhile, in a large pot of boiling water, cook rigatoni for 10 minutes or until tender but firm; drain. In a serving bowl combine pasta and sauce; toss well. Sprinkle with feta cheese; serve immediately.

12 oz	boneless leg of lamb, cut into 1-inch (2.5 cm) cubes	375 g
2 tbsp	all-purpose flour	25 mL
2 tsp	vegetable oil	10 mL
1 1/2 cups	sliced leeks	375 mL
1 1/2 cups	diced mushrooms	375 mL
1 1/2 cups	diced zucchini	375 mL
3/4 cup	diced red bell peppers	175 mL
2 tsp	minced garlic	10 mL
1	can (19 oz [540 mL]) tomatoes, with juice	1
1/2 cup	BEEF STOCK or CHICKEN STOCK (see recipes, page 50)	125 mL
1 cup	diced peeled sweet potatoes	250 mL
1 cup	canned cooked red kidney beans, rinsed and drained	250 mL
1 tbsp	chili powder	15 mL
1 1/2 tsp	dried basil	7 mL
1 tsp	dried oregano	5 mL
1/4 tsp	salt	1 mL
1 lb	rigatoni	500 g
3 oz	light feta cheese, crumbled	75 g

essential numbers

PER SERVING

Calories	575
Protein	32 g
Fat, total	10 g
Fat, saturated	4.2 g
Carbohydrates	89 g
Sodium	287 mg
Cholesterol	54 mg
Fiber	6 g

ask ROSE

Chili recipes are usually just variations on the same old ingredients — ground beef, red kidney beans and tomato sauce. B-o-o-o-o-ring! Now here's a twist on chili that's delicious and sophisticated enough to serve to company. I prefer leg of lamb in this recipe because it's milder than stewing lamb. (Just be sure you don't overcook the meat or it will dry out.) Paired with sweet potatoes, the lamb acquires a honeyed richness that is simple sensational!

cooking 101

Boneless leg of lamb is an inexpensive and tender cut of meat. Its mild flavor works well in stews like this one, but it's also terrific grilled on the barbecue. Buy a butterflied leg of lamb (cut so that it will lie flat). Or ask your butcher to make a pocket which you can stuff with your favorite filling and roast at 375° F (190° C) for 15 minutes per 1 lb (500 g).

pork fajitas
with salsa, onions and rice noodles

1 In a pot of boiling water, cook rice noodles for 5 minutes or until tender; drain. Rinse under cold running water; drain. Set aside.

2 In a nonstick frying pan sprayed with vegetable spray or on a preheated grill, cook pork tenderloin over medium-high heat, turning once, for 15 minutes or until just cooked through. Slice thinly.

3 In a nonstick frying pan sprayed with vegetable spray, heat oil over medium-high heat; add red onions and garlic. Cook for 2 minutes or until softened. Add green peppers and red peppers; cook, stirring frequently, for 2 minutes or until tender-crisp. Add green onion, rice noodles and pork; remove from heat. Add salsa and coriander; combine well.

4 Sprinkle tortillas with Cheddar cheese. Place about 1/2 cup (125 mL) filling in center of each tortilla. Add sour cream; fold bottom end up over filling. Tuck sides in; roll up tightly. Serve immediately.

3 oz	wide rice noodles	75 g
8 oz	pork or beef tenderloin	250 g
2 tsp	vegetable oil	10 mL
1 cup	thinly sliced red onions	250 mL
2 tsp	minced garlic	10 mL
1 cup	thinly sliced green bell peppers	250 mL
1 cup	thinly sliced red bell peppers	250 mL
1	large green onion, sliced	1
3/4 cup	medium salsa	175 mL
1/3 cup	chopped fresh coriander	75 mL
8	8-inch (20 cm) flour tortillas	8
3/4 cup	shredded low-fat Cheddar cheese	175 mL
1/3 cup	low-fat sour cream	75 mL

meat

177

essential numbers

PER SERVING

Calories	249
Protein	14 g
Fat, total	8 g
Fat, saturated	3.0 g
Carbohydrates	30 g
Sodium	292 mg
Cholesterol	29 mg
Fiber	2 g

ask ROSE

Order fajitas from a fast-food restaurant and chances are you'll feel pretty good about your choice. After all, they contain meat, vegetables and cheese — pretty much a complete, healthy meal, right? Don't kid yourself! Most fast-food fajitas are loaded with fatty cuts of meat, oil used to fry the vegetables, as well sour cream and cheese. My fajitas use lean pork tenderloin (5 g fat per 4 oz [125 g]) as well as low-fat sour cream and a small amount of light Cheddar cheese. Add in plenty of great vegetables and salsa, and you get all the flavor without the fat!

nutrition watch

Pork and B vitamins

Is true that B vitamins give you more energy? Sorry, but they don't — at least, not directly. Rather, B vitamins serve as coenzymes in the release of energy from the carbohydrates, fat and protein in foods. But if you're looking for a good source of these vitamins (and they are important), you can't do much better than pork. Pork's nutritional claim to fame is its high thiamin (vitamin B1) content — in fact, it's the best dietary source available; it's also a great source of other B vitamins, including niacin, riboflavin, B6 and B12.

tomatoes with barley
and pesto stuffing

1. In a nonstick saucepan over medium-high heat, bring stock to a boil. Add barley; reduce heat to medium-low. Cook, covered, for 45 minutes or until grain is tender and liquid is absorbed.

2. Meanwhile, in a small food processor or blender, combine basil, Parmesan cheese, pine nuts and garlic; process until finely chopped. Add water and olive oil; process until smooth, adding a little more water if necessary. Set aside.

3. Slice top 1/2 inch (1 cm) off tomatoes; reserve tops. Scoop out tomato shells. Save pulp for another use.

4. In a bowl combine roasted red peppers, pesto and cooked barley. Stuff tomato shells with mixture, mounding high. Sprinkle with Parmesan cheese; place stuffed tomatoes on baking sheet. Bake in preheated oven for 15 minutes. Serve hot, with tomato "lids" on, if desired.

PREHEAT OVEN TO 425° F (220° C)
BAKING SHEET

| 2 cups | VEGETABLE STOCK *or* CHICKEN STOCK (see recipes, pages 51 and 50) | 500 mL |
| 1/2 cup | pearl barley | 125 mL |

Pesto

1/2 cup	tightly packed fresh basil leaves	125 mL
1 1/2 tbsp	grated low-fat Parmesan cheese	20 mL
1 tbsp	toasted pine nuts	15 mL
1/2 tsp	minced garlic	2 mL
2 tbsp	water	25 mL
1 1/2 tbsp	olive oil	20 mL
4	large ripe tomatoes	4
1/4 cup	chopped bottled roasted red bell peppers	50 mL
1 tbsp	grated low-fat Parmesan cheese	15 mL

essential numbers

PER SERVING

Calories	183
Protein	7 g
Fat, total	7 g
Fat, saturated	1.6 g
Carbohydrates	25 g
Sodium	79 mg
Cholesterol	3 mg
Fiber	6 g

ask ROSE

Barley is a nutty, versatile grain (not just for soups anymore!) that makes a nice change from traditional accompaniments like rice or pasta. Generally, I prefer to use pearl barley, which has the husk, bran and germ ground away, and cooks in only 40 to 45 minutes. Scotch (or pot) barley has more of the bran left on — so it contains more fiber, but it must be soaked and left to simmer for at least 1 1/2 hours.

nutrition watch

Shades of vegetarianism
Being a vegetarian these days doesn't always mean swearing off all animal products. For many people, it simply means changing to a diet that focuses on plant foods. Here's a quick summary of the most common types of vegetarianism:
Semi vegetarians avoid red meat.
Pesco vegetarians avoid red meat and poultry.
Lacto-ovo vegetarians avoid meat, poultry and fish, but eat dairy and eggs.
Vegans avoid all animal products, including dairy and eggs — even honey, in some cases!

Serves 4

tortellini with garlic
and roasted red peppers

1. On prepared baking sheet, place garlic and red pepper. Roast in preheated oven, turning pepper often, for 30 minutes or until pepper is charred on all sides; let cool. Peel, stem and seed pepper. Squeeze roasted garlic out of skins.

2. In a food processor or blender, combine roasted red pepper, garlic, chickpeas, stock, coriander, tahini, lemon juice and olive oil; purée until smooth.

3. In a large pot of boiling water, cook tortellini according to package directions or until tender; drain. In a serving bowl combine tortellini and sauce; toss to coat well. Serve immediately.

PREHEAT OVEN TO 450° F (230° C)
BAKING SHEET LINED WITH FOIL

1	small head garlic, top 1/2 inch (1 cm) cut off, loosely wrapped in foil	1
1	medium red bell pepper	1
3/4 cup	cooked canned chickpeas, rinsed and drained	175 mL
1/2 cup	VEGETABLE STOCK *or* CHICKEN STOCK (see recipes, pages 51 and 50)	125 mL
1/3 cup	chopped fresh coriander	75 mL
3 tbsp	tahini (sesame paste)	45 mL
1 1/2 tbsp	fresh lemon juice	20 mL
2 tsp	olive oil	10 mL
1 lb	fresh or frozen cheese tortellini	500 g

vegetarian

181

essential numbers

PER SERVING

Calories	420
Protein	19 g
Fat, total	16 g
Fat, saturated	3.8 g
Carbohydrates	55 g
Sodium	414 mg
Cholesterol	20 mg
Fiber	7 g

ask ROSE

If you love the flavor of garlic, but not its lingering odor, you've got to try roasted garlic. It's less pungent than in its raw state, it's easier to digest — and it won't linger on your breath! Roasted garlic is great served as a vegetable alongside your main course or just squeezed out of its skin and spread over Italian or French bread. To keep the garlic from drying out, roast with the whole head wrapped in foil.

for the record

The skinny on chickpeas

Contrary to popular belief, chickpeas are not high in fat. In fact, only 12% of the calories in this legume come from fat. What's more, they're a great way to boost the protein content of a vegetarian meal. A 1-cup (250 mL) serving of chickpeas has 16 g protein, 84 mg calcium and 5.2 mg iron — and only 4 g fat!

quinoa wraps
with hoisin vegetables

1 In a small nonstick skillet, toast quinoa over medium-high heat for 2 minutes.

2 In a saucepan over medium-high heat, bring stock to a boil. Add quinoa; reduce heat to medium-low. Cook, covered, for 15 minutes or until grain is tender and liquid is absorbed. Set aside.

3 In a nonstick frying pan sprayed with vegetable spray, cook garlic, ginger, red peppers, snow peas and water chestnuts over medium-high heat for 3 minutes or until softened. Add green onions; cook for 1 minute. Remove from heat; add to quinoa.

4 In a bowl combine hoisin sauce, mayonnaise, honey and coriander; spread over tortillas. Place about 1/3 cup (75 mL) quinoa mixture in center of each tortilla. Fold right side over filling; roll up from the bottom. Serve.

1 cup	quinoa, rinsed	250 mL
2 cups	VEGETABLE STOCK *or* CHICKEN STOCK (see recipes, pages 51 and 50)	500 mL
1 tsp	minced garlic	5 mL
1 tsp	minced ginger root	5 mL
1/2 cup	diced red bell peppers	125 mL
1/2 cup	diced snow peas	125 mL
1/2 cup	diced water chestnuts	125 mL
1/4 cup	chopped green onions	50 mL
1/4 cup	hoisin sauce	50 mL
1/4 cup	light mayonnaise	50 mL
2 tbsp	honey	25 mL
1/4 cup	chopped fresh coriander or parsley	50 mL
8	6-inch (15 cm) flour tortillas	8

vegetarian

182

essential numbers

PER SERVING

Calories	264
Protein	7 g
Fat, total	6 g
Fat, saturated	0.8 g
Carbohydrates	46 g
Sodium	213 mg
Cholesterol	0 mg
Fiber	3 g

ask ROSE

Quinoa (pronounced KEEN-wah) may be unfamiliar to many North Americans, but it's not exactly new. In fact, it was a staple of the ancient Incas, who described it as the "mother grain." And it seems that they were right! Quinoa contains more protein than any other grain. I like to use it in soups, as part of a main or side dish, in salads and as a substitute for rice.

cooking 101

While it's incredibly nutritious, quinoa can have a slightly bitter taste. But you can eliminate the bitterness by rinsing the quinoa thoroughly, drying it and then toasting it lightly in a nonstick skillet.

Serves 4

polenta with chèvre
and roasted vegetables

1 In a deep saucepan over medium-high heat, bring stock to a boil. Reduce heat to low; gradually whisk in cornmeal. Cook, stirring, for 5 minutes. Pour into baking dish, smoothing top; chill.

2 In a bowl combine red pepper, yellow pepper, onion, zucchini and olive oil; transfer to prepared baking sheet. Wrap garlic loosely in foil; add to baking sheet. Roast vegetables in preheated oven, turning occasionally, for 45 minutes or until tender. Squeeze garlic out of skins; chop remaining vegetables. Transfer all to a bowl. Sprinkle with balsamic vinegar; toss to coat well.

3 Turn polenta onto cutting board; cut into 4 squares. In a large nonstick frying pan sprayed with vegetable spray, cook polenta over medium-high heat for 2 minutes or until golden. Turn; cook for 1 minute. Spoon polenta onto serving plates. Top with vegetable mixture; sprinkle with goat cheese. Serve.

PREHEAT OVEN TO 425° F (220° C)
8-INCH (2 L) SQUARE BAKING DISH SPRAYED WITH VEGETABLE SPRAY
LARGE BAKING SHEET LINED WITH FOIL

Polenta

3 cups	VEGETABLE STOCK *or* CHICKEN STOCK (see recipes, pages 51 and 50)	750 mL
1 cup	cornmeal	250 mL
1	medium red bell pepper, cut into quarters	1
1	medium yellow pepper, cut into quarters	1
1	medium red onion, sliced	1
2	small zucchini (about 8 oz [250 g]), cut in half lengthwise	2
1 tbsp	olive oil	15 mL
1	small head garlic, top 1/2 inch (1 cm) cut off	1
1 tbsp	balsamic vinegar	15 mL
2 oz	goat cheese (*chèvre*)	50 g

vegetarian

183

---

essential numbers

PER SERVING

Calories	253
Protein	8 g
Fat, total	9 g
Fat, saturated	3.1 g
Carbohydrates	39 g
Sodium	155 mg
Cholesterol	8 mg
Fiber	6 g

ask ROSE

Chèvre is a white, tart-flavored cheese made from goat's milk. At least, it's supposed to be — some cheese sold as *chèvre* contains cow's milk, so read the label carefully! Depending on the producer, goat cheese can be drier or creamier in texture. Either way, at only 15% M.F, it is a lower-fat cheese. And because it's so flavorful, a little goes a long way.

nutrition watch

Great garlic

It appears that garlic's sulfur compounds can help the liver detoxify carcinogens, stimulate immune function and kill certain cancer cells. The Iowa Women's Health Study followed 42,000 women for five years and found that those who ate 0.7 g garlic each day (less than 1 clove) had a 32% reduced risk of colon cancer compared with women who consumed no garlic. A Harvard study found that regular garlic consumption reduced the risk of colon cancer in men by 23%.

cheese manicotti
with wild mushroom filling

1. In a large pot of boiling water, cook manicotti shells until tender; drain. Rinse under cold running water. Set aside.

2. In a large nonstick frying pan sprayed with vegetable spray, cook onions and garlic over medium-high heat for 4 minutes or until softened and browned. Add mushrooms; cook, stirring occasionally, for 8 minutes or until mushrooms are tender and browned. Transfer mixture to a bowl; add ricotta cheese, mozzarella cheese, Parmesan cheese, pepper and egg. Set aside.

3. In a bowl combine tomato sauce and evaporated milk. Spread half the sauce over bottom of baking dish. Stuff each manicotti shell with about 3 tbsp (45 mL) filling; place shells in baking dish. Pour remaining sauce over stuffed shells; sprinkle with mozzarella cheese. Cover dish with foil; bake in preheated oven for 30 minutes or until heated through. Serve.

vegetarian

184

PREHEAT OVEN TO 350° F (180° C)
13- BY 9-INCH (3 L) BAKING DISH

12	manicotti shells	12
Filling		
1/2 cup	chopped onions	125 mL
1 tsp	minced garlic	5 mL
12 oz	wild mushrooms, finely chopped	375 g
1 1/2 cups	5% ricotta cheese	375 mL
1/3 cup	shredded low-fat mozzarella cheese	75 mL
3 tbsp	grated low-fat Parmesan cheese	45 mL
1/4 tsp	freshly ground black pepper	1 mL
1	large egg	1
Sauce		
1 1/4 cups	tomato pasta sauce	300 mL
2 tbsp	low-fat evaporated milk	25 mL
1/4 cup	shredded low-fat mozzarella cheese	50 mL

essential numbers

PER SERVING

Calories	390
Protein	23 g
Fat, total	12 g
Fat, saturated	6.6 g
Carbohydrates	55 g
Sodium	580 mg
Cholesterol	80 mg
Fiber	4 g

ask ROSE

Here's the perfect dish to feed a crowd! Just prepare a day ahead and refrigerate; next day, bring to room temperature and then bake.

For a real treat, try this dish with dried mushrooms. Just soak 1 oz (25 g) dried mushrooms in boiling water for 20 minutes; drain and chop. Reduce quantity of fresh wild mushrooms to 8 oz (250 g).

for the record

Terrific tofu

Looking for ways to eat more tofu? Try substituting it for ricotta cheese or cottage cheese in pasta recipes. It's a great way to add high-quality protein to a meatless meal — without a lot of fat! Just compare the numbers per 1/2-cup (125 mL) serving: firm tofu – 94 calories, 10 g protein, 5.9 g fat and 130 mg calcium*; 5% ricotta cheese – 124 calories, 10 g protein, 8 g fat and 224 mg calcium; 2% cottage cheese – 107 calories, 16 g protein, 2.5 g fat and 82 mg calcium.

*Calcium content of tofu ranges from 120 to 750 mg per serving, depending on how the tofu is processed.

linguine with bok choy
and snow peas in oyster sauce

1 In a bowl combine vegetable stock, oyster sauce, rice wine vinegar, cornstarch, sesame oil, brown sugar and Asian chili sauce. Set aside.

2 In a large pot of boiling water, cook linguine for 8 to 10 minutes or until tender but firm; drain. Meanwhile, in a nonstick wok or large skillet sprayed with vegetable spray, heat oil over medium-high heat. Add garlic and ginger; cook for 1 minute. Add bok choy, red peppers, carrots and snow peas; cook for 4 minutes or until vegetables are tender-crisp. Add sauce; cook for 1 minute or until thickened and bubbly.

3 In a serving bowl, combine sauce and pasta; toss well. Serve immediately.

Sauce

2/3 cup	VEGETABLE STOCK or CHICKEN STOCK (see recipes, pages 51 and 50)	150 mL
1/4 cup	oyster sauce	50 mL
1 tbsp	rice wine vinegar	15 mL
1 tbsp	cornstarch	15 mL
2 tsp	sesame oil	10 mL
2 tsp	packed brown sugar	10 mL
1 tsp	hot Asian chili sauce (optional)	5 mL
8 oz	linguine (regular or whole wheat)	250 g
1 tsp	vegetable oil	5 mL
1 1/2 tsp	minced garlic	7 mL
1 tsp	minced ginger root	5 mL
3 cups	thinly sliced bok choy	750 mL
1 cup	thinly sliced red bell peppers	250 mL
1 cup	shredded carrots	250 mL
1 cup	halved snow peas	250 mL

vegetarian

185

essential numbers

PER SERVING	
Calories	266
Protein	9 g
Fat, total	5 g
Fat, saturated	0.5 g
Carbohydrates	49 g
Sodium	222 mg
Cholesterol	0 mg
Fiber	6 g

ask ROSE

Bok choy is also known as pak choy or Chinese white cabbage — although it shouldn't be confused with Chinese cabbage, which is another name for napa cabbage. (I wish they'd get these names straightened out!) Anyway, it's a delicious vegetable — mild, with a nice crunch that makes it ideal for salads and stir-fries. Baby bok choy is, perhaps surprisingly, exactly what it sounds like: a more delicate (and sweeter) version of regular bok choy.

nutrition watch

The view on vitamin C

American researchers have linked the daily use of vitamin C pills to a lower risk of cataracts in women. They found that women who supplemented their diet for 10 years or longer had more than a 70% lower risk for early cataract formation. While the study didn't measure how much vitamin C was taken, your best bet is to eat at least one vitamin C rich food a day (e.g. citrus fruit, broccoli, bok choy, red pepper, tomato juice) and take a 200 to 500 mg supplement. This recipe provides a great start at 123 mg per serving.

acorn squash
with rice, pineapple and molasses

1 Microwave squash on High for 10 minutes or until tender; cool. Cut into half lengthwise. Scoop out cooked flesh; if desired, keep shell intact. Chop flesh.

2 Meanwhile, in a saucepan over medium-high heat, combine stock, white rice and wild rice; bring to a boil. Reduce heat to medium-low; cook, covered, for 20 minutes. Add carrots; cook, covered, for 10 minutes or until rice and carrots are tender and liquid is absorbed. (Wild rice will be crunchy.)

3 Add squash, pineapple, raisins, orange juice concentrate, molasses, brown sugar and cinnamon. Cook, uncovered and stirring often, for 5 minutes or until heated through. If desired, spoon squash mixture into reserved shell as a serving platter. Pour remaining squash into a serving dish.

1	acorn or pepper squash, slit several times with a knife	1
2 cups	VEGETABLE STOCK *or* CHICKEN STOCK (see recipes, pages 51 and 50)	500 mL
1/2 cup	long grain white rice	125 mL
1/2 cup	wild rice	125 mL
1 cup	diced carrots	250 mL
1 cup	canned crushed pineapple	250 mL
1/2 cup	raisins *or* dried cherries	75 mL
2 tbsp	orange juice concentrate	25 mL
1 1/2 tbsp	molasses	20 mL
1 tbsp	packed brown sugar	15 mL
1/2 tsp	cinnamon	2 mL

essential numbers

PER SERVING

Calories	330
Protein	7 g
Fat, total	1 g
Fat, saturated	0.3 g
Carbohydrates	77 g
Sodium	99 mg
Cholesterol	0 mg
Fiber	5 g

ask ROSE

Acorn squash is named for its oblong shape (think of an acorn without its "hat"). That's about where the similarity ends, however; acorn squash is deeply ridged, usually green (although it can be yellow, brown, orange and/or black), with yellow-orange flesh. Like most squash, it is pretty bland on its own. But here, with addition of pineapple, raisins and molasses, the squash comes alive — providing a wonderful sweet-and-sour complement to the rice.

nutrition watch

Make room for molasses

Not all sweeteners are empty calories. Take blackstrap molasses, for example. Just 1 tbsp (15 mL) gives you 144 mg calcium, 3.4 mg iron and 615 mg potassium. (It's a great source of calcium and iron for vegans.) Try swirling molasses into yogurt, adding it to baked beans or drizzling it over hot cereal.

artichoke cheese dill
sauce over rotini

1 In a large pot of boiling water, cook rotini for 8 to 10 minutes or until tender but firm; drain.

2 Meanwhile, in a food processor combine artichokes, stock, red onions, mozzarella cheese, Swiss cheese, dill, sour cream, mayonnaise, lemon juice and garlic; process until smooth. Transfer to a nonstick saucepan; cook over medium heat, stirring frequently, for 4 minutes or until heated through.

3 In a serving bowl, combine pasta and sauce; toss well. Garnish with fresh chopped parsley. Serve immediately.

12 oz	rotini	375 g
1	can (14 oz [398 mL]) artichoke hearts, drained	1
2/3 cup	VEGETABLE STOCK *or* CHICKEN STOCK (see recipes, pages 51 and 50)	150 mL
1/2 cup	chopped red onions	125 mL
1/2 cup	shredded low-fat mozzarella cheese	125 mL
1/3 cup	shredded low-fat Swiss cheese	75 mL
1/3 cup	chopped fresh dill (or 1 tsp [5 mL] dried)	75 mL
1/3 cup	low-fat sour cream	75 mL
2 tbsp	light mayonnaise	25 mL
2 tbsp	fresh lemon juice	25 mL
1 tsp	minced garlic	5 mL
	Fresh chopped parsley	

vegetarian

187

essential numbers

PER SERVING

Calories	310
Protein	14 g
Fat, total	7 g
Fat, saturated	3.2 g
Carbohydrates	49 g
Sodium	193 mg
Cholesterol	15 mg
Fiber	6 g

ask ROSE

When buying artichoke hearts for this recipe, be sure that they're packed in water, not oil. The oil-packed variety have double the calories and triple the fat — a huge difference!

cooking 101

While commercially prepared artichoke hearts are convenient, it's really not very difficult to make your own. Just buy 6 fresh artichokes and rinse them well; with scissors, trim off the thorny tough tops of the outside layers. Rub these surfaces with lemon. Place the artichokes right-side up in boiling water with a squeeze of lemon juice; reduce to a simmer and cook, uncovered, for 20 minutes or until a leaf pulls away easily. Remove leaves and, with a spoon, scrape off the "fuzz" to reveal the tender, delicious artichoke heart.

asparagus frittata
with roasted red peppers and linguine

1 In a pot of boiling water, cook linguine for 8 to 10 minutes or until tender but firm; drain. Rinse under cold running water; drain. Set aside.

2 In a 12-inch (30 cm) nonstick frying pan sprayed with vegetable spray, cook onions and garlic over medium-high heat for 5 minutes or until golden and tender. Add asparagus; cook, stirring often, for 2 minutes or until tender-crisp. Remove from pan; cool.

3 In a bowl combine eggs, egg whites, evaporated milk and Dijon mustard; whisk well. Add roasted peppers, dill, Brie cheese, pasta and cooled vegetable mixture.

4 Wipe out frying pan; heat oil over medium-low heat. Pour in frittata mixture; cook for 5 minutes. Gently lift sides of frittata, letting uncooked egg mixture flow beneath. Cook, covered, for 3 minutes or until frittata is set. Slip onto a serving platter; serve warm or at room temperature.

2 oz	linguine, broken	50 g
1/2 cup	chopped onions	125 mL
1 tsp	minced garlic	5 mL
1 cup	finely chopped asparagus	250 mL
2	large eggs	2
3	large egg whites	3
1/4 cup	low-fat evaporated milk	50 mL
1 tsp	Dijon mustard	5 mL
1/3 cup	chopped roasted red bell peppers	75 mL
3 tbsp	chopped fresh dill (or 1 tsp [5 mL] dried)	45 mL
2 oz	Brie cheese, chopped *or* feta cheese, crumbled	50 g
2 tsp	vegetable oil	10 mL

essential numbers

PER SERVING

Calories	131
Protein	8 g
Fat, total	7 g
Fat, saturated	2.5 g
Carbohydrates	10 g
Sodium	162 mg
Cholesterol	83 mg
Fiber	1 g

ask ROSE

Brie cheese is so rich and creamy, it just has to be packed with fat and calories, right? Not at all! In fact, 1 oz (25 g) has 100 calories and 9 g fat — about the same as (or slightly less than) other average-fat cheeses. The other good thing is that with a cheese as rich-tasting as Brie, you don't need to use much. In fact, this frittata, serving 6 people, has only 2 oz (50 g) Brie — a lot of flavor for only 3 g fat!

nutrition watch

Soy protein and heart health
If your blood cholesterol is high, consider adding soy foods — such as tofu, texturized soy protein, soy beverages and soy flour — to your diet. Studies have shown that a daily dose of soy can reduce LDL cholesterol (the "bad" kind) by 13% and blood triglycerides by 10%. And it appears that soy can also prevent blood vessel damage and the formation of blood clots. Soy's protective power comes from natural chemicals called isoflavones, which are found inside soybeans.

roasted garlic
and tomatoes with ricotta cheese over rotini

1 Place garlic and tomatoes on prepared baking sheet. Roast in preheated oven for 30 minutes or until tomatoes are charred; let cool. Squeeze garlic out of skins.

2 In a food processor or blender, combine roasted tomatoes (with their juices) and garlic; pulse on and off several times until combined but still chunky. Transfer mixture to a bowl; add ricotta cheese, feta cheese, basil, olive oil and pepper. Set aside.

3 In a large pot of boiling water, cook rotini for 8 to 10 minutes or until tender but firm; drain. In a serving bowl combine pasta and sauce; toss well. Serve immediately.

PREHEAT OVEN TO 450° F (230° C)
BAKING SHEET LINED WITH FOIL

1	head garlic, top 1/2 inch (1 cm) cut off, loosely wrapped in foil	1
5	large ripe plum tomatoes, cut in half crosswise	5
1/2 cup	5% ricotta cheese	125 mL
2 oz	feta cheese, crumbled	50 g
1/2 cup	chopped fresh basil (or 1 tsp [5 mL] dried)	125 mL
1 tbsp	olive oil	15 mL
1/2 tsp	freshly ground black pepper	2 mL
12 oz	rotini	375 g

vegetarian

189

essential numbers

PER SERVING	
Calories	310
Protein	12 g
Fat, total	7 g
Fat, saturated	3.1 g
Carbohydrates	49 g
Sodium	150 mg
Cholesterol	16 mg
Fiber	3 g

ask ROSE

Fresh basil is one of my favorite herbs — I just wish it stayed fresh a little longer! In the refrigerator, it keeps for a day or two. But that's about it. So try to buy basil no earlier than a day before you need it. And when you get home, don't wash the leaves; just put the basil in a paper bag (or perforated plastic bag). Basil also bruises easily — quickly turning from a beautiful green to an ugly brown-black color — so don't chop it until just before you're ready to add it to the recipe.

for the record

Lower-fat nut?
If you're looking for a healthy snack, try roasted soynuts — a tasty source of soy protein with only 136 calories and 6 g fat per 1-oz (25 g) serving. That's a lot less fat than you'll find in the same amount of peanuts (14 g fat), macadamias (21 g), walnuts (18 g) or cashews (15 g). Soynuts also contain more protein, and they're the only nut that contains health-enhancing isoflavones. Try them plain, barbecued, onion-flavored or garlic-flavored.

barley with tomato,
red onion, goat cheese and basil

1. In a saucepan over medium-high heat, bring stock to a boil. Add barley; reduce heat to medium-low. Cook, covered, for 45 minutes or until tender and liquid is absorbed. Transfer to a large serving bowl. Add tomatoes, red onions, basil and goat cheese; toss well.

2. In a bowl combine olive oil, lemon juice, balsamic vinegar and garlic. Pour over barley mixture; toss to coat well. Serve warm or at room temperature.

3 cups	VEGETABLE STOCK *or* CHICKEN STOCK (see recipes, pages 51 and 50)	750 mL
3/4 cup	pearl barley	175 mL
3 cups	chopped ripe plum tomatoes	750 mL
1 cup	chopped red onions	250 mL
3/4 cup	chopped fresh basil (or 1 tsp [5 mL] dried)	175 mL
2 oz	goat cheese, crumbled	50 g

Dressing

1 tbsp	olive oil	15 mL
1 tbsp	fresh lemon juice	15 mL
1 tbsp	balsamic vinegar	15 mL
1 tsp	minced garlic	5 mL

vegetarian

190

essential numbers

PER SERVING

Calories	253
Protein	10 g
Fat, total	8 g
Fat, saturated	3.0 g
Carbohydrates	38 g
Sodium	270 mg
Cholesterol	9 mg
Fiber	9 g

ask ROSE

What makes balsamic vinegar so sensational — and *expensive*? Well, it's made from one type of grape (Trebbiano), and aged for years (often 12 or more) in special casks, which give the vinegar its characteristic sweetness and purplish-brown color. In fact, the oldest balsamic vinegars are often more highly prized (and costly) than vintage wines! Such vinegars should be treated with respect and used sparingly to highlight simple foods — a plate of mixed greens or strawberries, for example.

cooking 101

Want to add a little variety to your salad dressings? Then try making your own flavored vinegars or oils. Just pour the oil (preferably olive oil) or vinegar (such as white wine or cider) into sterilized bottles. Then add your choice of spices or herbs (before adding herbs, they should be boiled for 1 minute to kill any bacteria). Apply sealed lids and then wait for a couple of weeks to obtain the best flavor.

Serves 6

teriyaki rotini
with bell peppers, snow peas and sesame sauce

1 In a bowl combine brown sugar, water, soya sauce, vinegar, flour, sesame seeds, sesame oil, garlic and ginger; whisk well. Set aside.

2 In a large pot of boiling water, cook rotini for 8 to 10 minutes or until tender but firm; drain. Meanwhile, in a nonstick wok or large nonstick saucepan sprayed with vegetable spray, cook peppers and snow peas over medium-high heat for 3 minutes or until tender-crisp. Add sauce; cook for 2 minutes or until thickened and hot.

3 In a serving bowl combine pasta and sauce; toss well. Sprinkle with green onions; serve.

Sauce

1/4 cup	packed brown sugar	50 mL
1/4 cup	water	50 mL
1/4 cup	light soya sauce	50 mL
3 tbsp	rice wine vinegar	45 mL
1 tbsp	all-purpose flour	15 mL
2 tsp	sesame seeds	10 mL
2 tsp	sesame oil	10 mL
2 tsp	minced garlic	10 mL
1 1/2 tsp	minced ginger root	7 mL
12 oz	rotini	375 g
1 1/2 cups	julienned red or yellow bell peppers	375 mL
1 cup	julienned snow peas	250 mL
1/2 cup	chopped green onions	125 mL

vegetarian

191

essential numbers

PER SERVING

Calories	296
Protein	9 g
Fat, total	3 g
Fat, saturated	0.5 g
Carbohydrates	58 g
Sodium	359 mg
Cholesterol	0 mg
Fiber	3 g

ask ROSE

Soya sauce is a big flavor booster in recipes. But if you're concerned about sodium, watch out — soya sauce is like bottled salt! What to do? Well, you can buy light soya sauce (which has 50% less sodium) or you can just dilute 2 parts regular soya sauce with 1 part water.

nutrition watch

Fight-o-chemicals?

We've all heard that eating plenty of fruits and vegetables can lower our risk of chronic disease, increase our energy levels and help us lose weight. In fact, over 200 studies from around the world have shown that such a diet lowers the risk of many cancers. Interestingly, however, the same benefits do not seem to result from taking single vitamin supplements. So what is so special about plant foods? It's their phytochemical content. These natural compounds act as antioxidants, natural antibiotics, and can inhibit cancer development.

oyster mushrooms,
warm spinach and oranges over rice noodles

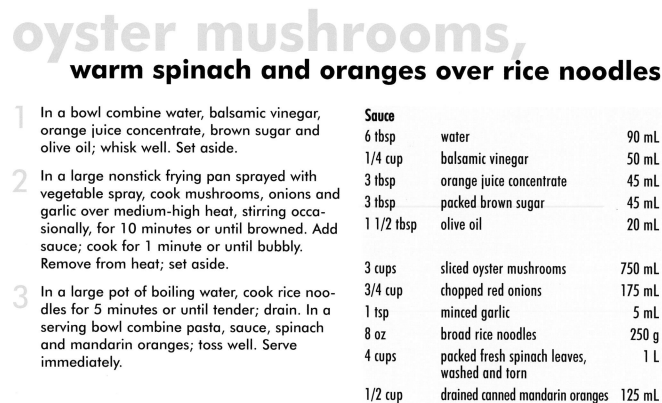

1. In a bowl combine water, balsamic vinegar, orange juice concentrate, brown sugar and olive oil; whisk well. Set aside.

2. In a large nonstick frying pan sprayed with vegetable spray, cook mushrooms, onions and garlic over medium-high heat, stirring occasionally, for 10 minutes or until browned. Add sauce; cook for 1 minute or until bubbly. Remove from heat; set aside.

3. In a large pot of boiling water, cook rice noodles for 5 minutes or until tender; drain. In a serving bowl combine pasta, sauce, spinach and mandarin oranges; toss well. Serve immediately.

vegetarian

192

Sauce

6 tbsp	water	90 mL
1/4 cup	balsamic vinegar	50 mL
3 tbsp	orange juice concentrate	45 mL
3 tbsp	packed brown sugar	45 mL
1 1/2 tbsp	olive oil	20 mL
3 cups	sliced oyster mushrooms	750 mL
3/4 cup	chopped red onions	175 mL
1 tsp	minced garlic	5 mL
8 oz	broad rice noodles	250 g
4 cups	packed fresh spinach leaves, washed and torn	1 L
1/2 cup	drained canned mandarin oranges	125 mL

essential numbers

PER SERVING

Calories	293
Protein	6 g
Fat, total	6 g
Fat, saturated	0.8 g
Carbohydrates	57 g
Sodium	60 mg
Cholesterol	0 mg
Fiber	3 g

ask ROSE

As kids, many of us grew up knowing that spinach made you strong. (You only had to watch a few Popeye cartoons to realize that!) But now, as adults, we understand why: Spinach is loaded with iron, as well as vitamins A and C. I like to use it often. In recipes where the spinach is well cooked, I substitute frozen spinach. With fresh spinach, I just wash it, place in a pot and cook, covered, for 2 to 3 minutes. The moisture on the leaves is all you need to steam it.

cooking 101

There's always plenty of frozen unsweetened orange juice concentrate in my house. I use it to make juice for my kids (who don't seem to appreciate fresh juice any better), and I use it for recipes such as this one. Be sure not to buy the type with added sugar; these are often labelled as orange juice "punch" or "cocktail."

A great substitute for orange juice concentrate is unsweetened pineapple juice concentrate.

pork fajitas with salsa, onions and rice noodles (page 177)

Serves 4

pasta quiche
with zucchini and cheese

1. In a pot of boiling water, cook pasta for 8 minutes or until tender but firm; drain. Rinse under cold running water; drain.

2. In a large nonstick frying pan sprayed with vegetable spray, cook onions, red peppers and zucchini over medium-high heat for 8 minutes or until tender and slightly browned. Set aside to cool.

3. In a food processor or blender, combine ricotta cheese, Swiss cheese, Parmesan cheese, dill, milk, egg whites, egg, mustard, garlic, salt and pepper; purée until smooth.

4. In a bowl combine pasta, cooled vegetables and cheese mixture; pour into prepared baking dish. Bake in preheated oven for 30 minutes or until set at center.

PREHEAT OVEN TO 350° F (180° C)
9-INCH (2.5 L) SQUARE BAKING DISH SPRAYED WITH VEGETABLE SPRAY

3 oz	small shell pasta	75 g
3/4 cup	diced onions	175 mL
3/4 cup	diced red bell peppers	175 mL
3/4 cup	diced zucchini (unpeeled)	175 mL
1 1/2 cups	5% ricotta cheese	375 mL
1/2 cup	shredded low-fat Swiss cheese	125 mL
3 tbsp	grated low-fat Parmesan cheese	45 mL
1/4 cup	chopped fresh dill (or 1 tsp [5 mL] dried)	50 mL
1/2 cup	low-fat milk	125 mL
2	large egg whites	2
1	large egg	1
1 tsp	Dijon mustard	5 mL
1 tsp	minced garlic	5 mL
1/4 tsp	salt	1 mL
1/4 tsp	freshly ground black pepper	1 mL

vegetarian

193

essential numbers

PER SERVING

Calories	368
Protein	26 g
Fat, total	16 g
Fat, saturated	9.1 g
Carbohydrates	31 g
Sodium	459 mg
Cholesterol	103 mg
Fiber	2 g

ask ROSE

What makes quiche such a high-fat food? Well, let's start with the crust, which uses butter or lard. And the filling? It gets even worse — typically 4 whole eggs and plenty of cream. That's a *lot* of fat. And the cholesterol — I don't even want to think about it! But not in my crustless quiche. Here we use a combination of whole eggs and egg whites, lower-fat cheese and low-fat milk to cut the fat by almost half.

nutrition watch

Quiche question

Do real men eat quiche? Sure — and real women, too! But unless you want to overload on fat, you'd better stick with this recipe. Just consider what you would be getting at your local bistro, where a typical serving of quiche has 27 g fat! Most of this fat is hidden in the crust. That's one reason why this "crustless" version is such a good choice.

polenta with chèvre and roasted vegetables (page 183)

barley risotto

with grilled peppers

1. Place red pepper and yellow pepper on baking sheet. Cook under preheated broiler, turning occasionally, for 20 minutes or until charred on all sides; remove from oven. When cool enough to handle, peel, stem and core peppers. Cut into chunks; set aside.

2. In a saucepan over medium-high heat, combine 2 cups (500 mL) stock with barley. Bring to a boil; reduce heat to low. Cook, stirring occasionally, for 30 minutes or until tender but firm. Set aside.

3. In a large nonstick frying pan sprayed with vegetable spray, cook onions and garlic over medium-high heat for 4 minutes or until softened. Add 1 1/2 cups (375 mL) remaining stock; bring to a boil. Add cooked barley and roasted peppers; bring to a boil, stirring often. Reduce heat to medium-low; cook, stirring often, for 10 minutes or until barley is creamy. Add extra stock as needed. Add Parmesan cheese and pepper. Serve immediately.

PREHEAT BROILER
BAKING SHEET

1	medium red bell pepper	1
1	medium yellow bell pepper	1
3 1/2 to to 4 cups	VEGETABLE STOCK *or* CHICKEN STOCK (see recipes, page 51 and 50)	875 mL to 1 L
1 cup	pearl barley	250 mL
1 cup	chopped onions	250 mL
2 tsp	minced garlic	10 mL
3 tbsp	grated low-fat Parmesan cheese	45 mL
1/4 tsp	freshly ground black pepper	1 mL

essential numbers

PER SERVING

Calories	253
Protein	10 g
Fat, total	4 g
Fat, saturated	1.5 g
Carbohydrates	47 g
Sodium	327 mg
Cholesterol	5 mg
Fiber	10 g

ask ROSE

To ensure that I always have some roasted peppers on hand, I prepare them in large batches. When cool enough to handle, I remove the skin and seeds, slice the peppers, and freeze them in airtight containers. When needed, they defrost quickly. This is a real time-saver — and much more economical than commercially prepared roasted peppers in a jar.

nutrition watch

Antioxidant all-stars
An American study ranked the ability of fresh produce to act as antioxidants and neutralize harmful free radicals. The winners...

Rank	Vegetables	Fruit
1.	kale	blueberries
2.	beets	strawberries
3.	red peppers	plums
4.	broccoli	oranges
5.	spinach	red grapes
6.	potato	kiwi
7.	sweet potato	white grapes
8.	corn	apples, tomatoes, bananas, pears and melons

Serves 8

tomato sauce

1. In a nonstick saucepan sprayed with vegetable spray, cook onions and garlic over medium-high heat for 3 minutes or until softened. Add tomatoes, leek, red peppers, carrots, brown sugar, basil, salt and pepper; reduce heat to medium. Cook, covered and stirring occasionally, for 30 minutes or until vegetables are tender and sauce is thickened.

2. Meanwhile, in a large pot of boiling water, cook pasta for 8 to 10 minutes or until tender but firm; drain.

3. In a food processor, purée sauce. In a serving bowl combine pasta and sauce; toss well. Sprinkle with Parmesan cheese. Serve.

1 cup	chopped onions	250 mL
2	cloves garlic, minced	2
1 1/2 lbs	ripe plum tomatoes, chopped	750 g
1	medium leek, white and pale green parts only, chopped	1
1 cup	chopped red bell peppers	250 mL
1/2 cup	chopped carrots	125 mL
2 tsp	packed brown sugar	10 mL
1 tsp	dried basil	5 mL
1/4 tsp	salt	1 mL
1/4 tsp	freshly ground black pepper	1 mL
1 lb	spaghetti	500 g
3 tbsp	grated low-fat Parmesan cheese	45 mL

vegetarian

195

essential numbers

PER SERVING

Calories	295
Protein	11 g
Fat, total	2 g
Fat, saturated	0.7 g
Carbohydrates	59 g
Sodium	123 mg
Cholesterol	2 mg
Fiber	4 g

ask ROSE

Ripe field tomatoes are great to eat. But they make a terrible sauce — watery and lacking flavor. So, for this recipe, be sure to use only ripe plum tomatoes in season; they're sweet, rich-tasting and retain their meat-like texture when cooked. Make a big batch of the sauce and preserve it in sterilized jars or freeze it in airtight containers. After defrosting frozen sauce, thicken by adding some tomato paste, then simmer for 10 minutes.

nutrition watch

When processed is better

Lycopene is a natural antioxidant in tomatoes that may help protect from prostate cancer. But to get more lycopene, did you know you're better off to eat processed tomato products rather than fresh tomatoes? Well, it's true. When processed, tomatoes are heated, which breaks down their fibrous cell walls, thereby releasing more of the available lycopene. And here's another suggestion: Add a little olive oil to your tomato sauce; it can help your body absorb even more lycopene!

feta grain burgers

with dijon sauce

vegetarian

1. In a saucepan over medium-high heat, bring stock to a boil. Add barley, brown rice and wild rice; reduce heat to medium-low. Cook, covered and stirring occasionally, for 45 minutes or until grains are tender and liquid is absorbed.

2. Meanwhile, in a nonstick frying pan sprayed with vegetable spray, cook mushrooms, red peppers, red onions and garlic over medium-high heat for 5 minutes or until tender. In a bowl combine vegetables and grains.

3. In a food processor combine grain mixture, bread crumbs, feta cheese, lemon juice, oregano, egg and egg white; pulse on and off just until combined.

4. Using wet hands, form each 1/2 cup (125 mL) of mixture into a patty (makes about 7 patties). Transfer to prepared baking sheet. Bake in preheated oven, turning halfway, for 15 minutes or until golden and heated through.

5. In a bowl combine sour cream and mustard; add a dollop of sauce to each burger. Serve.

196

PREHEAT OVEN TO 425° F (220° C)
BAKING SHEET SPRAYED WITH VEGETABLE SPRAY

Amount	Ingredient	Metric
3 cups	VEGETABLE STOCK *or* CHICKEN STOCK (see recipes, pages 51 and 50)	750 mL
1/3 cup	pearl barley	75 mL
1/3 cup	brown rice	75 mL
1/3 cup	wild rice	75 mL
1/2 cup	diced mushrooms	125 mL
1/2 cup	diced red bell peppers	125 mL
1/2 cup	diced red onions	125 mL
1 tsp	minced garlic	5 mL
1/4 cup	dry seasoned bread crumbs	50 mL
2 oz	light feta cheese, crumbled	50 g
1 tbsp	fresh lemon juice	15 mL
1 tsp	dried oregano	5 mL
1	large egg	1
1	large egg white	1

Sauce

Amount	Ingredient	Metric
1/3 cup	low-fat sour cream	75 mL
2 tsp	Dijon mustard	10 mL

essential numbers

PER BURGER

Calories	295
Protein	13 g
Fat, total	8 g
Fat, saturated	4.2 g
Carbohydrates	44 g
Sodium	263 mg
Cholesterol	74 mg
Fiber	5 g

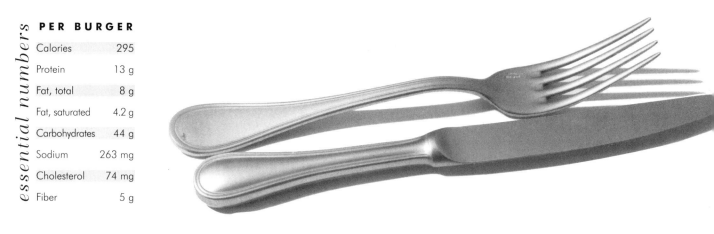

These grain burgers are the best I've ever tasted. In fact, they're so good, I'd seriously consider giving up beef burgers entirely! The secret is in the combination of barley, brown rice and wild rice. Try these burgers in a pita bread, loaded with tomatoes, onions, lettuce and alfalfa sprouts and drizzled with sauce.

Complementary proteins

A diet that includes meat, chicken and milk provides "complete proteins," since these foods have all the amino acids the body requires. But this is not the case for vegetarian diets, since plant foods (including beans, grains and vegetables) are missing one or more of these essential amino acids (thus providing "incomplete proteins"). At one time, it was believed that vegetarians had to combine grains with beans at the same meal to "complete" the protein. We now know that this is not necessary. As long as vegetarians eat a variety of protein foods throughout the day, they'll meet their amino acid requirements.

baba ghanoush
with coriander and red onions over penne

1. Place eggplants on baking sheet; bake in preheated oven for 40 minutes or until soft. When cool enough to handle, peel eggplants.

2. In a food processor combine eggplants, sour cream, stock, tahini, lemon juice, olive oil, garlic, cumin, pepper and salt; process until smooth.

3. In a large pot of boiling water, cook pasta for 8 to 10 minutes or until tender but firm; drain. Rinse under cold running water; drain.

4. In a serving bowl combine pasta, baba ghanoush, coriander and red onions; toss well. Serve immediately.

PREHEAT OVEN TO 425° F (220° C)
BAKING SHEET

2	eggplants (about 2 lbs [1 kg] total), pierced with a fork	2
1/2 cup	low-fat sour cream	125 mL
1/2 cup	VEGETABLE STOCK *or* CHICKEN STOCK (see recipes, pages 51 and 50)	125 mL
1/3 cup	tahini (sesame seed paste)	75 mL
2 tbsp	fresh lemon juice	25 mL
2 tbsp	olive oil	25 mL
1 1/2 tsp	minced garlic	7 mL
1/4 tsp	ground cumin	1 mL
1/4 tsp	freshly ground black pepper	1 mL
1/8 tsp	salt	0.5 mL
1 lb	penne	500 g
1/2 cup	chopped fresh coriander	125 mL
1/2 cup	diced red onions	125 mL

vegetarian

198

essential numbers

PER SERVING

Calories	460
Protein	16 g
Fat, total	16 g
Fat, saturated	3.2 g
Carbohydrates	73 g
Sodium	110 mg
Cholesterol	7 mg
Fiber	3 g

ask ROSE

Baba ghanoush — it sounds exotic, but it has been a standard in Middle Eastern cooking for centuries. And it's really quite a simple dish, consisting of cooked eggplant, tahini (sesame seed paste), lots of oil, garlic and lemon juice. Simple, but scrumptious! Here, I've eliminated a lot of calories by using low-fat sour cream and stock to replace some of the oil. Serve as a dip or, in the traditional manner, with pita bread.

cooking 101

A lot of people tell me they don't eat eggplant because it's bitter. And it's true — eggplant *can* be bitter, but only if it has been picked too late. Here's how to pick a young eggplant: just press it with your fingers; if the flesh doesn't spring back, it's too old. Choosing young eggplants eliminates the need to salt the flesh before using (a technique traditionally used to eliminate excess moisture and remove bitterness). Who needs all that extra sodium?

sweet potato gnocchi

with parmesan sauce

1. In a saucepan over medium-high heat, cover sweet potatoes with cold water; bring to a boil. Cook for 30 minutes or until tender when pierced with a fork; drain. When cool enough to handle, peel potatoes; mash. Add ricotta cheese, egg, cinnamon, pepper and salt; mash until well combined. Mix in flour.

2. On a lightly floured wooden board, roll about one-quarter of dough into a rope as thick as your thumb. With a sharp knife, cut into 3/4-inch (2 cm) pieces. Repeat with remaining dough. Keep gnocchi pieces separate to avoid sticking.

3. In a large pot of boiling water, cook gnocchi (in batches of about 20) for 3 minutes or until they rise to the top; cook for another 30 seconds. Remove with a slotted spoon to a warm serving dish.

4. Meanwhile, in a small nonstick saucepan, heat margarine over low heat. Add flour; cook, stirring, for 1 minute. Add milk and stock; bring to a boil, whisking constantly. Reduce heat to low; cook for 5 minutes. Remove from heat. Add Parmesan cheese.

5. In a serving bowl combine gnocchi and sauce; toss well. Serve immediately.

1 1/2 lbs	sweet potatoes, scrubbed	750 g
1/3 cup	5% ricotta cheese	75 mL
1	large egg	1
1/4 tsp	ground cinnamon	1 mL
1/8 tsp	freshly ground black pepper	0.5 mL
Pinch	salt	Pinch
1 1/2 cups	all-purpose flour	375 mL

Parmesan sauce

2 tsp	margarine *or* butter	10 mL
1 1/2 tbsp	all-purpose flour	20 mL
1 cup	low-fat milk	250 mL
2/3 cup	VEGETABLE STOCK *or* CHICKEN STOCK (see recipes, pages 51 and 50)	150 mL
3 tbsp	grated low-fat Parmesan cheese	45 mL

vegetarian

199

essential numbers

PER SERVING

Calories	241
Protein	8 g
Fat, total	4 g
Fat, saturated	1.8 g
Carbohydrates	43 g
Sodium	153 mg
Cholesterol	34 mg
Fiber	4 g

ask ROSE

My kids love gnocchi. But frankly, I rarely make the regular potato-flour variety myself; the pre-made ones sold in supermarkets are perfectly good. But this sweet potato gnocchi is different — unusual, easy to make and you can't find it in any store! When preparing this dish, be sure to pay attention to the texture of the dough; if it feels sticky, just add more flour and it will roll beautifully. Not too much, though; you don't want to overwork the dough. To save time, make a double batch and freeze half in freezer bags.

for the record

A high-calcium milk alternative
Want to add a little soy to your diet? Try replacing your next glass of milk with a calcium-fortified soy beverage. When it comes to bone-building nutrients, these products are comparable to milk. An 8 oz (250 mL) glass of a fortified soy beverage has 300 to 330 mg calcium and 100 I.U. of vitamin D. And if you use it to replace milk in cooking, here's a bonus: the phytoestrogens (isoflavones) in the soy won't break down when heated.

spinach gnocchi

with tomato sauce

1. In a large saucepan over high heat, cook spinach, covered, for 3 minutes. Toss spinach; cook, uncovered, for 1 minute or until wilted. Drain; squeeze spinach dry. If using frozen spinach, cook according to package directions; drain and squeeze dry.

2. In a food processor, combine cooked spinach, ricotta cheese, egg and salt; purée until smooth. Set aside.

3. In a saucepan over medium-high heat, cover potatoes with cold water; bring to a boil. Cook for 25 minutes or until tender when pierced with a fork; drain. When cool enough to handle, peel potatoes. In a bowl mash potatoes; add spinach mixture and flour. Mix well.

4. On a lightly floured wooden board, roll about one-quarter of dough into a rope as thick as your thumb, using extra flour as necessary. With a sharp knife, cut into 3/4-inch (2 cm) pieces. Repeat with remaining dough. Keep gnocchi separate to avoid sticking.

5. In a large pot of boiling water, cook gnocchi in batches (of about 20) for 3 minutes or until they rise to the top. Cook for another 30 seconds; remove with a slotted spoon to a warm serving dish.

6. Meanwhile, in a saucepan over medium heat, combine tomato sauce and evaporated milk. Cook for 3 minutes or until heated through. Pour sauce over gnocchi; toss well. Sprinkle with Parmesan cheese; serve immediately.

1	pkg (10 oz [300 g]) fresh or frozen spinach (if using fresh, wash and cook only with water clinging to the leaves)	1
1/3 cup	5% ricotta cheese	75 mL
1	large egg	1
1/4 tsp	salt	1 mL
1 lb	potatoes, scrubbed	500 g
1 1/2 cups	all-purpose flour	375 mL

Sauce

1 cup	tomato pasta sauce	250 mL
1/3 cup	low-fat evaporated milk	75 mL
3 tbsp	grated low-fat Parmesan cheese	45 mL

vegetarian

200

PER SERVING

Calories	179
Protein	8 g
Fat, total	2 g
Fat, saturated	0.9 g
Carbohydrates	33 g
Sodium	226 mg
Cholesterol	31 mg
Fiber	2 g

ask ROSE

If you love potatoes, then gnocchi is pasta made in heaven. Traditionally, it is served with lots of butter, cheese or cream sauce. (Feel those arteries starting to clog?) But in this recipe I have eliminated the need for all those calories with a delicious tomato sauce with a creamy texture that comes from low-fat evaporated milk.

nutrition watch

Slimming spuds

Believe it or not, the humble potato may actually help you lose weight. According to an Australian study, the spud is the most filling, low-calorie food. Why? Because potatoes contain a large amount of soluble fiber, which forms a gel in your stomach and gives you that feeling of fullness. (Insoluble fiber in bran and whole grains passes quickly through the stomach, but helps to keep you regular.) Foods rich in soluble fiber may also do more than help you control your weight — they're helpful in lowering LDL cholesterol and controlling blood sugar. Other good sources of soluble fiber include carrots, oats, cantaloupe, oranges and strawberries.

roasted vegetable lasagna

1. In a bowl combine sweet potato, red pepper, yellow pepper, red onion, zucchini and olive oil; toss well. Spread mixture over prepared baking sheet; add garlic. Bake in preheated oven for 45 minutes or until vegetables are tender; remove from oven. Squeeze garlic from skins; mash. Chop roasted vegetables; mix well with accumulated juices and mashed garlic. Set aside. Reduce oven temperature to 350° F (180° C).

2. Meanwhile, in a large pot of boiling water, cook lasagna noodles for 12 to 14 minutes or until tender; drain. Rinse under cold running water; drain. Set aside.

3. In a bowl combine ricotta cheese, mozzarella cheese, 1/3 cup (75 mL) milk, pesto and half the Parmesan cheese; set aside. In another bowl combine tomato sauce and milk; set aside.

4. Spread half the tomato sauce over bottom of prepared baking pan. Top with three lasagna noodles; trim to fit pan (discard trimmings). Add half the vegetable mixture, then half the cheese mixture; spread evenly. Top with three more lasagna noodles; repeat layers. Top with remaining tomato sauce; sprinkle with remaining Parmesan cheese. Bake, uncovered, in preheated oven for 30 minutes or until heated through. Serve.

PREHEAT OVEN TO 425° F (220° C)
BAKING SHEET LINED WITH FOIL
9-INCH (2.5 L) SQUARE BAKING DISH, SPRAYED WITH VEGETABLE SPRAY

1	medium sweet potato, peeled and cut crosswise into 1/2-inch (1 cm) slices	1
1	medium red bell pepper, quartered	1
1	medium yellow or green bell pepper, quartered	1
1	medium red onion, cut into wedges	1
1	medium zucchini, cut into half lengthwise	1
1 tbsp	olive oil	15 mL
1	medium head garlic, top 1/2 inch (1 cm) cut off, wrapped loosely in foil	1
9	lasagna noodles	9
1 1/2 cups	5% ricotta cheese	375 mL
3/4 cup	shredded low-fat mozzarella cheese	175 mL
1/3 cup	low-fat milk	75 mL
1/3 cup	CREAMY PESTO SAUCE (see recipe, page 204) *or* prepared pesto	75 mL
1/4 cup	grated low-fat Parmesan cheese	50 mL
1 1/2 cups	tomato pasta sauce	375 mL
1/4 cup	low-fat milk	50 mL

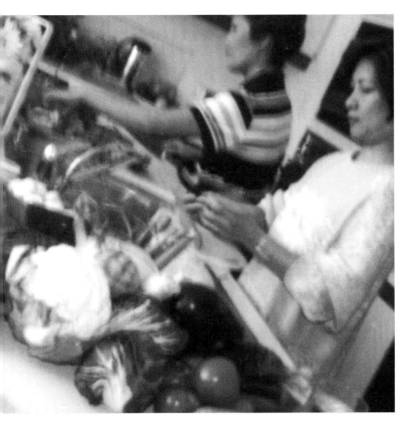

essential numbers

PER SERVING	
Calories	369
Protein	19 g
Fat, total	18 g
Fat, saturated	7.5 g
Carbohydrates	34 g
Sodium	497 mg
Cholesterol	36 mg
Fiber	4 g

ask ROSE

Traditional lasagna — with its layers of melted cheese and white cream sauce — is deliciously satisfying. But talk about high-fat food! There must be another way to enjoy this pasta dish. Well, here it is: a lasagna with loads of sweet roasted vegetables piled over low-fat ricotta and mozzarella cheese and homemade light pesto. Truly decadent — but light.

cooking 101

Once you taste the sweet richness of roasted vegetables, you'll never want them any other way. And the best part about roasting is that it's so easy! Just choose any vegetable you like, cut into large chunks, drizzle with 1 to 2 tbsp (15 to 25 mL) oil and roast, uncovered, at 425° F (220° C) for 45 minutes. Place in a bowl with the leftover juices and eat either hot or at room temperature. They also make great leftovers.

creamy pesto sauce

1. In a food processor, combine basil, sour cream, mayonnaise, Parmesan cheese, olive oil, pine nuts, lemon juice and garlic; process until smooth. Add 1 tbsp (15 mL) water if too thick.

1 cup	tightly-packed fresh basil leaves	250 mL
1/4 cup	low-fat sour cream	50 mL
2 tbsp	light mayonnaise	25 mL
1 1/2 tbsp	grated low-fat Parmesan cheese	20 mL
1 tbsp	olive oil	15 mL
1 tbsp	toasted pine nuts	15 mL
1 1/2 tsp	freshly squeezed lemon juice	7 mL
1 tsp	minced garlic	5 mL

vegetarian

204

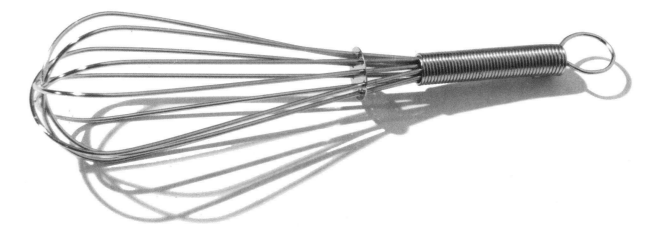

essential numbers

PER TBSP

Calories	33
Protein	1 g
Fat, total	3 g
Fat, saturated	1.0 g
Carbohydrates	1 g
Sodium	39 mg
Cholesterol	1 mg
Fiber	0 g

ask ROSE

Store-bought pesto is convenient, but it's loaded with fat and calories. Why? Commercial preparations contain huge amounts of oil, nuts and cheese. But not here! With this pesto sauce, I've replaced the oil with low-fat sour cream and mayonnaise. You could also use chicken or vegetable stock.

variation

Substitute the basil with parsley, spinach, coriander or dill, or select a combination. These variations are delicious — and economical, especially when basil is expensive in the winter months!

roasted gazpacho
vegetables with shell pasta

1. In a bowl combine tomatoes, green pepper, red pepper, red onion, zucchini and olive oil; toss well. Spread onto prepared baking sheet; add garlic. Bake in preheated oven for 45 minutes or until vegetables are tender.

2. Squeeze garlic from skins. In a food processor, combine garlic, roasted vegetables and juices, tomato juice, vinegar, lemon juice, pepper and salt; pulse on and off several times until combined but still chunky.

3. In a large pot of boiling water, cook shell pasta for 8 to 10 minutes or until tender but firm; drain. In a serving bowl, combine pasta, sauce and coriander; toss well. Serve immediately.

PREHEAT OVEN TO 425° F (220° C)
BAKING SHEET LINED WITH FOIL

1 lb	fresh plum tomatoes, cut in half crosswise	500 g
1	medium green bell pepper, quartered	1
1	medium red bell pepper, quartered	1
1	medium red onion, cut into wedges	1
1	medium zucchini, cut in half lengthwise	1
1 tbsp	olive oil	15 mL
1	head garlic, top 1/2 inch (1 cm) cut off, wrapped loosely in foil	1
1 cup	tomato juice	250 mL
1 tbsp	balsamic vinegar	15 mL
1 tbsp	fresh lemon juice	15 mL
1/4 tsp	freshly ground black pepper	1 mL
1/4 tsp	salt	1 mL
1 lb	medium shell pasta	500 g
1/2 cup	chopped fresh coriander	75 mL

vegetarian

205

essential numbers

PER SERVING

Calories	510
Protein	16 g
Fat, total	6 g
Fat, saturated	0.9 g
Carbohydrates	100 g
Sodium	137 mg
Cholesterol	0 mg
Fiber	7 g

ask ROSE

Gazpacho over pasta? Sure! This traditional summer soup, which originated in Spain, is made from a puréed mixture of fresh tomatoes, bell peppers, onions, celery and seasoning. So I thought, why not roast the vegetables, mix them with gazpacho flavors and serve over pasta? The results are sensational — a great meal for outdoor eating.

for the record

Wash away pesticides
If you wash your produce, there's little need to worry about pesticides. A study in Texas tested 17 popular fruits and vegetables for 22 common pesticide residues. Sixty percent had no detectable residues without washing. Residues were eliminated in another 21% by washing and, in some cases, peeling skins. For the rest, peeling and washing reduced residues by 30%. To play it safe, wash produce in a mixture of mild dishwashing liquid and water or, if you're still concerned, buy organically grown fruits and vegetables.

falafels with tahini

sauce over linguine

1. In a food processor, combine chickpeas, bread crumbs, coriander, green onions, lemon juice, tahini, garlic, egg, cumin and pepper; pulse on and off until finely chopped and well mixed. With wet hands, form each 1 tbsp (15 mL) mixture into a ball. Place on prepared baking sheet; flatten slightly. Bake in preheated oven for 15 minutes or until heated through and golden.

2. Meanwhile, in a clean food processor or blender, combine coriander, sour cream, water, tahini, mayonnaise, soya sauce, honey and sesame oil; purée until smooth.

3. In a large pot of boiling water, cook linguine for 8 to 10 minutes or until tender but firm; drain. In a serving bowl, combine pasta, falafels and sauce; toss well. Serve immediately.

206

PREHEAT OVEN TO 400° F (200° C)
BAKING SHEET SPRAYED WITH VEGETABLE SPRAY

1	can (19 oz [540 mL]) chickpeas, rinsed and drained	1
1/4 cup	dry seasoned bread crumbs	50 mL
1/4 cup	chopped fresh coriander	50 mL
1/4 cup	chopped green onions	50 mL
2 tbsp	fresh lemon juice	25 mL
2 tbsp	tahini (sesame seed paste)	25 mL
1 1/2 tsp	minced garlic	7 mL
1	large egg	1
1/4 tsp	ground cumin	1 mL
1/8 tsp	freshly ground black pepper	0.5 mL

Sauce

1/2 cup	chopped fresh coriander	125 mL
1/2 cup	low-fat sour cream	125 mL
1/2 cup	water	125 mL
1/4 cup	tahini	50 mL
3 tbsp	light mayonnaise	45 mL
2 1/2 tbsp	light soya sauce	35 mL
1 tbsp	honey	15 mL
2 tsp	sesame oil	10 mL
12 oz	linguine	375 g

essential numbers

PER SERVING

Calories	438
Protein	16 g
Fat, total	17 g
Fat, saturated	2.6 g
Carbohydrates	61 g
Sodium	813 mg
Cholesterol	40 mg
Fiber	8 g

ask ROSE

Falafels are a Middle Eastern specialty made from ground chickpeas and spices. Traditionally, these small patties are deep-fried, wrapped in a pita bread and smothered with a high-fat dressing. Delicious, but not exactly health food! Served this way, just two small patties can have over 250 calories and 15 g fat! The difference in this recipe is that the patties are baked and served with a low-fat, high-flavor dressing.

nutrition watch

Beans, beans, the magical fruit...

Love the taste of beans but afraid of their, ahem, after-effects? It's true that chickpeas, kidney beans and lentils cause flatulence in some people. That's because they contain certain sugars (raffinose and stachyose) that are difficult to digest. When they reach your large intestine, bacteria ferment them, producing gas and bloating.

Try the following tips to make you (and your friends) feel better:

- Soak dried beans for at least 4 hours before cooking. Discard the water, rinse the beans, then add fresh water for cooking.

- Rinse canned beans before using them.

- Sprinkle your meal with Beano. Available in drugstores, it's a natural enzyme that helps break down the gas-producing sugars.

- Don't give up. Keep eating beans in small portions to help your intestinal tract adapt.

leek pesto over linguine

1. In a nonstick frying pan sprayed with vegetable spray, cook leeks over medium heat for 4 minutes or until softened. In a food processor combine leeks, basil, Parmesan cheese, pine nuts, brown sugar, garlic, stock and olive oil; purée until smooth.

2. Meanwhile, in a large pot of boiling water, cook linguine for 8 to 10 minutes or until tender but firm; drain. In a serving bowl, combine pasta and pesto; toss well. Serve immediately.

1 cup	chopped leeks	250 mL
1 1/2 cups	tightly packed fresh basil leaves	375 mL
3 tbsp	grated low-fat Parmesan cheese	45 mL
3 tbsp	toasted pine nuts	45 mL
2 tsp	packed brown sugar	10 mL
1 tsp	minced garlic	5 mL
1 cup	VEGETABLE STOCK *or* CHICKEN STOCK (see recipes, pages 51 and 50)	250 mL
3 tbsp	olive oil	45 mL
8 oz	linguine	250 g

vegetarian

208

PER SERVING

essential numbers

Calories	358
Protein	11 g
Fat, total	17 g
Fat, saturated	2.9 g
Carbohydrates	44 g
Sodium	283 mg
Cholesterol	4 mg
Fiber	4 g

ask ROSE

While pesto is traditionally made from basil leaves, I've always liked to experiment with combinations of parsley, dill, spinach and coriander. Well, here's my latest idea — a vegetable-basil pesto! In this recipe I've combined basil with 1 cup (250 mL) leeks. (Don't use any more or the pesto will be bitter.) This combination works perfectly, and makes a great sauce for serving over chicken or fish.

cooking 101

Unless you like your pesto with crunchy grit, remember to wash the leeks thoroughly. To make sure you get all the dirt, slice the leeks lengthwise, open the leaves and wash well. Then chop and use as directed.

avocado-tomato salsa
over linguine

1. In a nonstick frying pan sprayed with vegetable spray, cook red onions over medium-high heat for 5 minutes or until softened. Add stock and chili paste; simmer for 1 minute. Remove from heat; cool. Add tomatoes, avocado, prosciutto, coriander, lime juice and garlic.

2. In a large pot of boiling water, cook linguine for 8 to 10 minutes or until tender but firm; drain. Rinse under cold running water.

3. In a serving bowl, combine salsa and linguine; toss well. Serve.

1 cup	sliced red onions	250 mL
1/2 cup	VEGETABLE STOCK or CHICKEN STOCK (see recipes, pages 51 and 50)	125 mL
1/2 tsp	hot Asian chili paste (optional)	2 mL
2 1/2 cups	diced ripe plum tomatoes	625 mL
Half	ripe avocado, diced	Half
2 oz	prosciutto, diced	50 g
1/2 cup	chopped fresh coriander	125 mL
1 1/2 tbsp	fresh lime or lemon juice	20 mL
1 tsp	minced garlic	5 mL
8 oz	linguine	250 g

vegetarian

209

essential numbers

PER SERVING

Calories	276
Protein	12 g
Fat, total	7 g
Fat, saturated	0.9 g
Carbohydrates	47 g
Sodium	311 mg
Cholesterol	7 mg
Fiber	4 g

ask ROSE

Traditional avocado or guacamole dip is high in calories and fat. And even though the fat in avocados is mostly of the "good" polyunsaturated variety, chances are you'd rather do without the calories (about 120 per 2 tbsp [25 mL]). Here, I have used only half an avocado and bolstered the flavor with plenty of meaty plum tomatoes and seasonings.

nutrition watch

High five!

Despite overwhelming evidence that fruit and vegetables provide substantial health benefits, many of us still fall short of the recommended 5 to 10 servings a day. Here are some tips to help you "strive for five": buy pre-chopped vegetables and "salad in a bag"; pick up fresh fruit or raw veggies from the salad bar; replace that diet pop with a vegetable juice; fill your sandwich with tomatoes, cucumbers and lettuce; add slices of lemon, lime or orange to water for flavor and a little vitamin C; and, top your frozen yogurt with a handful of berries.

cheese orzo bake
with sun-dried tomatoes and black olives

1. In a large nonstick frying pan sprayed with vegetable spray, cook fennel, onions, garlic and fennel seeds for 5 minutes or until softened. Add tomatoes (with juice), stock, sun-dried tomatoes, black olives, brown sugar and pepper. Bring to a boil, stirring with wooden spoon to break up tomatoes. Add orzo; transfer to casserole dish.

2. Bake, covered, in preheated oven for 25 minutes or until orzo is tender and most of liquid is absorbed. Sprinkle with feta cheese. Serve.

PREHEAT OVEN TO 425° F (220° C)
8-CUP (2 L) CASSEROLE DISH

1 1/2 cups	chopped fennel	375 mL
1 cup	chopped onions	250 mL
1 1/2 tsp	minced garlic	7 mL
1 tsp	fennel seeds	5 mL
1	can (19 oz [540 mL]) tomatoes, with juice	1
1 1/2 cups	VEGETABLE STOCK or CHICKEN STOCK (see recipes, pages 51 and 50)	375 mL
1/2 cup	chopped sun-dried tomatoes	125 mL
1/3 cup	sliced black olives	75 mL
2 tsp	packed brown sugar	10 mL
1/4 tsp	freshly ground black pepper	1 mL
1 1/3 cups	orzo or small-shaped pasta	325 mL
4 oz	light feta cheese, crumbled	125 g

vegetarian

210

essential numbers

PER SERVING	
Calories	278
Protein	11 g
Fat, total	11 g
Fat, saturated	4.9 g
Carbohydrates	37 g
Sodium	831 mg
Cholesterol	28 mg
Fiber	3 g

ask ROSE

Just the word "bake" says "comfort food" — and that description certainly fits this wonderfully satisfying orzo pasta dish, with its hearty tomato vegetable sauce and flavorful feta cheese highlights. Traditionally, this type of dish tended to be heavy with excess butter and cheese — which is comforting only until you think about all the fat calories! Here the comfort comes without a price.

cooking 101

Sooner or later, it seems that everything is recreated in a "light" version. And feta cheese has proved to be no exception. The light version of this tangy cheese has 40% of the fat removed, so 1 oz (25 g) contains only 60 calories and 4 g fat.

To soften sun-dried tomatoes, place in a bowl and cover with boiling water. Let sit for 15 minutes. Drain, then chop.

roasted fennel,
garlic and plum tomatoes over rotini

1. In a bowl combine fennel, tomatoes and oil; toss well. Spread over prepared baking sheet; add garlic. Bake in preheated oven for 45 minutes or until vegetables are tender. Squeeze garlic from skins; chop vegetables coarsely.

2. In a saucepan combine garlic, vegetables (with accumulated juices), stock, olives, pepper and salt. Bring to a boil; reduce heat to medium-low. Cook for 3 minutes or until heated through.

3. Meanwhile, in a large pot of boiling water, cook rotini for 8 to 10 minutes or until tender but firm; drain. In a serving bowl combine pasta and sauce; toss well. Serve immediately.

PREHEAT OVEN TO 425° F (220° C)
LARGE BAKING SHEET SPRAYED WITH VEGETABLE SPRAY

1	large fennel bulb, trimmed and cut into wedges	1
1 lb	plum tomatoes, cut in half crosswise	500 g
1 tbsp	olive oil	15 mL
1	head garlic, top 1/2 inch (1 cm) cut off, wrapped loosely in foil	1
3/4 cup	VEGETABLE STOCK or CHICKEN STOCK (see recipes, pages 51 and 50)	175 mL
1/3 cup	black olives	75 mL
1/4 tsp	freshly ground black pepper	1 mL
1/8 tsp	salt	0.5 mL
8 oz	rotini	250 g

vegetarian

211

PER SERVING

Calories	324
Protein	9 g
Fat, total	8 g
Fat, saturated	0.7 g
Carbohydrates	55 g
Sodium	192 mg
Cholesterol	0 mg
Fiber	4 g

essential numbers

ask ROSE

Fennel is a tremendously useful vegetable, in that you can eat both the bulb and the stalks. But it's the bulb — especially when roasted — that I love best. Its sweet, delicate flavor is a perfect complement to the garlic and tomatoes in this recipe.

for the record

Figuring out the fat

Wondering how to translate grams of fat on a nutrition label into something meaningful? A good rule of thumb is that 1 tsp (5 mL) fat (butter, margarine or oil) has 4 g fat. So that small bag of potato chips you were craving, with 21 g fat, translates into 5 1/4 tsp (26 mL) worth of oil. Ouch! That really hurts the intestine. Remember, the average healthy male should consume no more than 90 g fat and a healthy female should not exceed 65 g.

desse

tulip egg roll cups

with berries

1 Place egg roll wrappers in muffin cups, fluting sides decoratively. Spray inside of wrappers with vegetable spray. Bake in preheated oven for 10 to 12 minutes or until lightly golden. Set aside.

2 In a food processor combine thawed berries, juice and icing sugar; purée until smooth. Add blueberries or sliced strawberries.

3 In a bowl combine sour cream and icing sugar. Pour 2 tsp (10 mL) sauce in bottom of baked tulip cups. Add berry mixture; drizzle with remaining sauce. Serve.

PREHEAT OVEN TO 400° F (200° C)

12-CUP MUFFIN TIN SPRAYED WITH VEGETABLE SPRAY

12	large (5 1/2-inch [13.5 cm] square) egg roll wrappers	12

Filling

1 1/2 cups	frozen strawberries or raspberries (thaw, do not drain)	375 mL
1/4 cup	icing sugar	50 mL
2 1/2 cups	fresh blueberries or sliced fresh strawberries	625 mL

Sauce

1/2 cup	low-fat sour cream	125 mL
4 tbsp	icing sugar	60 mL

desserts

214

PER SERVING

Calories	144
Protein	4 g
Fat, total	1 g
Fat, saturated	0.5 g
Carbohydrates	30 g
Sodium	189 mg
Cholesterol	5 mg
Fiber	2 g

ask ROSE

I love the flavor of ripe fresh strawberries. But if you're just going to purée them (as we do here), why not save some money and use frozen berries? Your tastebuds will never know the difference!

If using raspberries, increase the icing sugar to 1/3 cup (75 mL).

nutrition watch

Good news from the stawberry patch

Aside from the fact that strawberries are low in calories, high in fiber and a great source of vitamin C, these succulent berries may play a role in cancer prevention. Strawberries contain ellagic acid, a natural compound that's been shown to inhibit cancers of the lung, liver, skin and esophagus in animals. This anti-cancer compound helps liver enzymes deactivate cancer-causing substances. Better yet, when you cook or freeze your strawberries, ellagic acid doesn't break down.

Serves 10

baklava wonton pouches
with honey lemon sauce

1   In a bowl combine raisins, nuts, brown sugar and cinnamon. Place 2 tsp (10 mL) filling in center of 1 egg roll wrapper; wipe corners with water. Draw edges up; press together into a pouch. Place on prepared baking sheet. Repeat procedure with remaining filling and wrappers. Bake in preheated oven for 10 minutes or until lightly browned.

2   Meanwhile, in a small saucepan, combine sugar, water, honey and lemon juice. Bring to a boil; reduce heat to low. Cook for 5 minutes or until syrupy; pour over hot pouches. Let stand for 10 minutes before serving.

PREHEAT OVEN TO 400° F (200° C)
BAKING SHEET SPRAYED WITH VEGETABLE SPRAY

2/3 cup	raisins	150 mL
2/3 cup	finely chopped pecans or walnuts	150 mL
1/4 cup	packed brown sugar	50 mL
1/2 tsp	ground cinnamon	2 mL
30 to 32	small (3 1/2-inch [8.5 cm] square) egg roll wrappers	30 to 32

Sauce

1/3 cup	granulated sugar	75 mL
3 tbsp	water	45 mL
2 tbsp	honey	25 mL
1 tbsp	fresh lemon juice	15 mL

desserts

215

PER SERVING

essential numbers

Calories	224
Protein	4 g
Fat, total	6 g
Fat, saturated	0.5 g
Carbohydrates	41 g
Sodium	158 mg
Cholesterol	2 mg
Fiber	2 g

ask ROSE

Traditional baklava, popular in Greece and Turkey, consists of several layers of butter-soaked phyllo pastry with loads of chopped nuts and a honey syrup poured over. High fat? You don't want to know! Better you should try this version, where we use small egg roll wrappers (delicious, if you've never tried them), eliminate the butter and end up with a fantastic "pop-in-your-mouth" dessert.

for the record

Sugar showdown
Looking for a more nutritious sugar? That may sound like an oxymoron, but take a look. You'll see that some sweeteners do have nutritional value beyond their calorie content.

1 tbsp (15 mL)…	calories	calcium (mg)	iron (mg)	potassium (mg)
White sugar	50	0	trace	trace
Brown sugar	34	0	0.3	31
Blackstrap molasses	45	144	3.4	615
Fancy molasses	53	35	0.9	193
Maple syrup	50	21	0.2	35
Corn syrup	56	4	0.7	9
Honey, liquid	64	1	0.1	11

Serves 12

egg noodle cake
with chocolate chip topping

1. In a pot of boiling water, cook egg noodles for 8 minutes or until tender but firm; drain. Rinse under cold running water; drain.

2. In a food processor, combine egg, egg whites, ricotta cheese, yogurt, brown sugar, cream cheese and cocoa; purée until smooth. Transfer to a bowl; add noodles, combining well. Pour into springform pan.

3. In a bowl combine brown sugar, chocolate chips and cocoa; mix well. Sprinkle over cake. Bake in preheated oven for 40 to 45 minutes or until set.

desserts

216

PREHEAT OVEN TO 350° F (180° C)

9-INCH (2.5 mL) SQUARE PAN SPRAYED WITH VEGETABLE SPRAY

8 oz	wide egg noodles	250 g
1	large egg	1
2	large egg whites	2
1 cup	5% ricotta cheese	250 mL
3/4 cup	low-fat yogurt	175 mL
1 1/4 cups	packed brown sugar	300 mL
2 oz	light cream cheese	50 g
1/3 cup	unsweetened cocoa	75 mL

Topping

1/4 cup	packed brown sugar	50 mL
2 tbsp	semi-sweet chocolate chips	25 mL
1 tbsp	unsweetened cocoa	15 mL

essential numbers

PER SERVING

Calories	227
Protein	9 g
Fat, total	5 g
Fat, saturated	2.6 g
Carbohydrates	37 g
Sodium	90 mg
Cholesterol	64 mg
Fiber	1 g

ask ROSE

There are many variations on this traditional Jewish holiday dessert — and just about all of them are high in fat and calories (thanks to sour cream, cream cheese and eggs). Well, here's a version that's light but satisfying — particularly if you love chocolate. The flavor secret is to use mostly cocoa with just a sprinkling of chocolate chips. A chocoholic's delight!

cooking 101

While both chocolate and cocoa powder are made from cocoa beans, the difference is that cocoa powder contains no cocoa butter, which chocolate does. There's a difference, too, in what each does to your waistline: 1 oz (25 g) chocolate has 130 calories and 9 g fat, while the same amount of cocoa has only 40 calories and 1 g fat!

Serves 6

double chocolate rice
pudding

1. In a nonstick saucepan over medium heat, combine milk, brown sugar, rice and cocoa; bring to a simmer. Reduce heat to medium-low; cook, partially covered and stirring occasionally, for 45 to 50 minutes or until rice is tender and mixture is thick. Cool slightly; add chocolate chips and coconut. Serve warm or at room temperature.

3 1/2 cups	low-fat milk	875 mL
3/4 cup	packed brown sugar	175 mL
1/2 cup	Arborio rice (risotto rice)	125 mL
1/4 cup	unsweetened cocoa	50 mL
2 tbsp	semi-sweet chocolate chips	25 mL
2 tbsp	toasted unsweetened coconut	25 mL

essential numbers

PER SERVING

Calories	210
Protein	8 g
Fat, total	3 g
Fat, saturated	1.5 g
Carbohydrates	43 g
Sodium	89 mg
Cholesterol	6 mg
Fiber	2 g

ask ROSE

Here we use brown sugar for its softer texture — a quality that derives from its molasses content. (Molasses is what makes brown sugar different from the white granulated type; the darker the sugar, the more molasses it has.) To keep brown sugar from hardening, put a piece of bread in the container and replace it every other week. You can also soften brown sugar by heating it gently in a microwave oven.

nutrition watch

Attention chocoholics!
Is chocolate truly addictive? Maybe. Scientists have learned that the ingredients in chocolate can affect the level of certain brain chemicals that make you feel good. Sugar in chocolate triggers the release of serotonin, a chemical that calms and relaxes. Then there's phenylethylamine, a compound that's used as a building block for dopamine, a brain chemical that makes you more alert. And some experts say that phenylethylamine stimulates feelings people experience when they're in love. Others argue that the craving for chocolate is purely sensory — a desire for its delicious, smooth taste. They've got that right. More Godiva, please!

cornmeal banana date muffins

1 In a food processor or blender combine sugar, oil, egg, vanilla and banana; purée until smooth. Transfer to a bowl.

2 In another bowl combine flour, cornmeal, baking soda and baking powder. Add to banana mixture alternately with yogurt. Add dates; divide among prepared muffin cups. Bake in preheated oven for 15 to 18 minutes or until tester inserted in center comes out clean.

desserts

218

PREHEAT OVEN TO 350° F (180° C)
12-CUP MUFFIN TIN SPRAYED WITH VEGETABLE SPRAY

3/4 cup	granulated sugar	175 mL
3 tbsp	vegetable oil	45 mL
1	large egg	1
1 tsp	vanilla extract	5 mL
1	medium ripe banana	1
1 cup	all-purpose flour	250 mL
1/4 cup	cornmeal	50 mL
1 tsp	baking soda	5 mL
1/2 tsp	baking powder	2 mL
3/4 cup	low-fat yogurt	175 mL
1/2 cup	chopped dates	125 mL

essential numbers

PER SERVING

Calories	159
Protein	2 g
Fat, total	4 g
Fat, saturated	0.5 g
Carbohydrates	29 g
Sodium	23 mg
Cholesterol	19 mg
Fiber	1 g

ask ROSE

Here's a little secret about how to create light desserts that still have plenty of flavor. Start by looking at a traditional "heavy" dessert; identify the ingredients that add fat, and replace them (or part of them) with low-fat substitutes. These substitutes include puréed banana, crushed pineapple, cooked applesauce, puréed dates or prunes, shredded carrots (which also release moisture after they're baked), as well as low-fat yogurt. Try them — you'll be amazed at how little you miss the fat!

for the record

Magnificent muffins

Here's a muffin you can enjoy — absolutely guilt-free! At 4 g fat, one of these treats has only a fraction of the fat found in most commercial muffins. That's right, folks. Your typical coffee-shop muffin has a whopping 16 g hidden fat — one-quarter of a woman's daily fat allowance.

rice pudding

with dates, apricots and cinnamon

1 In a nonstick saucepan over medium heat, combine milk, rice, sugar and cinnamon; bring to a simmer. Reduce heat to medium-low; cook, partially covered and stirring occasionally, for 50 minutes or until rice is tender and mixture is thickened. Add vanilla, apricots and dates. Serve warm or at room temperature.

3 1/2 cups	low-fat milk	875 mL
1/2 cup	Arborio rice (risotto rice)	125 mL
1/3 cup	granulated sugar	75 mL
1/2 tsp	ground cinnamon	2 mL
1 tsp	vanilla extract	5 mL
1/3 cup	chopped dried apricots	75 mL
1/3 cup	chopped dried dates	75 mL

desserts

219

essential numbers

PER SERVING	
Calories	200
Protein	7 g
Fat, total	2 g
Fat, saturated	0.5 g
Carbohydrates	43 g
Sodium	81 mg
Cholesterol	7 mg
Fiber	2 g

ask ROSE

My husband loves rice pudding. But most traditional recipes for this dish call for whole-fat milk, cream and eggs. So, to keep the spousal arteries clear, I created this version, which uses low-fat milk and creamy Arborio rice (the same type used for risotto). The higher starch content of this rice gives the pudding a texture very much like the old-fashioned variety. Adding dried fruit makes it even more delicious!

cooking 101

Unless you really enjoy spending money needlessly, avoid buying dried fruit in small packages. Purchase it in bulk and keep it in the freezer.

When chopping dried fruit, use a pair of sharp scissors. It's much faster than a knife!

egg roll cheesecakes

with chocolate sauce

desserts

1. In a food processor or blender combine cream cheese, ricotta cheese, sugar, egg and vanilla; purée until smooth. Add chocolate chips. Place one egg roll wrapper into each muffin tin; place 1/4 cup (50 mL) filling into center of each wrapper. Wet corners; squeeze together and twist. Bake in preheated oven for 15 to 18 minutes or until lightly browned.

2. Meanwhile, in a saucepan over medium-high heat, combine sugar, corn syrup, water and cocoa; bring to a boil. Reduce heat to low; cook for 5 minutes or until slightly thickened. Drizzle over warm egg rolls; serve. (If chocolate sauce thickens, gently reheat.)

PREHEAT OVEN TO 400° F (200° C)
12-CUP MUFFIN TIN SPRAYED WITH VEGETABLE SPRAY

4 oz	light cream cheese	125 g
3/4 cup	5% ricotta cheese	175 mL
3/4 cup	granulated sugar	175 mL
1	large egg	1
1 tsp	vanilla extract	5 mL
3 tbsp	semi-sweet chocolate chips	45 mL
12	large (5 1/2-inch [13.5 cm] square) egg roll wrappers	12

Sauce

1/3 cup	granulated sugar	75 mL
1/4 cup	corn syrup	50 mL
1/4 cup	water	50 mL
3 tbsp	unsweetened cocoa	45 mL

essential numbers

PER SERVING

Calories	218
Protein	7 g
Fat, total	4 g
Fat, saturated	2.0 g
Carbohydrates	40 g
Sodium	242 mg
Cholesterol	29 mg
Fiber	1 g

ask ROSE

Believe it or not, this chocolate sauce contains virtually no fat. But it's so good, I'm always making up new batches to keep in jars in the refrigerator. To serve, just loosen the lid and pop the jar in the microwave to make it pourable. It's delicious served over frozen yogurt, fruit and cheesecake.

lifestyle

These mini cheesecakes can be made in advance, and they taste great when reheated. Just place in a 300° F (180° C) oven for 10 minutes or until the cheese filling is warm.

rice paper apple strudels

1. In a nonstick frying pan, heat margarine over medium heat. Add apples, brown sugar and cinnamon; cook, stirring, for 3 minutes or until apples are tender and sugar is melted. Set aside.

2. In a bowl cover wrappers with cold water; let stand for 3 minutes or until softened. Pat dry; place on work surface. Place 1/4 cup (50 mL) apple mixture into center of each wrapper. Fold in sides; roll up tightly. Repeat with remaining wrappers and filling.

3. In a nonstick frying pan sprayed with vegetable spray, cook filled wrappers over medium heat, turning once, for 3 to 4 minutes or until golden.

4. In a bowl combine sour cream and sugar; drizzle over warm strudels. Serve.

2 tsp	margarine *or* butter	10 mL
2 cups	thinly sliced peeled apples	500 mL
1/4 cup	packed brown sugar	50 mL
1 tsp	ground cinnamon	5 mL
6	6-inch (15 cm) round rice paper wrappers	6

Sauce

| 1/4 cup | low-fat sour cream | 50 mL |
| 2 tbsp | icing sugar | 25 mL |

desserts

221

essential numbers

PER CRÊPE

Calories	199
Protein	5 g
Fat, total	4 g
Fat, saturated	1.5 g
Carbohydrates	38 g
Sodium	260 mg
Cholesterol	3 mg
Fiber	3 g

ask ROSE

Rice paper wrappers make wonderfully delicate desserts. Look for them in Asian markets, specialty food stores or in the Asian section of larger supermarkets. The wrappers need to be softened before using — preferably in cold water. (While wrappers take less time to soften in hot water, they also break more easily.) Once softened, it's best to dry them slightly before filling.

nutrition watch

An apple a day...

According to a Finnish study, people who eat a lot of apples have lower rates of lung cancer. The study focused on flavonoids — vitamin-like compounds found in fruits and vegetables that have an antioxidant effect. After reviewing the eating habits of almost 10,000 Finns, the researchers found that those with the highest consumption of flavonoid-rich foods had a 20% lower incidence of lung cancer. Interestingly, quercetin, a flavonoid specific to apples, accounted for 95% of the flavonoids consumed. Granny Smith anyone?

apple cinnamon orange
noodle pudding cake

1 In a pot of boiling water, cook noodles for 8 minutes or until tender but firm; drain. Rinse under cold running water; drain.

2 In a food processor combine egg, egg whites, ricotta cheese, yogurt, cream cheese, orange zest, orange juice, sugar, cinnamon and nutmeg; purée until smooth.

3 In a bowl combine apples, raisins, sugar and cinnamon. In another bowl combine brown sugar, flour, oats, margarine and cinnamon.

4 In a bowl combine noodles, ricotta cheese mixture and apple mixture; pour into prepared pan. Sprinkle with topping. Bake in preheated oven for 35 minutes or until set.

222

PREHEAT OVEN TO 350° F (180° C)
9-INCH (2.5 L) SPRINGFORM PAN SPRAYED WITH VEGETABLE SPRAY

8 oz	wide egg noodles	250 g
1	large egg	1
2	large egg whites	2
1 cup	5% ricotta cheese	250 mL
3/4 cup	low-fat yogurt	175 mL
2 oz	light cream cheese	50 g
1 tbsp	finely grated orange zest	15 mL
1/4 cup	fresh orange juice	50 mL
3/4 cup	granulated sugar	175 mL
1/2 tsp	ground cinnamon	2 mL
1/8 tsp	grated nutmeg	0.5 mL
1 cup	sliced peeled apples	250 mL
1/3 cup	dried raisins or cranberries	75 mL
1 tbsp	granulated sugar	15 mL
1/2 tsp	ground cinnamon	2 mL

Topping

1/3 cup	packed brown sugar	75 mL
1/4 cup	all-purpose flour	50 mL
3 tbsp	rolled oats	45 mL
2 tsp	margarine *or* butter	10 mL
1/4 tsp	ground cinnamon	1 mL

essential numbers

PER SERVING

Calories	175
Protein	6 g
Fat, total	3 g
Fat, saturated	1.0 g
Carbohydrates	33 g
Sodium	93 mg
Cholesterol	25 mg
Fiber	2 g

ask ROSE

Different varieties of noodle pudding — called *lukshenkugel* — are served at most traditional Jewish holiday meals. And high-fat occasions they are, too, because these puddings often contain as much as 2 cups (500 mL) sour cream, 1 cup (250 mL) cream cheese and 3 to 4 whole eggs. But in this recipe, we use a combination of ricotta cheese and cream cheese, 1 whole egg plus egg whites, and yogurt. The result: a low-fat version with about half the calories!

for the record

Is it really light?

When you buy light cream cheese, you probably assume it has less fat and calories than regular cream cheese. And in this case, you assume correctly: light cream cheese has almost half the calories and fat that you get in the regular version. But be careful. The term "light" on a label doesn't always mean a product is lower in fat or calories. It can mean light in color (light olive oil), light in texture (light brown sugar), lower in sodium (light soy sauce), or light in taste. When in doubt, check the label for specific information about fat and calories.

rice paper crêpes
with caramelized bananas and maple syrup

1 In a nonstick saucepan sprayed with vegetable spray, heat margarine over medium-high heat. Add bananas, brown sugar and cinnamon; cook for 2 minutes or until browned and slightly softened. Set aside.

2 In a bowl cover wrappers with cold water; let stand for 3 minutes or until softened. Pat dry; place on work surface. Place 4 tbsp (60 mL) banana mixture in the center of each wrapper. Fold in sides; roll up tightly. Repeat with remaining wrappers and filling.

3 In a nonstick frying pan sprayed with vegetable spray, cook filled wrappers over medium heat, turning once, for 4 minutes or until golden. Serve warm with maple syrup.

2 tsp	margarine *or* butter	10 mL
4	medium bananas, peeled and sliced	4
1/4 cup	packed brown sugar	50 mL
1 tsp	ground cinnamon	5 mL
12	6-inch (15 cm) rice paper wrappers	12
1/4 cup	pure maple syrup	50 mL

desserts

224

PER CRÊPE

essential numbers

Calories	200
Protein	4 g
Fat, total	3 g
Fat, saturated	1.0 g
Carbohydrates	40 g
Sodium	240 mg
Cholesterol	0 mg
Fiber	2 g

ask ROSE

If I didn't have to think about the fat, I'd use whipped cream as a topping all the time. But I do. So I don't. Still, I've discovered an amazingly good substitute. Just combine 1/4 cup (50 mL) low-fat sour cream with 2 tbsp (25 mL) icing sugar. Try it!

nutrition watch

Margarine or butter...
True or false: Margarine has fewer calories and less fat than butter. False. The fact is that both are 100% fat. And all fat, be it canola oil, margarine or butter, contains 9 calories per gram and 45 calories per 1 tsp (5 mL). The difference between these two spreads is in the type of fat they're made from. Margarine has a lot less saturated fat (the cholesterol-raising kind). Butter gets 63% of its calories from saturated fat, whereas margarine ranges from 13 to 19%, depending on the brand.

acorn squash with rice, pineapple and molasses (page 186)

tulip egg roll cups with berries (page 214)

Agnolotti. Similar to ravioli, usually semicircular or square in shape. It is filled with various ingredients such as cheese, meat, or vegetables. You can substitute any stuffed pasta, such as ravioli or tortellini.

Angel hair. *See Capelli d'angelo.*

Arborio rice. A short-grain Italian rice with an extremely high starch content that gives risotto is characteristically creamy texture.

Barley. A hearty grain traditionally used in soups, but now finding a much wider range of uses. There are a number of varieties available: pearl barley, which has had the bran removed, and cooks in the least amount of time; and pot barley, which has had only the outer husk removed and therefore requires more time to cook.

Bean-thread noodles (Cellophane noodles or Glass thread noodles) Unlike traditional noodles, which are made from wheat or rice, these white-transparent noodles are actually made from the starch of mung beans. Sold dried, they can be added directly to soups; otherwise they should be soaked before use.

Bow-ties. *See Farfalle.*

Buckwheat. Not a cereal, as its name would suggest, buckwheat is actually the seed of a herb plant native to Russia. It is ground to make flour that is familiar to North Americans as an ingredient for pancakes. Coarsely crushed buckwheat is known as kasha.

Bulgur. A centuries-old staple in the Middle East, bulgur is made from processed wheat kernels that have been crushed. (It is not the same as cracked wheat, however.) Its chewy texture makes it well suited to salads and various side dishes.

Cannelloni. Usually sold fresh as 4- by 5-inch (9 by 12 cm) flat pieces or as a dried pasta in rolled form. They can be filled with meat or cheese fillings and are usually baked in a sauce. They are smaller than manicotti, but can be used interchangeably with them. Use about 1 tbsp (15 mL) of filling in each.

Capelli d'angelo (Angel hair). Very thin strands of pasta, usually sold in coils.

Capellini. Similar to angel hair pasta, but slightly thicker.

Chow mein noodles. Thin wheat noodles, yellow in color, sometimes made with egg, available fresh in the refrigerated section of some supermarkets and most Asian specialty stores. Be sure you don't mistakenly buy the type of dried, deep-fried "chow mein" that is used primarily as a garnish for oriental salads. If you can't find any "real" chow mein, the closest replacement is angel hair pasta.

Conchiglie (Shells). Shaped like conch shells, ranging in size from small bite-size pasta to large shells that can be stuffed with meat, cheese, or vegetable fillings.

Cornmeal. Corn kernels that have been dried and crushed. Available in coarse, medium and fine grinds, it is typically yellow in color but can also be white or blue. Cornmeal is the principal ingredient of polenta.

Couscous. Originally from North Africa, couscous is made from semolina wheat. It cooks quickly and makes an ideal accompaniment to a number of dishes, as well as an excellent replacement for potatoes.

Ditali. Macaroni-like tubes of pasta, but very short and very small.

Egg noodles. Made with whole eggs or yolks, these wheat noodles are available fresh or dried.

Egg roll (wonton) wrappers. Square or round sheets of fresh wheat noodle dough, available in packages in Asian markets or the produce section of supermarkets. Extremely versatile, they can be used to encase a wide variety of fillings. They dry out easily, so cover with a damp towel until ready to use.

Elbow macaroni. *See Macaroni.*

Farfalle (Bow-ties). Shaped like bow-ties — or butterflies, if you like — they come in a variety of sizes. Most often used in the same way as a wide, flat noodle.

Fettuccine (Tagliatelle). Long, flat pasta, usually about 1/4 inch (5 mm) wide.

Fusilli (Spirals, Rotini). Shaped like twisted spaghetti or corkscrews, about 3 inches (7.5 cm) in length.

Gnocchi. Dumpling-like in appearance, but nevertheless a type of pasta. Make your own and freeze them, or buy the packaged gnocchi, which are usually excellent. Gnocchi is made from potatoes and flour, and can be served with a variety of sauces.

Lasagna. Sheets of fresh or dried pasta, usually measuring 13 inches (32.5 cm) long by 3 inches (7.5 cm) wide; usually cooked, layered with filling and sauce, and baked.

Linguine. A flat, strand-type pasta, like fettuccine, but not as wide.

Macaroni. Available as long, relatively thin tubes, but are most familiar in "elbow" form — that is, as short, crescent-shaped tubes of pasta used for casseroles or soups.

Manicotti. A rolled pasta like cannelloni, but larger; usually filled with a cheese mixture and baked with a sauce. You can buy them in dried form, or buy sheets of lasagna and cut to desired size, usually 5 by 4 inches (12.5 by 10 cm). Use about 1 tbsp (15 mL) filling for each shell.

Millet. Until recently, millet was sold in North America almost exclusively as feed for birds and animals. It is now being rediscovered as a mild-tasting grain that can be used like rice.

Orzo. Sometimes used as a substitute for rice, which it resembles, but is heavier and fuller. Good in soups.

Pearl barley. *See* **Barley**

Penne rigate. Quill shaped, tubular pasta, cut diagonally; comes in various sizes, but most often measuring 2 inches (5 cm) in length. Good with heavier meat sauces.

Quinoa (pronounced KEEN-wah). Sacred to the Incas, this fluffy grain is sold as whole grain or as pasta. It's lower in carbohydrate and higher in protein that most grains. Try it in pilafs, salads, casseroles and stir-fries.

Radiatore. An unusually shaped, bite-sized pasta, featuring fins like those of an old-fashioned hot water radiator.

Ramen noodles. Orginating from Japan, these thin, curled noodles are often packaged (with premixed seasonings) as instant meals. On their own (that is, without the seasonings), ramen noodles are a useful ingredient for soups and other dishes. Larger packages of ramen noodles, without the flavorings, are available at some Asian markets.

Ravioli. Square pasta, 1 to 2 inches (2.5 to 5 cm) across, filled with a small amount of cheese or meat filling and crimped at the edges. You can prepare your own or buy ready-made frozen. Serve with a sauce.

Rice noodles, dried (Rice stick noodles or **Rice vermicelli).** These noodles are available in a variety of widths. The wide type is flat and ribbon-like in appearance (similar to fettuccine) and grayish-white in color; they are quite common in Asian stores and many supermarkets. The thin type of rice stick noodles are not very stick-like, and are sold in bundles (like angel hair pasta).

Rice noodles, fresh. Made from strips of rice noodle sheets (see below), these noodles are typically quite wide. They require very little cooking, often no more than running hot water over the noodles before adding to a hot sauce.

Rice noodle sheets. Usually sold in rolls, these large white sheets of noodle dough are used to encase a variety of fillings. While gelatinous in texture, the noodles eventually dry out and become inflexible; however, dipping the roll quickly in hot water will soften it. Noodle sheets are typically available only in Chinese markets.

Rice paper wrappers. Made from a mixture of rice flour, water and salt, which is rolled thin and dried on bamboo mats. Typically sold in rounds or squares, these wrappers are extremely fragile and must be softened in hot water before using. They can be found in Asian markets and some supermarkets.

Rigatoni. Large, ridged tubes of pasta, usually about 1 1/2 inches (3 cm) long. Excellent with a chunky sauce.

Shanghai noodles. These wheat noodles are available in a variety thicknesses — ranging from thin (like spaghetti) to thick (like ziti) — but all are distinctively round in shape. They are easily overcooked (even sitting in a hot sauce), so prepare only just before serving. Available in Chinese markets and some grocery stores.

Shells. *See Conchiglie*

Soba noodles. These Japanese noodles are made from buckwheat, although they may also contain wheat flour. They can be found in health food stores, as well as Japanese and Asian markets. Some supermarkets cary them frozen in shrink-wrapped packages. Buckwheat soba, which is wheat-free, is often used in gluten-free diets. To preserve the texture of soba noodles, avoid overcooking; otherwise, they will become mushy.

Spaghetti. Best known of all pastas, often used as a generic term for any strand-type pasta, ranging from thin capellini to thick spaghettoni.

Spaghettini. Thinner than spaghetti, but thicker than vermicelli.

Stellini. Tiny, star-shaped pasta; good for soups.

Tagliatelle. See Fettuccine.

Thin wheat noodles. Similar in appearance to linguine, these flat noodles are often made with egg. Available fresh or dried, in a variety of sizes and widths, usually at Asian or ethnic markets.

Tubetti. Small, hollow tubes of pasta.

Tortellini. Similar to ravioli, but with a twisted, irregular shape; usually filled with cheese or meat. You can prepare your own or use ready-made. Fillings for this pasta are interchangeable with manicotti, cannelloni, or jumbo pasta shells.

Udon noodles. Long, thick, round white noodles originating from Japan. Available fresh, frozen (usually precooked) or dried.

Vermicelli. Thinner than spaghettini, but thicker than capellini.

Wheat berries. Whole kernels of wheat from which the more familiar cracked wheat is made.

Wheels. Circular, bite-sized pasta with various configurations of "hubs" and "spokes." Good in salads and soups.

Wide wheat noodles. Flat noodles, usually quite thick, similar in appearance to fettuccine (with which it can be replaced). Available at Asian markets and supermarkets.

Ziti. A tubular pasta similar to penne.

and health

LESLIE BECK, RD

Eat right, live well — so the saying goes. A diet that's low in fat and rich in vegetables, fruit and whole grains will give you plenty of vitamins and minerals. In fact, your body needs more than 45 such nutrients to stay healthy. And whole foods also offer many other natural compounds, like fiber and phyto (plant) chemicals, that help your body fight disease.

These days we're overloaded with information on the benefits of eating what's good for you, yet many of us still don't get enough vitamins and minerals. If you're on the go, under stress, or you're a haphazard eater, chances are you don't always eat right. Sometimes that fat-laden muffin is more convenient than a bowl of high-fiber cereal. Or pouring a jar of tomato sauce over pasta takes a lot less effort than preparing a stir-fry. Whatever the reason, nutrition surveys show that many of us fall short of important nutrients like calcium, iron and zinc.

Even if you are getting the daily recommended nutrient intake (RNI), there are certain vitamins you probably should get more of. Vitamins like C, E and folate, in amounts greater than the official RNIs, may reduce your risk for cancer, heart disease and other age-related illness.

To help you eat a diet that's brimming with protective vitamins and minerals, use the following guide to choose the right foods. If you're eating right, do you need a supplement? Well, if you want a little extra nutritional insurance, then a multivitamin and mineral pill is a wise idea. And when it comes to vitamin E, I strongly recommend a daily supplement to achieve an optimal intake. Vitamin and mineral supplements are meant to support and reinforce a healthy diet. For example, here's a safe and healthy supplement plan for your daily diet:

Multivitamin and mineral supplement, adults and children (choose one with 0.4 to 1.0 mg folic acid)

2 **Vitamin E**, 400 IU once daily

3 **Vitamin C**, 500 mg once daily

4 **Calcium citrate with added vitamin D**. Take a 300 mg supplement for every milk serving you don't get (you need 2 to 4 servings to meet your calcium needs).

For dosage amounts that meet your specific health and nutrient needs, consult your nutritionist or naturopathic physician.

fat-soluble vitamins

	what it does	best food sources	daily RNI[a]
Vitamin A	Needed for night and color vision; supports cell growth and development; maintains healthy skin, hair, nails, bones and teeth; enhances immune system; may help prevent lung cancer	*Vitamin A:* liver, oily fish, milk, cheese, butter, egg yolks *Beta carotene:* orange and yellow fruits and vegetables; dark green vegetables	Males: 1000 RE (Retinol Equivalents) Females: 800 RE
Vitamin D	Regulates body calcium levels; needed for calcium absorption; maintains bones and teeth	Fluid milk, fortified soy and rice beverages, oily fish, egg yolks, butter, margarine (Also made by body when exposed to sunlight.)	Males & Females:[b] 19 – 50: 200 IU 51 – 70: 400 IU Over 70: 600 IU
Vitamin E	Protects cell membranes; enhances immune system; strong antioxidant; needed for iron metabolism	Vegetable oil, margarine, nuts, seeds, whole grains, green leafy vegetables, asparagus, avocado, wheat germ	Males: 9 mg (13 IU) Females: 6 mg (9 IU)
Vitamin K	Essential for blood clotting	Green peas, broccoli, spinach, leafy green vegetables, liver	Males & Females[c]: 60 – 80 mcg

water-soluble vitamins

Vitamin C	Supports collagen synthesis and wound healing; strengthens blood vessels; boosts immune system; helps body absorb iron; antioxidant	Citrus fruit, strawberries, kiwi, cantaloupe, broccoli, bell peppers, Brussels sprouts, cabbage, tomatoes, potatoes	Males: 40 mg Females: 30 mg
B1 (Thiamin)	Needed for energy metabolism; maintains normal appetite and nerve function	Pork, liver, whole grains, enriched breakfast cereals, legumes, nuts	Males: 1.1 mg Females: 0.8 mg

	what it does	best food sources	daily RNI[a]
B2 (Riboflavin)	Used in energy metabolism; supports normal vision; maintains healthy skin	Milk, yogurt, cottage cheese, fortified soy and rice beverages, meat, whole grains, enriched breakfast cereals	Males: 1.4 mg Females: 1.0 mg
B3 (Niacin)	Used in energy metabolism; maintains skin, digestive system nerve function	Chicken, tuna, liver, peanuts, whole grains, enriched cereals, dairy products, all high protein foods	Males: 19 mg Females: 14 mg
B6	Needed for protein and fat metabolism; used to make red blood cells; supports brain serotonin production	Meat, poultry, fish, beans, nuts, seeds, whole grains, green and leafy vegetables, bananas, avocados	Males: 2 mg Females: 1.6 mg
Folate	Supports cell division and growth; used to make DNA and red blood cells; prevents neural tube defects in newborns; may prevent heart disease	Spinach, lentils, orange juice, asparagus, avocados, whole grains, seeds, liver	Males and Females:[b] 400 mcg
B12	Maintains nerve function; needed to make DNA and red blood cells	All animal foods, fortified soy and rice beverages	Males & Females: 1.0 mcg (adults over 50 should get B12 from supplement or fortified foods)
Biotin	Used for energy metabolism, fat synthesis, amino acid and carbohydrate metabolism	Kidney, liver, oatmeal, egg yolk, soybeans, brewer's yeast, clams, mushrooms, bananas	Males & Females:[c] 30 – 100 mcg
Pantothenic Acid	Needed to break down fats, protein and carbohydrate for energy; used to make bile, red blood cells, hormones, vitamin D.	Widespread in foods	Males & Females:[c] 4 – 7 mg
Choline	Necessary for fat metabolism and cell membrane structure; building block for acetylecholine, a chemical for brain and nerve function	Egg yolks, liver, kidney, meat, brewer's yeast, wheat germ, soybeans, peanuts, green peas	Males & Females:[b] 425 mcg

[a] Recommended Nutrient Intake (RNI) stated for adults over the age of 24 years. From Scientific Review Committee: *Nutrition recommendations*, Ottawa, Canada, 1990, Health and Welfare.

[b] Dietary Reference Intakes from Food and Nutrition Board, National Academy of Sciences – Institute of Medicine.

[c] No RNI established. This amount is considered to be safe and adequate.

vitamins & minerals

233

	What it does	Best Food Sources	Daily RNI[a]
Calcium	Needed for strong bones and teeth, muscle contraction and relaxation, nerve function, blood clotting; maintains blood pressure	Milk, yogurt, cheese, fortified soy and rice beverages, tofu, canned salmon (with bones), kale, bok choy, broccoli, chard	Males & Females: [b] 24 – 50: 1000 mg Over 50: 1200 mg
Magnesium	Involved in bone growth, protein building, muscle contraction, and transmission of nerve impulses	Nuts, legumes, whole grains, leafy green vegetables, meat poultry, fish, eggs	Males: 250 mg Females: 200 mg
Phosphorus	Maintains strong bones and teeth; used in metabolism; part of genetic material	Dairy products, meat, poultry, fish, egg yolks, legumes	Males: 1000 mg Females: 850 mg
Iron	Needed to transport oxygen to all cells; Supports metabolism	Red meat, seafood, poultry, eggs, legumes, whole grains, enriched breakfast cereals	Males: 9 mg Females: 13 mg
Zinc	Crucial for growth and reproduction; used to make genetic material, immune compounds, enzymes; helps transport vitamin A	Oysters, seafood, red meat, poultry, yogurt, whole grains, enriched cereals	Males: 12 mg Females: 9 mg
Iodide	Used to make thyroid hormones which regulate growth, development and metabolism	Iodized salt, seafood, plants grown in iodide rich soil	Males & Females: 160 mcg
Copper	Helps the body absorb iron; needed for nerve fibres, red blood cells, connective tissue and many enzymes	Liver, meat, shellfish, legumes, prunes	Males & Females: [c] 1.5 – 3 mg
Manganese	Part of many enzymes; facilitates cell metabolism	Coffee, tea, legumes, nuts, wheat bran	Males & Females: [c] 2.5 – 5 mg
Molybdenum	Used for metabolism; helps the body mobilize iron stores	Hard drinking water, meat, whole grains, legumes, green leafy vegetables, organ meats	Males & Females: [c] 75 – 200 mcg
Fluoride	Essential in formation of bones and teeth; helps prevent tooth decay	Drinking water (if fluoridated), tea, seafood	Males & Females:[c] 1.5 – 4 mg
Chromium	Helps insulin regulate blood sugar	Brewer's yeast, molasses, mushrooms, whole grains	Males & Females: [c] 50 – 200 mcg
Selenium	Antioxidant; works with vitamin E to prevent cell damage from free radicals	Seafood, meat, organ meats, grains, onion, garlic, mushrooms	Males: 70 mcg Females: 55 mcg
Sulfur	Necessary for body proteins, bones and teeth; activates enzymes; regulates blood clotting	Meat, organ meats, poultry, fish, eggs, legumes, dairy products	Not established

[a] Recommended Nutrient Intake (RNI) stated for adults over the age of 24 years. From Scientific Review Committee: *Nutrition recommendations*, Ottawa, Canada, 1990, Health and Welfare.

[b] Dietary Reference Intakes from Food and Nutrition Board, National Academy of Sciences – Institute of Medicine.

[c] No RNI established. This amount is considered to be safe and adequate.

Leeks:

    about, 142

    lamb chili with, 176

    and mango sauce with halibut, 142

    pesto over linguine, 208

    to wash, 208

Lentils:

    about, 57, 67

    soup

     with cheese tortellini, 67

     with sausage, 57

Light, use of word, 223

Linguine:

    and asparagus frittata, 188

    avocado-tomato salsa over, 209

    with bok choy and snow peas, 185

    calves' liver with onions over, 148

    falafels with tahini sauce over, 206

    leek pesto over, 208

    mussel mushroom, 129

    scallops and spinach over, 122

    varieties of, 129

Liver. *See* Calves' liver; Chicken, livers

Lobster Alfredo, over smoked salmon fettuccine, 123

Lutein, sources of, 53

Lycopene, about, 195

M

Macaroni:

    and cheese casserole, 124

    and shrimp salad, 77

    spaghetti squash with turkey Bolognese, 105

Mango(es):

    about, 86

    kiwi and apricots over rotini, 87

    -leek sauce over halibut and spaghettini, 142

    and ravioli salad, 86

    salsa, 136

Manicotti shells:

    with cheese and wild mushrooms, 184

    stuffed with beef, mushrooms and cheese, 149

    stuffed with pesto and cheese, 151

Maple chicken with peppers and mustard over rotini, 104

Maple syrup, about, 104

Margarine, fat content, 224

Marinade for flank steak, 156

Mayonnaise, about light, 100

Meatballs:

    beef, 164

    chicken pine nut, 96

    polenta, 65

index

246

index

index

255